BORN UNDER A LUCKY STAR

Reminiscences

Richard F. Staar

*for Corliss A. Tacosa, Ph.D.
in friendship

Richard F. Staar

2 December 2002*

University Press of America,® Inc.
Lanham · New York · Oxford

Copyright © 2002 by
University Press of America,® Inc.
4720 Boston Way
Lanham, Maryland 20706

12 Hid's Copse Rd.
Cumnor Hill, Oxford OX2 9JJ

All rights reserved
Printed in the United States of America
British Library Cataloging in Publication Information Available

Library of Congress Cataloging-in-Publication Data

Staar, Richard Felix, 1923-
Born under a lucky star : reminiscences / Richard F. Staar.
p. cm.
1. Staar, Richard Felix, 1923- 2. Polish Americans—Biography.
3. Diplomats—United States—Biography. 4. Historians—
United States—Biography. 5. World War, 1939-1945—Personal
narratives, Polish. 6. World War, 1939-1945—Poland.
7. World War, 1939-1945—Concentration camps.
8. Ex-concentration camp inmates—Biography. 9. Poland—
Biography. I. Title.

E184.P7 S68 2002
327.73'0092—dc21   [B]   2002028496 CIP

ISBN 0-7618-2381-6 (paperback : alk. ppr.)

∞™ The paper used in this publication meets the minimum
requirements of American National Standard for Information
Sciences—Permanence of Paper for Printed Library Materials,
ANSI Z39.48—1984

To

*the Seven Graces,
who shaped my life:*

*Agnes
Marie
Barbara
Jadwiga
Monica
Christina
Rachel*

Contents

TABLES vii

ACRONYMS ix

PREFACE xiii

INTRODUCTION xv

CHAPTER ONE
    Roots, War, and Return 1

CHAPTER TWO
    College and Graduate School 23

CHAPTER THREE
    Career Highlights 37

CHAPTER FOUR
    The 1980–81 Transition 65

CHAPTER FIVE
    Balance of Power 81

CHAPTER SIX
    The Vienna Talks 97

CHAPTER SEVEN
    Decision-making and Negotiations 119

CHAPTER EIGHT
Public Diplomacy 137

CHAPTER NINE
The "End of History?" 153

CHAPTER TEN
Back in "God's Country" 167

APPENDIX A
Executive Correspondence 177

APPENDIX B
Other Works by Author 183

NAME INDEX 205
SUBJECT INDEX 209
ABOUT THE AUTHOR 215

TABLES

1. Poland's Losses during World War II, 1939-45 xvi
2. Destruction of Warsaw 18
3. Movements with a "Socialist" Orientation in Third World Countries 84
4. World Socialist System, 1989 86
5. U.S. Ambassadors to MBFR and CFE 100
6. Soviet CFE-Limited Equipment in East-Central Europe 113
7. Naval Armaments, *USSR vs. NATO* 117
8. CPSU Political Bureau (1982) 120
9. Arms Control Commission of the CPSU 121
10. Soviet Expenditures for Propaganda 145
11. International Communist Front Organizations 148
12. USSR/Russia in Local Wars, 1946–2000 158

ACRONYMS

AAASS	American Association for Advancement of Slavic Studies
ACDA	U.S. Arms Control and Disarmament Agency
ACDUTRA	Active Duty for Training (USMCR)
AEI	American Enterprise Institute for Public Policy Research
AFL/CIO	American Federation of Labor/Congress of Industrial Organizations
AID	Agency for International Development
AK	*Armia Krajowa* (Home Army)
APSA	American Political Science Association
ASAT	Anti-Satellite Program
BBC	British Broadcasting Corporation
CBM	Confidence Building Measures
CDR	Commander
CFE	Conference on Armed Forces in Europe
CIS	Commonwealth of Independent States
CMEA	Council for Mutual Economic Assistance
CO	Commanding Officer
CPSU	Communist Party of the Soviet Union

CSC	Command and Staff College
CSCE	Conference on Security and Cooperation in Europe
DP	Displaced Person
DRS	Division of Research on the Soviet Union and Eastern Europe
EUCOM	European Command, U.S. Army
FSO	Foreign Service Officer
GDR	German Democratic Republic
Gestapo	*Geheime Staatspolizei* (Secret State Police)
GRU	*Glavnoe Razvedyvatel'noe Upravlenie* (Chief Intelligence Directorate)
GS	Government Schedule
ILAG	*Internierungslager* (internment camp)
INF	Intermediate-range Nuclear Forces negotiations
INR	Bureau of Intelligence and Research
IPSA	International Political Science Association
ISKAN	*Institut Soedinënnykh Shtatov Ameriki* (Institute of the USA)
KGB	*Komitet Gosudarstvennoi Bezopasnosti* (Committee on State Security)
KSČ	Komunističeská Strana Československa (Communist Party of Czechoslovakia)
LTC	Lieutenant Colonel
MAD	Mutual Assured Destruction
MBFR	Mutual and Balanced Forces Reduction talks
MCRRD	Marine Corps Reserve and Recruitment District
MX	Missile, Experimental
NAS	Naval Air Station

NATO	North Atlantic Treaty Organization
NIE	National Intelligence Estimate
NKVD	People's Commissariat of Internal Affairs (preceded KGB)
NSC	National Security Council
NSDD	National Security Decision Directive
OIR	Office of Intelligence Research
OPC	Office of Policy Coordination
Panzer	Tanks (German)
PAO	Public Affairs Officer
PLO	Palestine Liberation Organization
POW	Prisoner of war
PR	Public relations
PRC	People's Republic of China
RAF	Royal Air Force
RDJTF	Rapid Deployment Joint Task Force
RFE	Radio Free Europe
RL	Radio Liberty
ROTC	Reserve Officers Training Corps
RSO	Regional Security Officer
SA	*Sturmabteilungen* (Storm Units)
SDI	Strategic Defense Initiative
SLBM	Submarine-launched Ballistic Missile
Spetsnaz	*Otriady Spetsialnogo Naznachenia* (Special Forces)
SPG	Special Planning Group
SRI	Stanford Research Institute

SS	*Schutzstaffeln* (Protective Units)
START	Strategic Arms Reduction Talks
Stuka	*Sturzkampfflugzeug* (dive bomber)
SUNY	State University of New York
TASS	*Telegraficheskoe Agentsvo Sovetskogo Soiuza* (Telegraphic Agency of the Soviet Union)
TLE	Treaty-Limited Equipment
UN	United Nations
USIA	United States Information Agency
USIS	United States Information Service
VOA	Voice of America
VTU	Volunteer Training Unit
WTO	Warsaw Treaty Organization
ŻOB	*Żydowska Organizacja Bojowa* (Jewish Combat Organization)

PREFACE

There are many individuals whom I wish to thank in connection with this book. First, and above all, I will always be grateful to my wife, Jadwiga, for her personal support during our several decades of marriage. Her advice has always been the best and of the highest caliber. Without that support, we could never have surmounted the difficulties and problems in connection with various career choices and assignments.

Next, the two successive directors of the Hoover Institution (the late Dr. W. Glenn Campbell and Dr. John Raisian) were kind enough to provide me leaves-of-absence without pay and their personal support during both two-year "sabbaticals" in Vienna and Boston. They assisted me on many occasions prior to and after these assignments.

Dr. Richard T. Burress, senior fellow and former associate director at the Hoover Institution, provided me with excellent counsel regarding whether to remain in the federal government before returning to the United States from Austria. Over the years, he has given me other advice on many occasions, and I treasure our friendship.

Apart from the two successive secretaries of state, Alexander M. Haig, Jr. and George P. Shultz, under whom I served in Vienna; Professor Eugene Rostow (ACDA director) as well as his successor as acting director, Dr. James George; Ms. Pamela Stratton, personnel director for international organization affairs at the Department of State; Edwin Meese III, counselor to President Reagan; Ms. Wendy H. Borcherdt in the Office of Presidential Affairs; Richard V. Allen, national security advisor; Richard T. Kennedy, undersecretary of state for management—to all of these, I owe debts of gratitude.

I should also mention my predecessor in Vienna, Ambassador Jonathan Dean, with whom I had several long conversations; Ambassador R. James Woolsey, Jr., who finally negotiated the renamed CFE treaty and was kind enough to talk with me about this at an American Political Science Association annual convention in Washington, D.C. On several occasions, the former Soviet ambassador to the CFE talks in Vienna, Oleg A. Grinevsky, and I held conversations while he was a visiting scholar at the Hoover Institution.

Finally, it would be remiss not to single out Mrs. Margit N. Grigory, my research associate with whose help I could reenter the academic world in the course of two smooth transitions. Our joint work resulted in several conference volumes, resumption of editing the *Yearbook on International Communist Affairs* (discontinued after the 1991 volume), and also my volume on *The New Military in Russia* as well as the two editions of *Transition to Democracy in Poland*. Ms. Molly Molloy, Slavic reference librarian, has been of great assistance throughout most of these projects. Curator of the East European Collection Dr. Maciej Siekierski as well as Archival Specialist Zbigniew Stańczyk helped me with source material on Poland.

To all of the above and others who gave me their insights as well as information, I will always be indebted, and especially to Professor Whitfield Bell, Jr., who suggested that I write these reminiscences.

Richard F. Staar
Stanford, California

INTRODUCTION

When giving some thought to writing a book of reminiscences, I decided to begin chronologically with what I could remember from childhood in Ann Arbor. Those were carefree years in elementary school, slipping out of my bedroom to hear "The Shadow" on the radio at a classmate's home late in the evening and then climbing back through a window.

Another event in my memory is of an outing at a farm belonging to one of Dad's colleagues at the University of Michigan. That family had a boy about my age. Both of us climbed to the top of a wagon loaded with hay. The horses jerked the wagon to start hauling it into a barn. I lost my balance and landed on a rock. My left arm broke from the impact. Had that "lucky star" saved me from falling on my head?

After moving to Poland, my language deficiencies were the reason for placement three grades lower than in the United States. Being self-conscious also was rooted in the fact that I towered over the boys in class. The same was true, to a lesser extent, when I entered secondary school the following year.

I remember a fist fight with a larger, if not older, student whose last name was Lik. His face had been covered with mercurochrome when his mother brought the boy to see my mother. After German troops had occupied our city, this young man wore a Hitler *Jugend* uniform, with the swastika armband. I felt sorry that I had not beaten him harder when I had the chance.

In thinking back about the Second World War, being held in a Gestapo prison for six months, hiding in Warsaw during the following year, and the thirty months at two different German internment camps—all of these experiences probably saved my life. Otherwise, I could have ended up in one of the following categories:

Table 1: Poland's Losses during World War II, 1939–45*

No.	Cause of Death	Number of Victims	% of Population
1.	Military operations	644,000	2.4
2.	Concentration camps, pacification, executions, Ghetto actions	3,577,000	13.3
3.	Prisons, camps (epidemics, exhaustion, brutal treatment, etc.)	1,286,000	4.7
4.	Result of wounds, excessive labor, etc. (outside of concentration camps)	<u>521,000</u>	1.8
		6,028,000	22.2
	Population on September 1, 1939	**27,007,000	100.00

* J. Szafrański, "Poland's Losses during World War II," *Studia i rozprawy* (Poznań: Wydawnictwo Zachodnie, March 1960), VIII, 38.

** Includes only the Polish and Jewish population living within the borders of Poland on that date, but apparently *not* the Ukrainian, Belorussian, or Lithuanian minorities in the areas annexed during September 1939 by the USSR. The total population with the other minorities in 1939 numbered over thirty-two million.
Note: The above losses include those who suffered death in either the German or Soviet zones of occupation.

The circumstances under which I survived were nothing less than miraculous. Thinking back, it was as if some spirit were whispering into my subconscious what to do and what to avoid. How could there be any other explanation? Coincidence? Too much of that. I have used the metaphor "lucky star" in this book's title, because that is how I feel even today as well as about the future.

For some time, during my first internment camp experience, I still had nightmares. In one of these, I would see Mr. Romanowski (my former music teacher) playing Chopin's funeral march on his violin while leading a group of Polish high school students to the guillotine. The violin is taken from him, and he is forced to place his head on the block. Then, the sharp blade drops. The next person in line is a lovely blonde former high school student with long braids, to whom the same is done. Would my emaciated father be at the end of this line? I wake up in a cold sweat.

My nightmares included Mother and baby sister Barbara being arrested by the Gestapo and deported from occupied Poland to a slave labor camp in Germany (which never happened). I also dreamed about the two German-Jewish boys who had gambled on survival as Latin American citizens and lost. Once in the hands of the Gestapo, they could not have survived.

The internment camps were not extermination sites, for which I always counted my blessings. In the second one, it was possible to play "catch-up" for the six years of schooling that would have been lost during the Second World War. The British civilian internees had already set up a tutoring system, before the Americans were transferred from Tittmoning to Laufen. An opportunity to take the University of London matriculation exam in the camp proved that my lucky star was still there.

Even prior to those experiences, the chance meeting at Warsaw with two Methodist missionaries led to an unbelievable opportunity for resumption of my formal education back in the United States. Marriage to my "dream girl," who has inspired me ever since, resulted from her acquaintance with my father in a displaced persons' camp at Aversa, Italy. My lucky star was shining, when we met in New York for the first time.

An interlude of three and a half years at the U.S. Department of State allowed me to write and successfully defend my dissertation. That diploma or "union card" gave me the opportunity to qualify for a position in academia. A chance meeting with the departmental chairman at Emory University led to an associate professorship there. Coincidence?

That same lucky star next brought us to California, as a result of my paper at an international conference of the Mont Pelerin Society in Belgium. We have been here at the Hoover Institution on War, Revolution, and Peace ever since—with two double-sabbatical leaves-of-absence in between. My fairy godmother said, "Open sesame," and a stream of publications resulted at this preeminent research center.

Involvement with the presidential campaign during 1980 and *pro bono* work in the transition period at Washington, D.C., led to ambassadorial rank as chief of mission to the conventional arms reduction talks in Vienna.

It reminded me of the "lateral transfer" opportunity during my first "tour of duty" at the Department of State. This second time, we started at the top of the promotion ladder. Coincidence or something else?

We returned to the Hoover Institution two years later, and our life resumed in academia. Every time I would be invited to speak or to write an article, it was as if a shot of adrenaline had entered my bloodstream. That is what happened when the Center for East European Studies at the University of Warsaw invited me to present the inaugural lecture at the opening of its summer school on 1 July 2002. This presentation will be published in the Center's academic journal, *Przegląd Wschodni*.

I have also been encouraged to apply for the distinguished Fulbright Chair in East Central European Studies at the University of Warsaw for the 2003–2004 academic year, with the rank of a university professor. Whether or not this materializes is unknown at this time. Jadwiga and I would welcome such a finale, a prestigious appointment ending where it all began. However, if it is not to be, we will thank my lucky star for that decision too.

CHAPTER 1

ROOTS, WAR, AND RETURN

Naturalization Certificate No. 250245 states that Alfred Staar, my father, received his American citizenship at age twenty-nine in King's County, New York. In addition, the certificate lists the names of his wife Agnes and daughter Marie (the latter then being only nine months old) as "with him" in Bridgeport, Connecticut. Alfred's country of birth is given as Russia. As is typical of such documents, however, no mention is made of how or why he reached the United States.

Alfred was born in a part of Poland that had been incorporated by the tsarist Russian empire during partitions at the end of the eighteenth century. Although predominantly made up of Polish people, other ethnic groups and faiths were well represented there. Russian, of course, was the official *lingua franca*. Nonetheless, Alfred spoke Polish with his family, being quietly home-schooled by his parents in the language, history, and culture of Poland. To study anything other than Russian and the approved tsarist curriculum was considered subversive.

By age fourteen, Alfred discovered that he had a talent for tutoring children. He began clandestine teaching of the Polish language to local boys and girls. In part, this was a public service: A good many of them could not be admitted to tsarist schools because they lacked "proper" shoes (most walked barefoot or wore wooden clogs). In part, it also became a matter of ethnic pride. Alfred and his approving parents were determined to keep their traditions alive.

At sixteen, Alfred began to publish an eight-page biweekly underground newspaper in the Polish language for high-school girls and boys. Within a year, he joined Józef Piłsudski's political movement for Poland's independence from the Russian empire. He also began the dangerous task of smuggling revolutionary literature from Western Europe.

One Christmas Eve, when Alfred was already twenty years old and in his last year in the Russian equivalent of junior college, the son of a Russian gendarmerie captain (a boy whom he had once tutored) came to warn him of imminent arrest. That same evening, Alfred fled on foot across the border into Prussia and made his way to Hamburg. He sailed from there in steerage to New York. It was January 1905 and a tsarist court back in Russia had sentenced him *in absentia* to fifteen years of hard labor in Siberia for his "revolutionary" activities. This threat to him disappeared at the end of World War I, when the Russian revolution brought down the tsarist empire.

Back in the United States, however, an incomplete junior college education from a Russian school had not provided Alfred with the skills required for his new life. The young immigrant wandered the streets of New York, ending up on the lower East Side. It was here that a Jewish shoemaker gave him work. They had only one thing in common: the Russian language. Alfred would remember that kindness and repay it many years later during World War II, as would his son thereafter.

Within eighteen months of arriving in New York, Alfred had already established himself. He organized preparatory courses for admission of Polish workers to study at Cooper Union, a technical institute on the corner of Bowery and East Seventh Street. Friends later provided him with a $5,000 loan to cover tuition at Columbia University, from which he received a master's degree in mechanical engineering.

Alfred's wife, Agnes, came from another part of Russian-occupied Poland—the sub-Carpathian region east of Kraków. As a small child, because of famine in this region, she was sent to live with an aunt and uncle in the state of Massachusetts. This little girl, wearing a cardboard sign with her name and the address of the relatives, traveled across the Atlantic Ocean all alone and then by bus to reach her final destination.

Agnes attended American schools and soon spoke English without a trace of a foreign accent. She also briefly attended Valparaiso University in Indiana. One evening, Agnes happened to attend a meeting at which Alfred gave an impressive speech. "The next thing I knew," she used to say to me, "I found myself married."

During the war years of 1914 to 1918, Alfred taught in the school of engineering at the University of Toledo. With approval from its president, Monroe Stowe, he organized and gave courses during his spare time in shop work, mathematics, and machine drawing for 120 Polish immigrant factory workers who could not afford college tuition. After the end of World War I, Alfred decided to return to Poland. He helped establish and organize the machine tool industry, an engineering school, technical libraries, and a bank.

Childhood

In due course, I was born in Warsaw, at an address on Krucza Street. My own American citizenship was inherited at birth from both parents (*ius sanguinis*) rather than from being born in the United States (*ius soli*). Ironically, I did not learn to speak the Polish language at that time. Only English was spoken at home, as my parents wanted to Americanize their children and prepare them to be educated in U.S. public schools. The family returned to Michigan when I was eleven months old.

My father then joined the engineering faculty at the University of Michigan. I began the first grade at age five and completed all six grades at Burns Park Elementary School, within walking distance of the family house near Stadium Boulevard. Beyond that boundary were farming communities, replaced by the urbanized East Ann Arbor of today.

My older sister, Marie, had enrolled in the University of Michigan at age sixteen. She received an M.Sc. degree in bacteriology and later taught chemistry in senior high school. A younger sister, Barbara, was born in Ann Arbor. At times, our mother would tell me to take the baby around the block in her carriage. Although not happy with this chore, refusal never seemed to be a real option for me: my father, the revolutionary, would brook no challenge to his authority as *pater familias*. At home, I would do as I was told.

My father could express himself silently as well. One afternoon, he returned early from the campus and caught me with a neighborhood pal behind the garage, smoking homemade cigarettes with corn silk rather than tobacco. I dropped everything and ran across the street into the open fields beyond. Dad pursued, although he never caught me. When I returned home long past supper time, nothing was said to me. However, no food appeared on my plate that night.

It was at Burns Park that I learned how to play tennis, with the help of my classmate, Jack Dumond, and his athletic French mother. During the winter, the nets came down and the courts were flooded so that kids could play ice hockey. Those lessons and my natural endurance proved valuable during later years.

My parents never gave me an allowance. Before going to a matinee movie on a Saturday morning, I had to mow a neighbor's lawn or shovel snow from a sidewalk and save that money. One day, Mother took me to a butcher shop. I found a twenty dollar bill in the sawdust which covered the floor. Mother gave the money to the butcher, who promised to hold it for a week, in case the owner were to claim it. Nobody did, so I bought my first brand new bike with those twenty dollars. It would have taken me a long time and many manicured lawns and cleaned sidewalks before I could have saved up such a sum on my own.

After I completed the sixth grade, the family moved to Cleveland Heights, Ohio. Dad had accepted an offer to teach at Case Institute of Technology (now Case-Western Reserve University). Marie remained in Michigan, where she worked as a bacteriologist. I enrolled in Roxboro Junior High School and, the following year, joined the Boy Scouts.

Then, one day before the end of the school year, Dad announced that the family would be taking a "vacation" in Europe. What he wanted to do, apparently, was return to his roots. His aged mother was still alive, and he wanted to see and care for her. Marie, who had just been married, drove to Cleveland with her husband, Harold, and declared that she would be staying in the United States. This was a blow to Dad, who had strong feelings about family and had always regarded his first child as his favorite. Harold, of course, did not speak a word of Polish and had no interest in such an adventure overseas with his new in-laws.

Without my older sister, the rest of us traveled that summer to Halifax, Nova Scotia. Then we boarded the *M.S. Stefan Batory* for the trip across the Atlantic and into the Baltic Sea. We landed at the new port of Gdynia, not far from the old historic port at Gdańsk. Dad apparently had decided to go into semi-retirement, made possible by a most favorable rate of exchange of five Polish *zloty* for one U.S. dollar. The purchasing power of these two currency units was about the same in their respective countries.

Neither my younger sister, Barbara, then only five years old, nor I, spoke or understood any of the new language we would soon be forced to learn. At least Barbara would be starting in the first grade of elementary school. My case was more complicated.

A shy twelve-year-old boy, I entered the Polish elementary school that first day and was told by a teacher to stand outside a door with a large number "4" painted above it. As soon as the teacher left, I walked to the end of the corridor and waited under the number "6." After all, I would have been entering eighth grade in Cleveland Heights!

The teacher returned and led me back to the classroom with the number "5" above its door. At least that was not as bad as being placed in the fourth grade. My parents hired several tutors, including a university student, who came to our house every day after school. These private sessions lasted several hours. I also had a violin teacher, who gave me lessons about once per week. Unfortunately, violin never excited me.

While still in the fifth grade, one of my assignments involved writing an essay in class about the late Marshal Józef Piłsudski, who had died in May of the previous year. It happened to be raining outside, so I wrote that the angels in heaven were weeping on this anniversary of *Dziadek's* ("Grandfather's") death. The teacher had tears in her eyes when she read my story to the class. I received the highest grade of "5" for the composition—despite my errors in spelling and faulty syntax.

Dad remembered the principal of the local high school from their days together back in Russian junior college. The following year, he prevailed on the man to accept me as a student there, even though I would have completed only the fifth grade. I remember taking an examination, although the results were never revealed to me. Shortly thereafter, I was admitted and got to wear a navy blue uniform, with the state secondary school number on a shoulder patch. No girls went to this high school, of course; they all attended their own *gimnazjum*.

Private tutors continued to help me master a most difficult language. The rigorous secondary school course of study included history, geography, mathematics, and science, as well as three languages: Polish, German, and Latin. I never felt comfortable either in the classroom or among classmates after school. This, to me, was an alien culture, and I felt that my own roots were back in the United States. The fact that I did not socialize very well probably saved my life in the long run.

As I struggled through school, Dad was writing yet another technical book. Two years after arrival in Warsaw, he had been asked by the Polish Manufacturers' Association to organize technical courses for machine tool operators. This work led him eventually to establish a school as well as a monthly technical magazine. Dad always had a talent for supplying what was needed. Since there were no textbooks available, Dad wrote three volumes of a *Handbook for Metal Workers*. A fourth volume was underway when Germany invaded Poland on 1 September 1939. My older sister

Marie had returned to the United States from a visit with us just before the war broke out.

Life during the Second World War

The armed forces of Poland, in existence for less than twenty years, were no match for the combination surprise attack by German *Stuka* dive bombers and massive armored *Panzer* formations. Polish defensive positions were quickly overrun, and the *Luftwaffe* methodically bombed Warsaw into submission. It did not restrain the Germans that the Polish capital had been declared an "open city," i.e., undefended and allegedly protected from such wanton destruction under international law.

Then, seventeen days later, the Red Army struck from the east. This attack by an old enemy came as a result of the secret treaty between Hitler and Stalin, which had been signed the preceding month. Our family resided in the part of Poland occupied by the German *Wehrmacht*. Almost immediately, all public and private schools were closed. Teachers as well as professors were arrested. Regardless of religion, training, or social status, every Polish citizen was considered an *Untermensch* (subhuman being) by the Nazis. As future slave-laborers for the Third Reich, they did not require any further education.

Dad immediately became involved with the political resistance. He also organized an "underground railroad" that began to smuggle Jews from German-occupied Poland into then still independent Lithuania, which only later came under Soviet occupation. At the same time, Polish army officers who had been interned in that country since the fall of 1939 were also brought in secret from Kaunas to Warsaw—that is, in the opposite direction—by the underground Home Army (*Armia Krajowa*).

Mother and I accompanied one of these camouflaged deliveries to Lithuania, conducting our own personal kind of "intelligence gathering." Our Jewish traveling companions, hidden under the hay, were also being smuggled across the border in this horse-drawn wagon. They were met by our contacts upon arrival and taken to other hiding places in Lithuania. Mother and son then headed for the U.S. legation at Kaunas. Barbara had stayed at home with our father.

It would have been possible at that time to book passage back to the United States on the *M.S. American Legion*. We could have traveled across the three Baltic states and Finland by rail to the northernmost port of

Petsamo (now Pechenga, Russia) and from there been on our way to New York. My older sister, Marie, had already agreed to pay all our expenses, and the four of us had earlier received new U.S. passports from the American embassy in Berlin. The one in Warsaw had been forced to close by the Germans because, in their eyes, Poland did not exist.

After re-crossing the border into German-occupied Poland at night, my mother and I reported on the above possibility to Dad. He decided that, for the time being, we would not avail ourselves of this opportunity for escape. Dad seemed to enjoy the excitement of the underground organization, helping others in more danger than he, and apparently wanting to witness what would happen in Europe.

That northern "window of opportunity" soon closed, however, when the Red Army occupied the three Baltic republics of Estonia, Latvia, and Lithuania in 1940 and incorporated them into the USSR. The underground railroad had to be discontinued, and so we were compelled to forfeit the chance of returning to the United States via that route.

A second possibility almost materialized. Dad took me with him by train to the American embassy in Berlin, where he explored another option. I can still remember opening our hotel windows at night and watching the RAF drop bombs on the city. It seems that ships were still leaving from Lisbon for New York. This was April 1941, about eight months before Hitler declared war against the United States. Even if we had booked passage immediately for a July sailing, though, we could never have made the trip. Fate had other plans for us.

Before dawn one day in early May 1941, the German secret police (*Gestapo*) arrived to arrest me. It was still dark, and the scene resembled a horror movie: each of these thugs wore the silver death's head insignia designed to instill fear. It worked! A search of the house uncovered US$307, which was confiscated. No other incriminating evidence could be found, except for a shortwave radio. No one cared that we were American citizens and completely harmless people. That same night, some 150 of my former high school classmates were arrested as well. Three days later, the *Gestapo* came for Dad too. It was no comfort to know that he was somewhere in the same prison.

I spent six months incarcerated by the *Gestapo*. They did indeed beat young prisoners repeatedly as part of our interrogation, but pain gave way to resolve within me. Although I knew of some "crimes" and indeed had participated in one clandestine smuggling operation into Lithuania, I kept my mouth shut and did not reveal anything about my father's "subversive" political activities. The *Gestapo* had accused him of being the political adviser for a clandestine anti-Nazi group. Allegedly, the latter had been collecting weapons in preparation for an uprising. The weapons part, in this charge of subversion, carried an automatic death sentence. Fortunately, the "underground railroad" we had been involved with remained a completely separate operation. We knew nothing—and could admit to nothing—about it.

Among the people arrested had been a secondary school teacher and my godmother, Janina Paszkiewiczówna. She had apparently become actively involved with the anti-German underground movement. After repeated torture, this courageous woman hanged herself in the isolation cell rather than risk revealing information to the *Gestapo*. There were many such heroines and heroes in the resistance movement throughout Poland during those desperate times.

One morning, just before dawn, I was awakened in my prison cell (which I shared with more than fifty other inmates) by the sound of aircraft flying overhead toward the east. The date was 22 June 1941, a Sunday. On this day, "Operation Barbarossa" had suddenly been launched by Nazi Germany against its Soviet "ally." Only naive, wishful thinking made me hope that the USSR might prevail immediately and free all political prisoners as a result. Instead, it would take almost four years before the Red Army could reverse direction and march through Poland toward Berlin.

Dad's Ordeal

Most of those arrested were tried subsequently by a notorious "People's Court" (*Volksgericht*) in Königsberg, Prussia. My father's crime came under the category of *Hochverrat*, or high treason. Dad learned enough German in prison, so that he could defend himself in that language during the trial, and that was the extent of his legal representation. Although he had never been a German citizen, the "people's judge" was still empowered to pronounce the death sentence on him, an American. Among his group, nineteen men and five women (between seventeen and sixty-seven years of age) were sentenced to death and then executed by the guillotine.

Fortunately for us, my sister Marie had contacted U.S. senators and congressmen as well as Dr. W. Wickenden (President at Case Institute of Technology), Professor Walter Rautenstrauch at Columbia, Professor Felix W. Pawlowski at Michigan, Professor Stanley Ault at Purdue, and Dr. A.

N. Goddard of the company bearing his name. The U.S. Department of State, through the Swiss embassy in Berlin, offered a captured German saboteur in exchange for Dad. In anticipation, perhaps because of the forthcoming exchange, Dad's sentence was "reduced" to seven years at hard labor in a penitentiary.

Despite repeated visits by a Swiss diplomat to the *Zuchthaus* at Wartenburg in East Prussia (on 16 October 1944, before the trial, and again on 10 January 1945), the actual exchange never took place. The winter offensive by the Red Army was about to break the *Wehrmacht*'s resistance and overrun the area in which Dad was incarcerated. I did receive a letter from him, dated 20 August 1944, which was how I knew he was still alive.

All inmates of this penitentiary were evacuated on foot, with those initially unable to walk shot and left in the snow. This "march" took place after almost four years of imprisonment. Dad survived his ordeal but was left near a small town in East Prussia with others who could not maintain the pace. With the Soviet troops pursuing them, the German guards finally fled, rather than waste time by executing the remaining prisoners. Dad could hear artillery fire in the east, and it was in that direction he chose to walk. When arriving at the first Red Army unit, the soldiers were surprised to hear the escapee speak to them in fluent Russian. An astonished TASS correspondent soon came by and interviewed Dad.

This camaraderie lasted only until military intelligence later arrived on the scene. These men obviously considered my father to be a spy who had been dropped by parachute close to Red Army lines. They told him that he would be sent under armed escort to the Lubyanka prison in Moscow for interrogation. He responded by reminding them that the United States and the USSR were officially allies in the war against Nazi Germany and that a TASS reporter had already filed a newspaper story about the liberation of an American professor by the Red Army, which fact by then was known throughout the world. To arrest him now would surely be a propaganda disaster.

Persuaded by this logic, the Soviet intelligence officers readily facilitated Dad's transportation to Odessa. There, he boarded a British troop ship with former POWs being repatriated to England. After entering the Mediterranean, the ship stopped at Naples, where Dad disembarked.

He had to wait until space became available before he could return to the United States: Demobilized U.S. troops had priority, of course. However, for the first time in years, my father had good reason to be hopeful for the future.

Richard's Saga

In my own case, I spent six months in a German prison. Upon my release, a *Gestapo* officer instructed me to report every Friday afternoon to secret police headquarters on Aleja Szucha No. 25 in Warsaw. I did so only once, quickly realizing that the German secret police could rearrest me on any one of those future reporting days. I must have looked like a scarecrow to them: tall and thin, with a limp from my injured left leg. In addition, one of my eardrums had been shattered.

What to do next presented quite a challenge. I spoke Polish with a definite American accent and was truly a stranger to this area. Nevertheless, the superintendent of the Methodist Church in Warsaw, a Dr. Gaither Warfield, along with his wife Hania, found a family who offered me a bedroom in exchange for tutoring their two young children. The German occupation authorities had kept closed all Polish educational facilities, as described above. In addition, I gave private English lessons to adults for money, although that sum barely covered the cost of my meals.

The particular public streetcar transportation which I used, as well as the side streets I walked, seemed immune, for some reason, from the frequent raids by uniformed German police. Those caught in the dragnets elsewhere were executed—at the rate of one hundred Polish men for each German official assassinated by the underground movement. The names of these unfortunate men were posted in public places throughout the city. I could easily have been recognized from the picture in my U.S. passport (which the *Gestapo* had kept, although they gave me a photographic copy) or even from my foreign pronunciation of Polish words. Clearly, I was living on borrowed time and good luck.

The German police frequently stopped streetcars or individual pedestrians to check their identification papers. They had, of course, lists of fugitives like myself. At times, their purpose was simply to fill a quota for slave workers to be incarcerated at forced labor camps in the *Reich*. When riding on a streetcar, therefore, I always stood or sat up front, so I could detect the presence of the police or spot their preparations to stop the vehicle. If trouble seemed imminent, I would run to the back and jump off into the crowd to avoid arrest.

Despite the high anxiety associated with such trips, it was nonetheless possible to travel this way from the suburbs by streetcar to the office of the Methodist Church on the corner of *Plac Zbawiciela* (Square of the Savior) in the center of Warsaw. Miss Ruth Lawrence, the secretary, had the telephone number of my Polish benefactors in case of an emergency. The Warfields would always invite me to share a meal in their apartment. This generosity made all the difference for me: Not being registered with the German authorities, I received no ration coupons, so I could not purchase even the limited variety of food available at the grocery stores. In addition, through the Methodist Church, a bowl of soup was made available every day at a local restaurant.

The Warfields wrote a book[1] on their wartime experiences. At one point they relate how Hania had asked Gaither "what if he [Richard] is a spy?" After seeing me eat "in silence and with concentration," however, they both decided that my story must be true. In these memoirs, they refer to me as Paul Squire. This, too, was an act of generosity: it concealed my identity while I was still hiding in Warsaw, even after they had already departed for the United States.

It is from their recollections that I can retrieve what I had blocked out of my memory during the intervening years. They quote me as having told them that "the prison cell held 52 men although built for only twelve. During summer, the cell was stifling, the heat unbearable. The food was rotten beets and turnips. It was a red letter day, when potatoes were served. He got dysentery, but remained on the same diet and in the same cell. The worst of it was that a number of inmates were degenerates and hardened criminals. The Gestapo cynically forced this association on them."

"Paul was beaten and tortured. He had pulled through, however, and as time went by his cracked leg mended, and the cuts on his body became scars. Only the broken eardrum could not heal. In November, they let him out. His father remained in prison."

This wonderful couple surely saved my life during that critical period of 1941–42. I believe that they would have adopted me if I had been an orphan. They, too, knew what it was to face danger: Gaither was interned immediately after Hitler declared war against the United States and was sent to the civilian internment camp at Laufen in Upper Bavaria. Hania and their young daughter, Monica, were reunited with Gaither in Berlin during mid-June 1942. All three returned to the United States on the *M.S.*

---

1. Hania and Gaither Warfield, *Call Us to Witness: A Polish Chronicle* (New York: Ziff-Davis Publ. Co., 1945), pp. 330–332.

Drottningholm at the end of that month, after being exchanged for German civilians interned by the U.S. government.

The compassion of the Warfields extended not only to non-Methodists like myself but also to a young Jewish woman, Krystyna Leser. She lived with Mrs. Warfield's parents as their daughter in the foothills of the Carpathian mountains and survived the war there in relative safety. These people also made it to the United States soon after the war ended.

My own "free" existence, fraught with danger, ended one morning at 5 a.m. when the telephone rang. The father of the two young tutorees pounded on my door. The *Gestapo* had called, ordering me to report in person immediately at their headquarters. I explained in the German language that streetcars did not begin to operate until 6 a.m. Since I was located on the outskirts of Warsaw, it would be impossible to report before 7 a.m. Miraculously, the police found this explanation acceptable.

In the meantime, as I gathered my few belongings, the father of the children attempted to convince me that I should go into hiding with the clandestine Polish *Armia Krajowa*. Among other things, they could supply me with forged identity papers. A tempting offer. I declined, however, knowing full well that the *Gestapo* would execute this man and his wife and probably the two children as well, for helping an enemy to escape. So, back to prison for me.

The timing of these events is noteworthy. In late October 1942, approximately one year since my release from the *Gestapo* prison, not only U.S. citizens (who had avoided the first roundup and internment after Hitler declared war against the United States in December 1941) but also those with Latin American passports were being arrested throughout German-occupied countries in Europe.

Internment Camps

Fortunately, I spent only several weeks at the notorious Pawiak political prison in Warsaw. It was here that *Armia Krajowa* members suffered torture and execution around the clock. Finally, the American internees were moved under armed guard to the central railroad station. A special train with bars on the windows took us to Tittmoning, Upper Bavaria, where we were housed in a crumbling castle-fortress.

It was in this camp that I began learning the Russian language from a Costa Rican citizen who had been born in Moscow before the 1917 revolution. I also continued my study of Latin with a Roman Catholic priest, Father Śledź. This man had come from the United States to attend the Jagiellonian University in Kraków before the war. Either the student or the teacher proved inadequate, since this Latin instruction could not be absorbed fully. In fact, it proved to be my only deficiency on the matriculation exam I later took for admission to the University of London.

In return for these wonderful opportunities, I began teaching English to young American citizens interned with me. They had all been born in the United States and then taken as infants or small children by parents to their native countries in Eastern Europe. These young men had never had an opportunity to learn the English language. What a thrill it was for me to share the knowledge that had come from my American schooling.

Among my students at Tittmoning was a young boy, several years junior to me, who had been interned with his father. Conrad M. Curtiss, after being repatriated, earned a degree in mechanical engineering at the University of Illinois, worked on the Apollo space program, and later joined the Lockheed Corporation. I admired his drive to succeed and am also proud of the small part I played in sustaining the ambition to continue his education.

"Schoolwork" and "medieval castle" notwithstanding, we were still prisoners and lived as such. An M.D. from Puerto Rico who had studied medicine in Brussels analyzed the caloric content of the food provided to us internees. We were subsisting on *ersatz* (synthetic) coffee and a slice of sawdust-fortified bread with *ersatz* jam for breakfast; a bowl of "thin" soup with a few floating cabbage leaves at lunch; and another slice of bread with "margarine" and the same coffee in the evening. No fruit, vegetables (other than cabbage leaves), meat, or fish, ever! This added up to a maximum of 600 calories per day, which was leading to slow starvation.

Fortunately, the internees did receive irregular deliveries of American Red Cross food packages. These almost certainly saved our lives. However, the huge railroad yards at Munich were being bombed frequently at this time (during the day by the U.S. Air Force and at night by the British RAF). This meant that relief as well as German supplies were being literally stopped in their tracks. All of us cheered whenever we heard the explosions, however, even though we knew full well that no food parcels could then be delivered to us for some time. I will always be grateful to the American Red Cross for the hope it offered, as well as its humanitarian efforts.

At one point, something most unusual occurred: Two young Germans joined our complement of civilian internees. Dressed in *Hitler Jugend* (youth) uniforms, albeit without the insignia, which had been torn off, they told us that they held Costa Rican passports. As neither one could speak Spanish, it was likely that their parents had purchased those documents for them at that country's embassy in Berlin.

One morning neither one of the newcomers appeared in the courtyard for the usual body count. The non-commissioned officer had the nickname of *"Fünf-a-fünf"* (five by five), because he would run back and forth, shouting those words to line us up in that fashion. When the two German youths could not be found on the grounds, a search began by guards throughout the castle.

All of us hoped and prayed that the young men were well on their way to Switzerland, since they both spoke fluent German. Unfortunately, they were discovered hiding in one of the attics. Dragged down the spiral staircase and beaten mercilessly, they were taken away in a black *Gestapo* sedan. We assumed, since both were German Jews, that they would be sent to one of the death camps.

Our internment camp at Tittmoning included several Jewish intellectuals from Eastern Europe who also had managed to acquire, some way or another, Latin American passports. Although known to many of us, this information never reached the German camp authorities. In this way, these men survived the Second World War. They were all well educated, as well as cultured, and must have made extraordinary contributions in South America after the war.

One evening, we prisoners were awakened by the arrival of another large black sedan in the castle courtyard. I climbed up to the fourth level of the stacked wooden bunk beds and peered through the window. Out came Heinrich Himmler, the dreaded head of the *Gestapo*. I could see the silver skull insignia on his cap. He went inside to speak with the camp commandant.

Immediately a rumor started circulating about an imminent transfer of all internees to a redoubt, then allegedly under construction in the Bavarian Alps for Hitler's last stand. We would become hostages, to be executed just before the fortress fell to the U.S. Army. This, of course, did not ever happen. What actually occurred involved our transfer in May 1944 to another camp at Laufen, also in Upper Bavaria. It was located across the Salzach River from the village of Oberndorf, where the famous carol

"Silent Night" had been composed by the local parish priest. Here, I could write and receive a limited number of letters.

The new camp was populated by British civilian internees from the Channel Islands and other German-occupied territories in Western Europe. By the time I arrived, these well-educated men already had a school in operation, run by former professors and civil servants. Some of these gentlemen had simply been vacationing on Jersey or Guernsey, when these two islands were overrun by the *Wehrmacht* after the fall of France in June 1940.

The inmates totaled approximately 1,000 men, about half British and half American. There were twenty-five teachers at Laufen; they lectured on mathematics, English grammar and literature, history, geography, art, mechanical and artistic drawing, engineering, economics, pharmacology, navigation, French, Spanish, German, Latin, etc. Students ranged from sixteen to sixty years of age. Many were studying for examinations in camp, some for "London Matriculation." Twenty languages were spoken.

Although internees had no access even to German newspapers, the British in Laufen must have been listening to a clandestine shortwave radio. Every evening, between supper and "lights out" at 10 p.m., a person from their part of the camp would appear in our building and brief me on the news of the day. I would memorize their news updates and pass them on to other Americans in the camp. In this way, at least we knew the overall picture of the war from the BBC. That proved to be a real morale booster, especially after the war's tide had turned in favor of the Allies.

Three of the British internees later compiled a book about life in the camp at Laufen. Here again, what starving people remembered most vividly was the food. The German quartermaster would provide daily rations of vegetables and "very little meat." This would be transformed by internee cooks into a thick soup at noon and a thin soup for supper. The worst meals were served on Saturday evenings and Sunday mornings: "two potatoes boiled in their jackets and a couple of spoonfuls of sauerkraut."[2] At least they offered a little more nutrition than the "food" of the previous camp.

---

2. F. B. Riggs, F. G. Leoni, and J. Whittaker (comps.), *The Bird Cage: ILAG-VII* (Hälsingborg: Aktiebolaget Boktryck, 1945), pp. 64–65.

The Two Warsaw Uprisings

I knew about establishment of a ghetto by the Germans in Warsaw at the beginning of 1942. They had imprisoned behind high walls as many as 400,000 Polish Jews. All of these people were forced to wear the yellow Star of David. Prior to the Second World War, only the poorest among them had lived in that particular neighborhood. During the night of 21–22 July, 1942, German elite *Waffen SS* troops began killing Jews indiscriminately in order to terrorize those still living in the ghetto prior to their total deportation to death camps. I was still "free" in Warsaw at the time and learned about these horrors from adults whom I tutored in English.

The Germans falsely promised deportees that they would be transported to safe areas, where they would be offered work and lodging. The underground Home Army resistance movement, fearful of disaster, offered the Jews weapons and ammunition, instead. The elderly leaders of the community, however, rejected these proposals. They believed it would be impossible for the Germans to kill almost half a million people.[3]

Many Jewish children were smuggled out of the ghetto and survived with Christian families that "adopted" them. Most adults, however, ended their deportation at the Treblinka death camp. They were told to enter shower rooms, which turned out to be the infamous gas chambers. However, tens of thousands of Jews had hidden below ground and were prepared to fight. By then, I had been arrested by the *Gestapo* and incarcerated at the Pawiak prison before being transported to the first internment camp in Germany.

The clandestine Jewish Combat Organization (ŻOB—*Żydowska Organizacja Bojowa*) decided to offer resistance. Just before Christmas, a delegation from ŻOB contacted the Home Army for weapons. Revolvers, rifles, machine guns with ammunition and about one thousand hand grenades as well as explosives for production of mines were delivered into the ghetto. Jews also began systematically to rob German supply trains. The Home Army showed the ŻOB how to produce anti-tank explosives with a mixture of gasoline and sulfuric acid in bottles.

At the beginning of 1943, the Germans resumed their attempt to exterminate all remaining Jews. They were surprised to be met with bullets

---

3. See Tadeusz Bór-Komorowski, *Armia Podziemna* (London: Studium Polski Podziemnej, 1979), fourth edition, pp. 99–101.

and hand grenades from the remaining 80,000 inhabitants of the ghetto. Deportations temporarily stopped. On 29 March, all Jews of American extraction were "invited" by the Germans to report for transfer abroad to a neutral country. Those who trusted this promise were taken, instead, to the Jewish cemetery and shot. The *Gestapo* then designated 19 April as the final date to liquidate the ghetto. The night before, German soldiers began pulling Jews out of their apartments. The invaders were met with bullets and hand grenades, supplied by the Home Army.

Next came the elite SS troops, who encountered machine gun fire at close range and were forced to retreat. German armored vehicles commenced firing into homes at point-blank range. Finally, artillery batteries began to destroy entire buildings. In return, Jews set fire to factories within the ghetto that had produced German uniforms, boots, etc. After three days of fierce fighting, the SS began burning down one house after another.

The Home Army organized several assaults in the German rear, with the purpose of providing open spaces through which Jews could flee the ghetto. After these were blocked, the Home Army occupied other exit points throughout the underground sewage system. Escapees were taken to a forest near Otwock and then hidden throughout the region. Many of them continued to fight as members of the Home Army resistance.

The last week of May, after Germans had completely leveled the ghetto, no sound could be heard from that neighborhood.[4] None of this was known to us at the time in the first internment camp at Tittmoning, but when we later learned about it, we could readily imagine the brutality and ferocity of these events.

During that time, the underground Home Army had been preparing for an armed uprising. Toward the end of July 1944, the Red Army offensive had pushed the Germans almost to the Vistula river. The Soviet forces already controlled six airfields in Poland, one of which was located only twenty minutes' flying time from Warsaw. Russian radio transmissions openly called for a Polish uprising, and it seemed that the hour for liberation had arrived.

General Tadeusz Bór-Komorowski, commander-in-chief of the Home Army, issued an order for this to commence at 5 p.m. on 1 August 1944. From that moment, however, the Soviet Army stood still. Stalin refused to drop any weapons, ammunition, or food for the 40,000 men and 4,200

---

4. Ibid., pp. 95–106.

women insurgents who had taken on the fight. When he finally relented, no parachutes were attached to the supplies, making the drops a total loss. The Germans utilized this period of inactivity to transfer the troops facing the Soviets and redirect them into the battle for Warsaw.

This wildly unequal struggle lasted sixty-four days, with the Red Army occupying the other side of the Vistula and refusing to move or render any assistance to the Polish soldiers. Even the RAF, which flew the long distance from England to drop supplies by parachute, was refused landing privileges at the Soviet-held airfields just across the river. Many of the British and Polish pilots lost their lives when German anti-aircraft artillery shot down their bombers on these flights from or back to England.

During 4 and 5 October 1944, the remnants of the Home Army surrendered to the Germans, who had agreed to treat them as prisoners of war under the Geneva Convention. It has been estimated that two-thirds of Warsaw city was completely leveled in the course of German military operations. The "official" destruction was calculated, as follows:

Table 2: Destruction of Warsaw

Time Frame	Percentage
1. During September 1939	9.5
2. Destruction of ghetto, 1943–1944	15.0
3. Warsaw uprising, 1944	34.3
4. Planned destruction by withdrawing Germans (5 October 1944–1 January 1945)	7.9
TOTAL	66.7

Source: Bór-Komorowski, *Armia Podziemna*, p. 353.

Rumors, hyperbole, and propaganda run rampant in wartime, and not all reports should be believed. However, a man who suffered torture at the hands of the *Gestapo* and survived was sent by the *Armia Krajowa* to England and then to the United States during World War II. He had been able to enter the Warsaw ghetto clandestinely and talk with Jewish leaders. Upon reaching London, this courageous individual told Foreign Secretary Anthony Eden about the transportation of Jews to death camps. He subsequently met with President Franklin D. Roosevelt in the United States. Neither one of these statesmen did anything to help the Jews.[5] Perhaps the sheer barbarity of the Germans was still beyond imagination.

The internees at the Laufen camp did not know any of the foregoing details. We did realize, however, that the Nazis were completely ruthless. On one occasion, a USAF pilot (whose plane had been shot down during a bombing raid over Munich) landed by parachute on a tree not far from our camp. Instead of helping him disentangle and climb down for transportation to a POW camp, one of the brown shirts (SA, or Stormtroopers), simply pulled out his gun and shot the American through the head. The crowd of Bavarian farmers cheered, according to a German witness who relayed the information to one of his contacts in our camp. The story may have been passed on to us to discourage attempts at escape or to demoralize us further. In either case, it had the desired effect.

Continuing Life and Education

Given the war and my time in prison and the camps, I had never actually finished high school. Fortunately, the second camp at Laufen provided an opportunity to fill the huge gaps in my education. One of my favorite tutors was David A. Savage, a civil servant, whom my wife and I later visited when the war was over. Through him, I was able to catch up in history, English, mathematics, and the rest.

As the war was ending for us, a miracle happened: before being repatriated to the United States, all qualified American civilian internees at ILAG VII-Z had the opportunity to "sit" for the University of London matriculation exam at the camp in Laufen. Results subsequently were received from England, with an unexpected welcoming letter that I could enroll as a student after the war, provided that I improved my scores in Latin during the first year of study there.

Little did we know how providence had been watching over the entire family. After the arrests of myself and my father, mother and sister Barbara had moved to the foothills of the Carpathian mountains in 1942. They lived in constant fear that Barbara would be taken away during one of the periodic round-ups by German police and sent to the *Reich* as a slave

---

5. Jan Karski, *Story of a Secret State* (Boston: Houghton Mifflin, 1944), pp. 320–354 and 380–389.

laborer. One time German soldiers broke into their home at midnight, thoroughly looted the place, and threatened to kill both mother and child unless they revealed the hiding place of nonexistent family heirlooms. Fortunately, a singularly compassionate German sergeant intervened, and the two were saved. This man probably had a family back in Germany, perhaps also a wife and daughter.

Mother and Barbara were taken, two years later, to an internment camp for American women at Liebenau near Lake Constance on the German side of the Swiss border. I knew about this and prayed that we would go home together. They were, indeed, picked up by the same repatriation train on which I was traveling. What a joy to see them again after so many years of forced separation! It was in Switzerland that the exchange took place for German civilians who had been interned in the United States.

This exchange of civilian internees had been based upon an agreement between the U.S. and German governments that neither side would be permitted to accept any of the repatriated citizens into its respective armed forces. This obviously worked against the latter, since Berlin was suffering from a manpower shortage.

After several nights of sleeping on straw in a Swiss high school gymnasium, for which hotel prices were later charged, the group boarded a train that would take us across southern France (already liberated by American troops). From there, we would travel to Spain and finally Portugal. In Lisbon, the former internees then boarded the Swedish passenger ship *M.S. Gripsholm* on the last exchange voyage she would make. Less than three months later, the war in Europe ended in May 1945 with the German surrender.

The U.S. government had prepaid for the "hotel" accommodations in Switzerland as well as steamship tickets and railroad fare from New York to Detroit, Michigan. All of these charges were reimbursed in full by my sister Marie and her husband Harold. Mother and Barbara then lived with them and their young son Tommy until Dad returned several months after the war had ended. Those four years had certainly taken their toll on my poor father. Prior to his arrest in May 1941, he had weighed 179 pounds; on release, his weight had dropped to a mere 95 pounds.

For me, the return to America also meant a reunion with my dear friends, the Warfields, in their home at Frederick, Maryland. I immediately took a job as a manual laborer at Hood College. This involved outdoor work on the campus grounds, which helped me regain my strength. The most I could hope for, however, without a high school diploma or a trade, would have been to become a carpenter's apprentice at one of the Levittowns being built along the East Coast.

If I were to have the life I wanted, I would have to find a way to go to school. That situation certainly made me appreciate my father's struggles decades earlier as he first tried to make his way in America! But the lucky star that had been shining down on all of us continued to light my way. Unexpectedly, the door of opportunity was about to swing wide open for me.

Chapter 2

College and Graduate School

Just as they had done in Europe, Dr. and Mrs. Warfield once again made a normal life possible for me back in the United States. This time they had guidance and opportunity to offer, as well as more of their great kindness and compassion.

Dr. Warfield had been graduated from Dickinson College in Carlisle, Pennsylvania. At his suggestion and with his assistance, I applied to Dickinson to begin undergraduate work.

My admission to college anywhere would have been problematic. I had never completed high school. After the war, the *gimnazjum* I had attended was no longer in existence, and thus, nobody could provide me with a transcript of grades. Instead, I had only the letter of acceptance ("Certificate of Provisional Matriculation") from the University of London, as described previously, and my own burning desire to study.

The admissions committee at Dickinson carefully examined this document and gave weight to my wartime experiences as well as the solid personal recommendation put forth by Dr. Warfield. In the end, the Dickinson administrators suggested only that I make up my deficiency in Latin by taking two years of further study in that language. They then admitted me, and I, happily armed with their full tuition scholarship, a bunk bed in a dormitory room, and plenty of chances for part-time jobs after classes, set out on my new life.

Days at Dickinson

By the close of that first summer term, I had already made substantial academic progress. In addition to the eighteen units of credit just earned,

I had received twelve more hours for my competence in German. While the German I had learned was hardly that of Goethe or Schiller, it was completely adequate to pass oral and written examinations. Later, this knowledge would prove useful in many respects. By the fall of 1945, therefore, I commenced studies as a sophomore. Not surprisingly, I was determined to make up for lost opportunities and was driven to excel.

The outstanding Latin requirement was soon satisfied. The professor, Dr. William Bishop, also proved to be an astute adviser. He steered me away from applying for a Rhodes scholarship, for instance (perhaps recognizing that my interest in Oxford was not so much academic as it was based on my interest in the country that had offered me college admission during my internment days). He and my English and history professors (John Hepler, Herbert Wing, Jr., and Whitfield Bell, Jr.) all encouraged me to read widely, write regularly, and be precise and accurate in my research.

Professor Hepler wrote an unsolicited letter by my Dad about me. He said, among other things, that "Dick probably needs less study than his colleagues, and yet he studies hard. . . .Dick stands head and shoulders above all the other students I have taught. Incidentally, his English is almost perfect." This letter delighted my father, who had been quietly anxious about my ability to readjust and get started at school. I found out about it, though, when my father then wanted to know, "What's this *almost* perfect about?!"

My willingness to do all the required class readings and take voluminous notes also made me the "man to know" at my fraternity house. Here, the family "gene" for tutoring seemed to express itself, and I was happy to help my fellow fraternity brothers cram for Professor Wing's world history exams. Having been blessed with a good memory, I found I had a talent for recalling details. Once, for instance, when I alone could name correctly all the official titles (plural) of Emperor Haile Selassie, my classmates burst into applause.

I had been very pleased when the Kappa Sigma fraternity invited me to become one of its pledges. I accepted, because Dr. Warfield had been a "Kappa Sig" while at Dickinson. That first night spent in a bunk bed at the frat house included an unbelievable noise level, the likes of which I (who had spent time in a cell with fifty other inmates) had never before experienced. The next morning, I went to Dean Ernest A. Vuilleumier's office and requested permission to return to the dormitory space that I had occupied during the previous summer. The dean graciously granted my request, after hearing the reason.

I really could not blame my fraternity brothers for "letting off steam." The great majority of them had served in the armed forces during World War II. They had been pilots, armored vehicle drivers, infantrymen, and so on. Our Kappa Sigma chapter president, William F. Borda, had been a gunner on a tank. Many of these veterans kept a bottle of bourbon on the chest of drawers in their rooms. In those days, there were no regulations that banned liquor from fraternity houses; such rules could not have been implemented, in any event.

Probably because of this atmosphere, I went out for football and joined the junior varsity. The coach put me into only one varsity game, at left tackle. We were playing Washington and Jefferson College from Washington, Pennsylvania. After the snap, the ball was handed to the W&J fullback, who must have weighed at least two hundred pounds, if not more. This giant came rushing in my direction and knocked me flat on my rear end. He made a substantial gain before being tackled. The coach immediately pulled me out of the line and sent me back to the junior varsity after that game. What an experience!

I spent the last two years in Biddle House, on the corner of Louther and College streets. This residence was at the edge of the main campus and just across the street from the library. My roommates included two other Kappa Sigs, both of whom subsequently were graduated from Dickinson School of Law and became practicing attorneys. The third student, a member of Phi Delta Theta, had a quiet and studious demeanor. During the senior year, I arranged for my first class to meet at 11:30 a.m., which allowed me to "hit the books" until 4 a.m. every weekday night.

In the chemistry class taught by Dean Vuilleumier, I could follow the lectures fairly well, although I frankly had little enthusiasm for the subject. At one point, the professor asked what the word *Zylinder* meant in the English language. I raised my hand and translated literally: "top hat." That was correct, of course, but for purposes of chemistry, it meant "cylinder," which has a similar shape. My response impressed the dean with my knowledge of the German language, which he, as a Swiss, spoke fluently. Activities in the laboratory did not excite me. I received a "B" for this required course of study.

I received only a "C" in College Algebra and a "D" in Plane Trigonometry (both required for graduation); these were my two lowest grades. No credit was given for the latter. I had fulfilled the requirement and did not have to take trigonometry over again. However, this experience made me realize that even if I had wanted to, I would not have been able to follow in my Dad's footsteps and become a mechanical (let alone an aeronautical) engineer. My talents lay in a different direction.

One day, at the beginning of our junior year, Professor Wing invited me and his son Gilman to the office for a chat. He suggested that each of us consider working toward eligibility for election to Phi Beta Kappa, the national scholastic honor fraternity. In addition, if we completed a special research project and a substantial term paper, we might qualify for graduation with honors.

Somehow, we succeeded at both, because those were the two distinctions that accompanied our B.A. degrees, which were conferred in June 1948. That ceremony took place exactly three calendar years after I had enrolled as a freshman at Dickinson College. Gilman Wing went on to graduate school, received an M.A. degree, and then chose a diplomatic career as a foreign service officer.

When notified about election to Phi Beta Kappa by "Brother" Rogers, a Kappa Sig who served as an instructor in the chemistry department's laboratory, I asked what the gold key would cost. I then refused the invitation with regret, because my meager budget had already been allocated for essentials. Mr. Rogers offered to pay for the key and be reimbursed after graduation, when the money became available. What a wonderful fraternity brother!

Another one of my friends at Dickinson was Andrew Wilson Green, a student of the law school, which was separate from although adjacent physically to the campus. After only two years at Princeton, he had taken and passed the U.S. foreign service examination. Instead of becoming a diplomat, however, Andy (after only two years of college) entered law school, from which he was graduated with distinction, and then went into the practice of law. What a fabulous achievement!

The only coed I dated was Elsbeth Walch, a foreign student from Switzerland. We attended a few free concerts. At one of these, my eyes filled with tears when the "Warsaw Concerto" was being played. Not able to afford a corsage, I never asked Elsbeth to a college dance. Besides, I had no experience with that kind of recreation. When told that she would be returning to Geneva, I kissed her on the cheek and gave her a hug. We had always conversed in German, which I would miss.

I feel a strong tie to Dickinson College as well as to Kappa Sigma. One of my fraternity brothers, Walter E. Beach, received his degree in 1956. Although much younger than I, we have maintained contact over the years. A native of Washington, D.C., he worked as an administrator at the prestigious Brookings Institution for many years and is now a senior fellow at an educational foundation in the District of Columbia. We see each other whenever I am on the East Coast. Another graduate of Dickinson with whom I am in contact is Colonel Sherwood D. Goldberg, class of 1963. He served on the staff of General Alexander M. Haig, Jr., in Vietnam as well as becoming his aide when the latter was Secretary of State.

As soon as able to do so financially, I began donating money to Dickinson. This did not amount to much at first, although some property in northern Indiana went to the college through me as part of an inheritance. Education, of course, brought eventual financial stability as well as other kinds of good fortune in my life. But frankly it is only now that I can look back with some nostalgia at the many odd jobs during my college years. "Tray scraper and washer" in the dormitory dining hall did not pay very well, for example, but for someone who had survived near-starvation during the war, the free half watermelon for dessert was a bonus beyond measure. Similar work at the women's dining hall also gave me insight regarding the idiosyncrasies of my fellow students. For instance, the senior "hasher" there would not allow members of his crew to earn more than $600 per year on the job. More than that amount would legally have to be reported to the IRS, and this fellow was determined both to avoid paperwork and to keep all of us from having to pay taxes to the federal government.

Yet another part-time job helped me to determine what I most definitely did not wish to do in life. This was my work as an orderly at the county hospital outside of Carlisle. The M.D. who supervised me was nice enough: he would include me in evening rounds during my 4 p.m.–midnight shift and carefully explain the nature and details of each patient's illness. Nonetheless, employment at this hospital did not excite me at all. It was with some relief that I was finally able to secure work as a salesman at a local department store, instead.

Although happy with all of my work experiences and opportunities, I have never forgotten that it was due to the generosity of my friends the Warfields that college became possible for me. With them in mind, Jadwiga and I were pleased to establish the Hania and Gaither Warfield Scholarship Fund at Dickinson a few years ago (its first recipient, international studies major Elizabeth S. Chassin, will graduate in 2003). With eventual donation of part of our residual estate to this fund, we hope to make additional prizes available for such students also in the future.

Yale University

Having worked hard at Dickinson, I had a solid foundation for graduate school. As luck would have it, Yale had just announced a new program in international studies. I applied for admission as well as for a scholarship, not really expecting to receive the latter, even though my Graduate Record Examination scores were high. The notice of admission arrived, together with a letter that I had been awarded a $600 fellowship for the following academic year. It occurred to me that I could live quite comfortably on $50 per month for a full twelve months. What a fantastic opportunity!

After arrival in New Haven, Ct., by bus, I presented the letter at the bursar's office. The official told me that $450 would be deducted for tuition and then asked how I would like to receive the remainder. *Sotto voce*, I replied, "Fifty dollars a month?" I soon found a small, furnished bedroom for five dollars per week, rented from an elderly widow, across the railroad tracks in the Italian neighborhood.

The landlady also rented most of the second floor to a dentist, and we would have discussions about world politics. Although frequently disagreeing, a friendship soon developed. I will never forget one conversation, when he quoted *"What is hateful to yourself, do not do to others!* That is the whole Torah; the rest is commentary!" When I told this gentleman that I would be leaving at the end of the academic year, he offered me a loan to cover full tuition for study toward a Ph.D. degree. I remembered the shoemaker who had helped Dad on the lower east side of New York but politely refused the offer.

At that time, I was an expert at making do. A large bowl of spaghetti at an Italian restaurant across the main street cost only 50 cents, so I became a pasta lover. I would make a sandwich and take a thermos bottle of cold milk for lunch each day. Two part-time jobs in the university library, evenings, and at a local drugstore as a cashier, on weekends, helped make ends meet. I also worked as a guide for groups of senior high school students who would visit companies in New Haven regarding career opportunities.

I came to graduate school with a developed sense of appreciation for the twists of fate in recent world history. After all, during the previous decade, I had been part of the group consigned by Hitler to be the slave laborers for the Reich. The whole of Poland, of course, had been intended to serve as a prison labor system. Some six million Poles, half of them

Jews, had died as a result of foreign occupation and oppression during the Second World War. I had also seen, first hand, that the "workers' paradise" promised by communism was not being built in the USSR or its satellites. For these reasons, the fate of Eastern Europe was a natural—and passionate—concern of mine. And Yale had outstanding professors to encourage and develop my interests in history and foreign policy.

Professor William T. R. Fox stands out in my memory. At first, I could not comprehend the specialized vocabulary used in the seminar on "Introduction to Power Analysis." It was filled with words I had never heard before as an undergraduate. From the long list of assigned articles and books, however, I quickly began to comprehend that I would have to learn and use expressions that were completely new to me. Professor Arnold Wolfers offered a seminar on "Foreign Policy and the Strategy of Peace," which continued on the foundation built by Professor Fox. From them, I gained appreciation for the "science" part of political science.

Another well-known scholar, George Vernadsky, who taught Russian history at Yale, had fled to Czechoslovakia after the 1917 Bolshevik revolution and arrived in the United States before World War II. His graduate seminar on "Russian Foreign Policy, 1850–1950" lasted a full year. I expected at least half of it to deal with the Soviet period. To my dismay, however, Professor Vernadsky never even reached World War I. Although we did not cover the historical years of greatest interest to me, I did gain a solid appreciation for events of the nineteenth century.

Yale was not at all an ivory tower, however. Professor Frederick C. Barghoorn was later arrested by the KGB "as a spy," having spent years earlier as a press attaché at the American embassy in Moscow. President John F. Kennedy responded to Dr. Barghoorn's arrest by declaring that the U.S. government did not use American academicians for espionage and demanded Barghoorn's immediate release. In response, Nikita S. Khrushchev replied in public that he could not comprehend why such a fuss was being made over a mere professor. This Soviet leader had boasted in one of his speeches that only under communism could a peasant like himself, with four years of elementary school, become leader of the country! Somehow, this argument did not impress the Harvard-educated Kennedy or the rest of the "attentive" public in the United States.

During my year in New Haven, Professor Barghoorn taught a graduate seminar on "Government and Politics of the Soviet Union." I wrote a paper for him about the political administration of the Red Army. This required a visit to the Library of Congress in Washington, D.C., for research in

Russian-language materials not available in New Haven or at the New York Public Library. I received an "Honors" grade in this seminar, which thrilled and encouraged me.

Another prominent professor at Yale was Bernard Brodie, author of *The Absolute Weapon* and strategic thinker par excellence. He taught a seminar on "Problems of Strategic Analysis." Brodie once invited a visiting Canadian general to one of our afternoon sessions. Most of the students in this class were active duty military officers, sent to receive an M.A. degree. They all wore civilian clothes. During the discussion, First Lt. James Garrett was addressed as "captain," Captain Roger Hilsman became a "major," and Major Jack Dwan was promoted to "colonel" by Professor Brodie. Garrett later taught as a professor at a college in Pennsylvania, and Hilsman served as assistant secretary of state for East Asian affairs. I may have been the only student present without any such rank, since my military service was yet to come. The grade received from Dr. Brodie also was "Honors."

Although I passed the written and oral exams for the M.A. degree at Yale, I had a bad moment during—of all things—the German language proficiency test. Professor Gabriel Almond, later of Stanford University, passed out an article from a German newspaper that reported on forthcoming national elections in Italy. We would have to translate the text into English. The article began, "Die Würfel sind geworfen!"—literally, "the dice have been tossed." Surely this was not an article about gambling in Italian politics! Then, all of the "remedial" Latin came to my rescue, and I recognized these German words as Caesar's famous "Alea iacta est" as his troops crossed the Rubicon into Italy. The rest was a breeze, and I received a very high mark. My own die had also been cast!

Overall, my final grades at Yale were a source of pride and reassurance. As a person who had once become reconciled that he would never get to college, I had proven myself alongside some of the brightest graduate students from all over the United States. That said, however, it was clearly time to have a personal life. And not long after that, my "lucky star" led me to meet the extraordinary individual who would have so monumental an influence on me "until the end of time."

Meeting Jadwiga

The remarkable woman who was to become my wife, Jadwiga [first name], was born in the Kaszuby lake region and attended private school at Grudziądz in northern Poland. As a teenager, she demonstrated natural ability with languages and became fluent in German. With the occupation of Poland during World War II, Jadwiga served as a teenage courier for the Polish resistance movement and deftly tapped into the telephone lines of the local Gestapo headquarters, reporting on all their incoming and outgoing calls.

Although arrested and tortured for information, she nevertheless revealed nothing about the activities of the underground. Finally, she was sent to a slave labor camp. Here, she worked on the assembly line at a German submarine construction plant at Danzig (now again Gdańsk). There, too, Jadwiga engaged in sabotage by producing flawed screws that did not fit properly into parts of the U-Boot. Other Polish prisoners would add sand to the ball bearings or other sensitive areas.

Liberated when the *Wehrmacht* withdrew from that area of northern Poland and before the Red Army had reached this part of the Baltic Sea coast, Jadwiga joined a group of former POWs from England who had walked out of their camp when German guards fled before the advancing Russians. They provided her with a British army uniform and false identification papers as "Nurse Nelly Smith." In this way, on the ex-POW train she reached Odessa, where a British troop transport awaited the group.

Her severe case of double pneumonia necessitated that the ship make port in Naples. Jadwiga was transferred to a local hospital and then to a displaced persons camp. It was at the Aversa DP camp that my father met this young woman, who was now working as a nurse. He had been waiting for repatriation but was delayed because demobilized U.S. military personnel had priority for return to the United States. He gave Jadwiga the address of my sister, Marie, in Michigan and urged her to contact him if she ever came to the United States.

When Jadwiga arrived in New York several years after the war in Europe had ended, she did just that. My father then immediately wrote to me. He suggested that I drive to New York from Washington, D.C., to meet her, then find a way for Jadwiga to receive a scholarship to resume her studies in the United States. Despite my own success with school, I did not really have much "pull." Nonetheless, I decided to do my utmost for this young woman who had suffered so much during the war.

It was love at first sight! The image of a slender, willowy blonde with blue eyes and an engaging smile will always remain in my mind. I could not understand why she was turning on all the lights in the living room. She apparently must have been affected by something in my demeanor, as well. In any event, we hit it off exceptionally well from the very start. Instead of trying to arrange a scholarship to college for Jadwiga, I proposed after several dates and then suggested that we travel to Michigan so she could see Dad again and meet my mother and my sisters.

She agreed and, during that visit, we were married in Wyandotte. It was years later before we could take our honeymoon at Niagara Falls, however. But since that time, Jadwiga has remained the woman of my dreams, an inspiration and a partner who helped us achieve whatever we did accomplish in life. In addition to becoming the mother of our two daughters, Monica and Christina, she worked full-time as a nurse at the University of Michigan hospital during my graduate studies there. Later, Jadwiga also studied English, American history and government as well as other subjects at George Washington University, when we lived in the nation's capital. She subsequently received a bachelor's degree with distinction from Emory University in Atlanta. No wonder that she passed her test for American citizenship with flying colors! Her earlier diplomas in language and literature had been awarded by the Sorbonne as well as by the universities in Munich and Pisa. She is fluent in English, French, German, Italian, and Polish!

After we moved to California, Jadwiga worked professionally as a research analyst for Stanford Research Institute (SRI International) and subsequently at Sun Microsystems, both located in Silicon Valley. She is a person of many talents and tremendous character.

More Graduate Study

Although married and looking forward to a family, Jadwiga and I both decided that I should continue my graduate studies. For this, we moved to Ann Arbor and the University of Michigan. It seemed as if life had come full circle, from six years of elementary school in this small town to enrollment in the Ph.D. program through the department of political science. Resumption of my former residence in the state of Michigan (interrupted by World War II and its aftermath) avoided payment of much higher fees charged to out-of-state students, and for this we were both grateful. The difference in tuition was, indeed, substantial.

We rented a room near campus, and Jadwiga began full-time work at the university hospital. In this way, she became the major breadwinner. I also had a job at the checkout desk every evening in the Chemistry Department library. We lived frugally and somehow managed to stay solvent. I find that even today I still prefer to take a sandwich from home for lunch!

My Ph.D. program required demonstrated competency in yet another foreign language. For many reasons, the obvious choice for me was Russian. With my background in Polish, I accomplished this without too much difficulty.

During oral and written examinations for the Ph.D. degree, I performed well. Before the orals, I waited in the political science departmental secretary's office for Professor James K. Pollock, the chairman. When the latter arrived, he asked me whether I would like something to drink. I replied, *"Ein Schnaps, bitte!"* We both laughed. He had meant water, of course.

The written test in Russian history was given in that department's office, where I spent the entire afternoon writing brief essays on questions covering events of the previous one hundred years. The professor in charge (André Lobanov-Rostovsky) liked to be called "Professor Lobanov," it was rumored, because a relative (Prince Lobanov) had been foreign minister of the tsar when the so-called Lobanov Treaty was signed with Japan.

Several days later, I happened to see Professor Lobanov walking toward me on the campus. I asked about the results of my written examination. The answer was in general quite positive, although he told me that the bibliographic question had been inadequately covered. It involved primary source materials "in *foreign* languages consulted by the student, with a brief paragraph about each one." I had done this for French, German, and Russian language materials.

Professor Lobanov seemed perplexed why nothing had been written in my answers about basic sources that had appeared in English. I replied that English was my *native* language, which by definition excluded such primary collections from my answer. Professor Lobanov thought for a moment and then replied simply, "I see." In fact, he may have been impressed by this response.

A most noteworthy seminar was offered on the government and politics of West Germany. This was taught by Professor Pollock and assisted by Henry Bretton. This man later received his doctorate and subsequently taught political science at a State University of New York (SUNY) campus. One of the term papers I wrote had to be submitted for the seminar on a certain date. I began typing it the night before, with one finger of each hand. This ordeal lasted until 6 a.m. When Mr. Bretton told me later that I had received an "A+," the effort and the ache in my fingers seemed eminently worthwhile.

Professor Pollock had served as political adviser to General Lucius D. Clay, U.S. Army, in the American Zone of occupation, after the end of World War II. When U.S. Senator Arthur Vandenburg died, there were rumors that our departmental chairman might receive a recess appointment to succeed him. That this did not come to pass was actually a fortunate event for me: Professor Pollock became my mentor and provided excellent advice on career opportunities, as well as letters of recommendation. A few years later, he asked me to teach at Michigan, provided that the state legislature would vote additional funds for a new position dealing with Eastern Europe. Unfortunately, the lawmakers decided against that increase.

Faculty members on my doctoral committee included Walter O. Filley (chairman), Lawrence Preuss, James K. Pollock (co-chairman), Edward S. Brown, James H. Meisel, and Russell H. Fifield. I had a straight "A" record in all eight seminars, with an "A+" for the "International Law Survey" compensating the "A-" for "Scope and Methodology in Political Science." Professor Meisel supervised the writing of my dissertation, which later became a book.

One of the pleasant circumstances of graduate school at the University of Michigan involved the proximity of my parents as well as both sisters, Marie and Barbara. The latter two lived with their families in Wyandotte and Livonia, respectively, only forty-five minutes to an hour's drive from Ann Arbor. We could, thus, visit them from time to time on a holiday or weekend. These outings offered a welcome break from the seminar and study routine.

It was in Ann Arbor that our first daughter, Monica, was born at the University of Michigan hospital where Jadwiga had been working as a nurse. Because of her employment, all charges for the birth were waived. What a break for us! I now required a full-time position to support a family. Responding to an announcement about professional positions at the U.S.

Department of State, where knowledge of two Slavic languages was required, I requested that my name be placed on the roster of applicants for an intelligence research analyst position.

I was offered, and accepted, this position and while working full-time also commenced research for my thesis at the Library of Congress in Washington, D.C. Professor Meisel, in the meantime, had moved to Italy for his sabbatical. This coincided with the writing of my dissertation. Dr. Meisel would receive my draft chapters as they were completed, for critical comments and suggestions. Nothing ever was lost, either in the United States or Italian mails, although I always kept a carbon copy of every chapter as insurance. Completion of the manuscript coincided with the end of Professor Meisel's sabbatical year. I owe him a debt of gratitude for his conscientious advice, which certainly took many hours from his own research project.

Eventually, it was time to prepare a defense of the doctoral dissertation on "The Political Framework of Communist Poland" back at the University of Michigan. All of my professors on the committee would be invited to this event, and I attempted to be ready for any possible question. Most sources for the thesis were in German, Polish, or Russian as well as a few memoirs that had been translated into English. My emphasis on primary source documentation could be seen from the fourteen pages, single-spaced in the printed book's bibliography, when it appeared several years later.

The friendly welcome I received when walking into the examination room made me optimistic. Obviously, the typescript had been thoroughly read over by the professors. They appeared to be quite impressed with the amount of primary source research I had done for this dissertation. Eventually, it became a 300-page printed volume, subsequently published by Louisiana State University Press in 1962 and reprinted by Greenwood Press in 1975.

As I recall, my examining committee also seemed to know that I had already been promoted from analyst to intelligence research specialist at the U.S. Department of State. This probably meant something in my favor, too.

The defense I feared might become my academic demise instead turned into a very spirited conversation about my approach to the subject matter, how the results compared with other books on related topics, and whether I intended to continue writing for publication. Having passed and received the committee's *imprimatur*, i.e., the privilege of having my dissertation published as a book, I could now look forward to a life of teaching at some time in the near future.

CHAPTER 3

CAREER HIGHLIGHTS

The path to my research position in Washington, D.C. began with a telephone call from Stanley Wilcox. This gentleman had an impressive alphabet soup of acronyms in his job title: National Intelligence Survey (NIS) Coordinator for the Division of Research on the Soviet Union and Eastern Europe (DRS) in the Office of Intelligence Research (OIR) at the U.S. Department of State.

Dr. Wilcox was delighted that I could do research in German, Polish, and Russian, as these were three of the major languages in the DRS geographic area of responsibility (specifically, the [East] German Democratic Republic, the People's Republic of Poland, and the Union of Soviet Socialist Republics). He offered me an entry-level position at the end of our telephone conversation. However, by mutual agreement, the final decision would be postponed until we met toward the end of April 1951 in Washington, D.C.

Since Professor and Mrs. Preuss were planning to attend the annual conference of the American Association of International Law at that time, I offered to drive them in my second-hand 1947 Ford club coupe from Ann Arbor to the nation's capital and back. We were late getting started on our trip, however: at best, we could reach Maryland by midnight. My passengers decided that we should stop at a motel. Unfortunately, the proprietor had only one room left. Professor Preuss looked at his wife (many years younger than he), then at me, and said: "We are good friends, but not *that* good!" In the interest of future amity, we decided to continue driving to Washington, D.C., which we entered during the early hours of the next day.

U.S. Department of State

My initial interview with Dr. Wilcox was very straightforward. We exchanged pleasantries, and I was glad to have looked up my interviewer in the State Department's *Biographic Register*. Dr. Wilcox received his Ph.D. from Yale and had a strong background in classics, which he also taught. During World War II, however, he worked on Soviet armed forces' order of battle in the U.S. Department of the Army.

As I sat down, he pulled out an old copy of *Pravda* from his desk and asked for a sight translation of a particular article. Knowing about his background, I interspersed the oral translation with comments about the peculiarities of Russian syntax. My approach was apparently effective, because the GS (Government Schedule) -7 position was offered to me for a second time at the end of the interview. Now, I accepted. That was the entry level for an intelligence research analyst with an M.A. degree and no other experience.

As soon as I had passed my oral and written examinations at Michigan, the Staar family packed its belongings into the car and drove east. Our baby girl Monica occupied the back seat all by herself.

We found an apartment on "E" Street, NW, overlooking the Potomac River and only a short walk from the office in State Annex 1. My work area was shared with three other analysts: Steven Fischer-Galati, Irene Jaffee, and Mitchell Stanley. The Staar family later moved to a small, two-bedroom, detached house in Kensington, Maryland. My first supervisor was Richard Tims (Ph.D., Columbia), who taught all of us at DRS a great deal about preparing intelligence reports for the government. He had served in Poland with the U.S. foreign service and spoke the Polish language fluently.

At this time, the Wriston Report (named after the president of Brown University who had chaired the commission) was released. It recommended that the number of career foreign service officers be raised from 1,300 to 3,900 by means of more aggressive recruitment as well as augmentation through lateral transfer (from positions such as mine). We later heard that our top intelligence research expert on Soviet agriculture went through this procedure and was sent, for some reason, to Singapore. That did not augur well for the rest of us!

Although I spent full-time as a research analyst, I was also a Ph.D. candidate with my own work to pursue. During a three and a half year period, most evenings and all weekends were occupied with the latter. My dissertation was defended successfully during a visit back in Ann Arbor and the Ph.D. awarded in February 1954. Despite promotions from GS-7 to GS-9 and later to GS-11, as well as the birth of a second daughter (Christina) at the George Washington University hospital, we decided it was time to look for a position in teaching. College jobs were scarce at that time, however.

In the meanwhile, both of my parents died. Dad was the first to pass away, at age seventy-four, after several strokes. His health had been broken during the years in a German penitentiary. I sat next to his bed in the hospital on that fateful night. He probably did not even know about my presence. His breathing was heavy, and after midnight it became weaker. Suddenly and quietly, it stopped. In response to my hitting the buzzer, a doctor and nurse came running into the room. They tried to revive him, although without success.

Mother left us three years later, at age sixty-seven, in the University of Michigan hospital. My sister Marie called to tell me that she too had suffered a brain hemorrhage. The doctor injected a dye to see which side had been affected, but diagnosis and treatment offered little help, and Mother died. Both parents are buried next to each other at a cemetery in southern Michigan.

Radio Free Europe

After these sad events, I received an invitation to the New York headquarters of Radio Free Europe for an interview. RFE needed a chief for its new program analysis section in Munich. I was introduced to a retired U.S. Army lieutenant general, who had been a classmate of Dwight D. Eisenhower at West Point. He did not mind at all putting the "new recruit" on the spot and greeted me with, "Dr. Staar! What kind of a *doctor* are you?" He had, of course, read my resumé.

I answered, "General, I am not a *real* doctor, like an M.D. I am only a Ph.D., which stands for 'phony doctor'." The interviewer liked that, and a lively conversation ensued. As the RFE position involved travel, interesting projects, and outstanding research opportunities, I readily accepted the job offer. The Staars packed up their few belongings and departed for Munich, Germany.

RFE and its sister station RL (Radio Liberty) were established during the Cold War as a response to the huge Soviet propaganda machine. RL broadcast in Russian and was also housed in Munich. The two were exceedingly effective: Moscow found it had to spend some $35 million per year in its attempt to jam RFE/RL transmissions, which was twice the cost to operate both of these American radio stations.

We were met at the Munich airport and taken to a furnished apartment on the Südliche Auffahrtsallee. This was certainly a better situation than the last time I had lived in Bavaria! Soon we moved to a small house across the river from RFE in a quiet residential neighborhood. Each morning, a driver came to take me to work and would bring me back in the evening. Both girls attended the U.S. Army kindergarten and elementary school at Perlacher Forst. They were picked up by a military bus, with Christina returning alone earlier in the afternoon by passenger car with an enlisted military driver. In other respects, too, life here resembled a posting at a military base.

Although it was a quiet and orderly existence, the realities of the Cold War were always with us. While we were there, Romania's communist dictator, Nicolae Ceaušescu, ordered the murder of his RFE critics; the mysterious deaths of three successive Romanian station directors (Noel Bernard, Mihai Cizmaresco, and Vlad Georgescu) have yet to be clarified. In addition, a deadly poison was discovered by U.S. counter-intelligence operatives in the cafeteria salt shakers during our stay. Later, a bomb exploded at the Munich office, the damage from which cost $2 million to repair.

The RFE director at that time was Erik Hazelhof, a naturalized American citizen of Dutch extraction who had served as a fighter pilot in the Royal Air Force during World War II. I reported directly to him, as I organized and supervised the new Program Analysis Section. Recruitment of analysts was done by the New York office from experts on Bulgaria, Czechoslovakia, Hungary, Poland, and Romania. Vlad Pascaleff, Hugh Elbot, Paul Schell, and Antoni Ostrowski were the initial appointees. It took longer to find a qualified and willing Romanian, for obvious reasons.

Monitoring of news and information programs occurred as they were being transmitted from Holzkirchen, outside of Munich, to La Gloria near Lisbon. Several hours would elapse before they could then be retransmitted eastward into the target areas. The angle of these signals, when they bounced off the ionosphere, would have been too sharp (and thus ineffective) had they come from Munich, due to the close proximity of listeners behind the Iron Curtain.

Those few hours gave our new section members time enough to analyze the content and appropriateness of the programs. The broadcasts could be heard over headsets as the transmissions were being relayed to Portugal. The individual analysts listened carefully for violations of daily policy guidelines. Specifications were received from the political adviser, Dr. Reuben Nathan, at RFE in New York, and discussed every morning at policy meetings with desk chiefs in Munich.

One example of what we did *not* transmit was the following: a military analysis being broadcast to Poland which stated that the entire area between West Germany and the USSR would be completely destroyed in the event of a nuclear war. What a terrifying message for Polish listeners! The RFE desk chief for programs to Poland as well as the RFE director agreed to "kill" that particular script and substitute an hour of music, instead.

I had never lost my enthusiasm for teaching, so I resumed this activity, as well, during 1958–59 for the University of Maryland's overseas program in West Germany. I taught evening college-level courses at Augsburg (to which I traveled by train) as well as successively at Bad Tölz and Bad Aibling. Students included both U.S. Army officers as well as enlisted personnel who were studying for bachelors' degrees. At Augsburg, Lieutenant Colonel Patrick W. Laurie (chief of military police) would send a car and driver to pick me up and return me after class to the railroad station. These experiences convinced me that I did not really want to spend the rest of my career outside of academia, despite the pleasant surroundings near Munich.

While at RFE, Professor Pollock from Michigan invited me to attend a conference sponsored by the International Political Science Association at Opatija, on the Adriatic coast of Yugoslavia. I traveled there by train from Munich and brought along a bottle of the professor's favorite Scotch whiskey. By coincidence, he had dropped his own bottle while debarking from a ship, and it shattered. That meeting included outstanding experts from the United States and Europe. It gave me great pleasure to "rub elbows" with these world renowned-authorities and share a drink with my former professor.

Emory University

In addition to being good company, Professor Pollock continued to be a helpful adviser. A few years earlier I had met the department chairman at Emory University during an annual meeting of the American Political Science Association in Denver, Colorado. We introduced ourselves at a bus stop for the airport and then sat together on the plane. Before leaving to make his connection, Dr. Lynwood M. Holland told me that I would make an excellent candidate for a future position in his department and that we should remain in contact.

During spring 1959, Professor Holland wrote to me in Munich about an associate professorship that would become available in the fall and asked about my availability as an applicant. I was immediately interested, and my name entered the pool of candidates. However, not having visited Atlanta or the Emory campus, I immediately contacted Professor Pollock at Michigan and asked for his opinion. He replied that a former colleague from a different department had moved to Emory and found the milieu as well as university to be most agreeable.

When a letter offering the appointment arrived, after a discussion with Jadwiga, I approached Dr. Hazelhof about leaving Munich in the coming fall. RFE would then have six months to find a successor to head an operation that appeared to be running smoothly and without any friction.

Munich had been a wonderful experience for the Staar family. Nonetheless, the opportunity to reenter teaching at a first-rate university could not be passed up. The salary of $7,500 (and an additional $1,500 for the summer) represented about one-third of that at RFE, after including the furnished house and other "perks." However, nobody goes into teaching for the money!

It was time now to establish a publications record. My first book came out with Louisiana State University Press, entitled *Poland, 1944–1962: The Sovietization of a Captive People*. Soon afterward I received tenure at Emory as well as a subsequent promotion. During my ten years there I also served as interim departmental chairman. It was a comfortable life. The family lived across the street from the golf course on Clifton Road, both girls attended Fernbank Elementary School, and Jadwiga became a student at Emory.

Atlanta in the 1960s was a city coming into its own. Although full of tradition, with peach trees and southern charm, it was also a site of civil rights activity, economic modernization, and cultural development. Emory reflected the new vitality in the region, attracting excellent faculty and very capable students. After having taught there for several years as an associate professor, however, I was approached by the chairman of the political science department at the University of Georgia with an offer of a promotion and a $3,000 salary increase. He told me that Athens was only fifty miles away from Atlanta. I thought to myself, "Yes; but it would be another fifty miles back." Nevertheless, Jadwiga and I visited the campus and gave some thought to the possible change.

When the official offer came in writing, I took the letter to the dean at Emory, who decided to match the promotion as well as the salary increase. Later, I promised myself never to do this again. What if the dean had shaken my hand and congratulated me on my new position at the University of Georgia? When I told this story to my good friend in the political science department, Charles D. Hounshell, he just laughed and said that I had been lucky. This man himself later became the dean at Emory.

My classes in the political science department included International Relations, Foreign Policies of the Major Powers, and The Soviet Sphere. The introductory IR course had to be divided into two sections because of unusually high enrollment.

During 1961–62, a new upper-division course was added under the title of "Soviet Foreign Policy" (Poli. Sci. 267). Among the names in my grade book is that of Newton L. Gingrich, who did extremely well despite the fact that he had not taken the prerequisite IR class. This brilliant young man went on to receive a Ph.D. degree and to become Speaker of the U.S. House of Representatives. I was delighted to see him again, when he was named a Distinguished Visiting Fellow at the Hoover Institution in 1999.

The War Colleges

Word apparently spread that I would be taking a one-year leave-of-absence from Emory to become a visiting professor at the U.S. Naval War College in Newport, Rhode Island, during 1963–64. For this reason, enrollment in International Relations (Poli. Sci. 260) increased to 101 students. We were forced to move the class into an auditorium, since I wanted to accommodate all of these young people. One of my students of that time was Catherine E. Rudder, who subsequently received her Ph.D. from Ohio State University. She later became executive director of the

American Political Science Association, and today she is a professor at George Mason University as well as director of its new program in public policy.

Yet another student, who proudly wore his Air Force ROTC uniform to my IR class, was Richard O. Keller. He later served on active duty with the Judge Advocate General's Corps. Captain Keller subsequently entered the private practice of law and became a Superior Court judge for Alameda County, California.

During a summer conference for young American political science faculty members held at the University of North Carolina, I met an Italian economics professor, named Bruno Leoni, from the University of Turin. He and his wife subsequently attended a convention of international economists in Atlanta. Jadwiga took good care of Signora Leoni, who did not speak any English, and the Leonis dined at our home on Clifton Road.

I later published several articles in *Il Politico*, the journal edited by Professor Leoni. He then invited me to present a paper at The Mont Pelerin Society's annual meeting in Knokke-sur-Mer, Belgium, on 13 September 1962. The paper dealt with the Kennedy Trade Expansion Act. My presentation was criticized by Professor Gottfried von Haberler from Harvard. I was very pleased that Professor Milton Friedman from the University of Chicago, who later won the Nobel Prize in economics, came to my defense.

Dr. W. Glenn Campbell, director of the Hoover Institution, had also attended this meeting and was favorably impressed with the paper as well as the ensuing discussion. Before the conference ended, he invited me to spend a year in California doing research on a book about Eastern Europe. However, since a total of six years of teaching qualified me only for a sabbatical at half-salary, it would have been impossible at that time. Furthermore, I had already agreed to the other commitment at the Naval War College.

The 1962–63 academic year was spent on leave-of-absence without pay from Emory to occupy the Fleet Admiral Chester W. Nimitz chair of political and social philosophy at the U.S. Naval War College (NWC) in Newport, Rhode Island The commandant at that time, Vice Admiral B. L. Austin, was a most gracious southern gentleman. He was nicknamed "The Count," because of his impeccable manners. Admiral Austin subsequently chaired the inquiry on the *Thresher* submarine tragedy.

My students at NWC proved to be an impressive group, and many of the graduates from that class attained flag rank or the equivalent for civilian government officials. I also taught evenings in the graduate program offered by George Washington University on the NWC campus. These seminars could eventually lead to an M.A. degree, since GW gave credit also for graduation from the resident year at Newport.

In December 1962, the annual meeting of the American Association for Advancement of Slavic Studies (AAASS) was held in New York. I came down from Newport by train. It was here that I happened to meet Professor Witold S. Sworakowski, then assistant director of the Hoover Institution in charge of library and archives. During our conversation, I mentioned Dr. Campbell's earlier invitation. I asked whether it would be possible for me to come out to California for one summer of research rather than the full year. That was arranged, with a welcome stipend of $1,500, which I had not expected.

Upon arrival in California with my family, we found a furnished condominium in graduate student housing at Escondido Village on the Stanford University campus. This meant that "home" was within walking distance of the Hoover Tower. A corner office in the basement had been reserved for me. This was how I spent the summer of 1965: in an unbelievable ivory (colored) tower filled with magnificent books, priceless and unique archival collections, as well as a plethora of serial publications and government documents in all languages. Truly a researcher's paradise!

A full three months were devoted to collecting and analyzing primary source materials for my new book, entitled *Communist Regimes in Eastern Europe*. This was published by Hoover Institution Press two years later. The volume went through another four revised and updated editions during the next twenty-one years. As a textbook, it was quite a success, being adopted by 169 different colleges and universities, including Stanford, as well as the U.S. Foreign Service Institute. In addition, the book was translated into Spanish (Mexico City and Madrid), German (Stuttgart), Korean (Seoul), and Chinese (Taipei).

After my productive summer at Hoover, I organized a conference at Emory. Papers and discussion there resulted in a volume on *Aspects of Modern Communism*, published in 1965 by the University of South Carolina Press. Participants attended from the Federal Republic of Germany, the Republic of China, South Vietnam, the Republic of Korea, and different areas of the United States. I wrote the preface and one of the papers, served as a discussant for another paper, and edited the entire volume. The hardback edition sold out completely.

I took yet another leave-of-absence without pay from Emory during the 1967–68 academic year. I spent the time as visiting professor of foreign affairs at the National War College (NWC) on the campus of Fort Lesley J. McNair in Washington, D.C. Here, too, my students were an accomplished mixture of military and civilian talent: many later made flag rank, and some rose to be ambassadors or the equivalent.

The commandant, Lieutenant General Andrew J. Goodpaster, U.S. Army, invited me to remain at the NWC for a second year in order to "break in" the other new civilian professors who would be joining the faculty. Fortunately, Emory agreed to extend my year of leave. General Goodpaster was certainly a difficult man to turn down. He was a top-notch soldier and a fine scholar: earlier, he had been sent to Princeton for an M.A. degree, and then also received a Ph.D. before his assignment to Ft. McNair. From there, his orders to Vietnam as deputy to General Creighton Abrams were followed by the position of Supreme Allied Commander at NATO and a fourth star.

During these two years, I had the opportunity to serve as faculty adviser for successive study tours of East Asia and Latin America. Both were most instructive, due to the high-level military and civilian officials with whom we met. The first group avoided stopping at Saigon, however, because the Vietcong had blown up the U.S. Army hotel the previous year, only one day after the NWC students and faculty had departed the area.

A few days after accepting General Goodpaster's invitation to extend the "tour of duty" at NWC, Dr. Campbell called from the Hoover Institution to tell me that I had ended up at the top of the list for the position of principal associate director. (I am certain that the letters of recommendation on my behalf from professors Barghoon and Pollock as well as General Goodpaster made an impression.) Would I accept? Unfortunately, as mentioned above, the commitment to remain at NWC for a second year had been made orally to General Goodpaster and could not be broken. Besides, the academic year at NWC was about to begin in June.

I suggested to Dr. Campbell that he offer the position to the next candidate on his "short list." The immediate response was that the Hoover Institution would wait another year before filling the vacancy. I was delighted! With this news, I then notified the president of Emory University that the family would not be returning to Atlanta after all and thanked him again for having granted me the two successive leaves-of-absence.

Soon after I had decided to accept the position at Hoover, Dr. Warren Nutter called me from the Pentagon. He had just been appointed assistant secretary of defense for international security affairs (ISA). I had known him as a distinguished economist and professor at the University of Virginia. He invited me to pay him a visit. Upon entering his office, I saw a table of organization that took up an entire wall. After some pleasantries, Professor Nutter came right to the point. He asked me to select the position I would like to occupy from among those on the chart. This was quite an offer!

I explained about the situation at the Hoover Institution and the one-year extension that Dr. Campbell had already given me. Professor Nutter suggested that I might receive another year's extension. Not likely, I thought to myself, and replied that I could not ask for that.

Hoover Institution

We did maintain contact during Professor Nutter's stay at the Pentagon, and I was appointed a consultant to ISA with a Top Secret clearance. This consulting resulted in several contracts for studies at the Hoover Institution dealing with international security affairs. I personally co-authored a projection through 1990–2000 for the northern tier of Eastern Europe (East Germany, Czechoslovakia, and Poland) for the Research Analysis Corporation in McLean, Virginia. This was then sent to the U.S. Department of Defense in February 1970. Its total of 143 pages was classified.

Another joint project for Sandia National Laboratories in Albuquerque, N. M., dealt with the results of possible fragmentation of the energy infrastructure during 1991–92 in the USSR, which had just collapsed. Other universities also took part in this study, which had been commissioned by the U.S. Department of Energy. Our contribution (with Ms. Anne Garvey, who did the write-up) from the Hoover Institution was part of a coordinated effort with faculty members at the universities of New Mexico and Washington, as well as other experts.

Having previously spent one summer at the Hoover Institution, the locale and surrounding areas were familiar. In 1969, the family rented a furnished home for the first year in neighboring Los Altos. Monica had been accepted at Wellesley, where she completed her freshman year, and later transferred to Stanford as a sophomore. Christina attended Los Altos High School, graduating in mid-year, which allowed her to take spring and summer courses at Foothill Junior College. These credits were subsequently accepted at Stanford. Both daughters were graduated from that university.

All of a sudden, I found that I had truly "come up in the world": from the previous summer's basement accommodations, I moved into a spacious corner office on the eleventh floor of the Tower across the hall from Mr. Hoover's former office. This area was in turn adjacent to that of Director Campbell. From the fifteenth-floor platform near the top of the Tower, on a clear day, one could see San Francisco, some forty miles away. With its famous carillon (a gift from post-World War I Belgium for the relief aid received through Herbert Hoover) and the surrounding scenic beauty of "the Farm" (as Stanford is known), the Institution was a very pleasant place to work.

The Scholars

Dr. W. Glenn Campbell, a Canadian by birth, had received his Ph.D. in economics from Harvard, where he also had been an instructor. He became co-founder with William Baroody of the American Enterprise Institute for Public Policy Research (AEI), a "think tank" in Washington, D.C. Appointed director of the Hoover Institution on War, Revolution, and Peace at Stanford University in 1960, Dr. Campbell served in that capacity for almost thirty years.

What attracted scholars, apart from the resident ones, were the library and archival collections. After Dr. Campbell became director, the research and acquisition programs were revitalized. Professor Sworakowski, mentioned above, was "one of the greatest collectors and bibliographers in the history of the Hoover Institution," where he served more than three decades.[1] The monumental effort of collecting archival materials was overseen by six expert curators. They covered Africa (Peter Duignan), East Asia (Ramon Myers), Eastern Europe (Wayne Vucinich), the Middle East (George Rentz), the USSR/Russia (the well-known British scholar Robert Conquest), and Western Europe (Agnes Peterson). Professor Vucinich held a joint appointment with the history department at Stanford (a half-time teaching assignment). He established and edited the "Studies of [non-Soviet] Nationalities" series, which have resulted in ten volumes being

---

1. Peter Duignan, "The Library of the Hoover Institution," *Library History*, vol. 17 [July 2001], p. 109.

published between 1978 and 2001 (Crimean Tatars, Volga Tatars, Georgians, Uzbeks, Estonians, Azerbaijan Turks, Kazakhs, Latvians, Moldovans, and Slovaks).

Unfortunately for the Hoover Institution, Professor Vucinich received an endowed chair at Stanford University and transferred back full-time to its history department. Several of the authors in the above series had been his graduate students. He continues to supervise the series even after retirement and remains a valued friend of the Hoover Institution. It was our good fortune to have worked with this scholar, who has an international reputation. Professor Vucinich was succeeded by Dr. Maciej Siekierski (Eastern Europe), an eminent authority in his field.

Even before I was being considered for the deputy directorship position at Hoover, Dr. Campbell had approached me to prepare a study of the Social Science Research Council in the United States. The data upon which my survey was based came from annual reports and published studies at this center. The twenty-six and one-half–page, single-spaced, typewritten analysis was mailed on 1 June 1966.

The results were read by Drs. Campbell and Baroody. Their joint appraisal in a letter to me stated, "It is excellent and just what the doctor ordered!" When asked about my fee for the work, I replied that there were only $122.34 in expenses and that the analysis had been prepared *pro bono*. It was a labor of love, and I personally benefited from gathering as well as analyzing this information. Besides, it had been fun! (And, I must also confess, it really had not occurred to me that I could charge AEI at that time!)

My first meeting with senior staff members as the new associate director took place in the De Basily Room on the ground floor of the Tower. I was introduced by Dr. Campbell and asked to say a few words about myself. I began by stating jokingly that I had been brought up in Ann Arbor, Michigan, where all of my relatives belonged to the *Mishugene* tribe of Indians. Afterwards, one of the senior research fellows (Bertram D. Wolfe) came up to me and said that the word in Yiddish was *meshuge*, which I knew meant "crazy."

During that same meeting, one of the secretaries interrupted the session by entering the room and saying in a distinct voice that "the White House" was calling Dr. Staar. I excused myself and left to take the telephone in an adjacent office. The caller was Roger Freeman, then on leave of absence from Hoover for public service. His office was located in the Old Executive Office Building, which used the adjacent White House telephone exchange.

He merely wanted to wish me well on the new appointment, but it certainly didn't hurt my standing with my new colleagues to have them think that the President of the United States might have been on the line!

In addition to being Dr. Campbell's deputy, I was given the responsibility for the library and archives as well as the International Studies research program. The latter was in its infancy and required not only more funding but also recruitment for scholars in residence as well as shorter-term fellows. This program also gave me the opportunity to engage in my own research and writing.

My first secretary was Laverne Klebofski, whom I "inherited" from Professor Sworakowski when he retired. She had a degree from the University of California at Berkeley, took shorthand, and typed like a machine gun. When Mrs. Edith Fabinyi retired as executive assistant to Dr. Campbell, the latter asked me for Laverne as her replacement. The same thing happened, after Mrs. Louise Doying was requested from me to succeed Mrs. Klebofski when she left to get married.

What did these two ladies have in common? Both were excellent stenographers. When I realized that, I began looking for somebody without any knowledge of shorthand. I did not want to "lose" my next assistant. At this point, I met Mrs. Margit N. Grigory. Although she had an M.A. in English literature as well as a fluent speaking knowledge of Hungarian, German, and French, she did not take dictation. Consequently she would not be transferred to the director's office. What a treasure!

The Yearbook

Mrs. Grigory proved to be of invaluable help for an ongoing major project, the *Yearbook on International Communist Affairs*. This series had been started by Richard V. Allen, who later became national security adviser to President Ronald Reagan. Professor Sworakowski compiled and edited the basic volume, *World Communism: A Handbook, 1918–1965*, for which I had written the profile on the Communist Party of Czechoslovakia prior to joining the Hoover Institution. Beginning with 1969 and ending in 1991, I took this task seriously and edited as well as contributed to a total of twenty-three annual volumes. This operation moved from an in-house production by a dozen full- or part-time analysts to one with more than ninety outside contributors. Through the yearly update format, we ultimately provided a history of communism in virtually every country in the world.

The remaining in-house production staff comprised six resident scholars who recruited outside contributors, wrote regional introductions and, at times, provided individual country profiles. Each had his own research projects, apart from the *Yearbook*. This editorial board included scholars Thomas H. Henriksen (Sub-Saharan Africa), William Ratliff (the Americas), Ramon H. Myers (Asia and the Pacific), Robert Conquest and Richard F. Staar (the Soviet Union and Eastern Europe), James H. Noyes (Middle East and North Africa), and Dennis L. Bark (Western Europe). The last, twenty-fifth-anniversary volume totaled 689 double-column pages and came out in 1991. With the dissolution of the Soviet Union and the independence of the former Eastern bloc nations, the project naturally drew to a close.

Without the able and totally dedicated assistance of Margit N. Grigory, who had become the managing editor of the *Yearbook*, this project would never have been accomplished so smoothly or with such integrity. The Central Intelligence Agency purchased fifty copies of each volume every year, and the U.S. Department of State likewise ordered many copies as well.

One afternoon, the U.S. naval attaché at our embassy in Brussels called to ask whether I would be available to present a paper at a conference commemorating the one hundredth anniversary of the *École de Guerre* during 28–29 September 1970. I responded in the affirmative. Next, an official letter of invitation came, asking whether my wife would also attend. I replied in the affirmative. My paper appeared as one of the chapters in a handsome hard-cover volume published in English, with summaries in Dutch and French.

In addition, I also edited two other series of books. The first was called "Histories of the Ruling Communist Parties" (in North Korea, North Vietnam, the Soviet Union, Poland, Mongolia, Hungary, Czechoslovakia, Romania, Afghanistan, Bulgaria, China, and Laos). These appeared between 1978 and 1986. They were authored, primarily, by contributors to the *Yearbook* who had the requisite expertise.

The other series appeared under the general title "Hoover International Studies." These volumes included *The Panama Canal Controversy*; *Imperialist Revolutionaries*; *South Africa: War, Revolution, or Peace?*; *Two China States*; *Persian Gulf Security*; *Soviet Strategy for Nuclear War*; *Science, Technology, and China's Drive for Modernization*; *The End of the*

Tito Era; *Japan Debates Defense*; *The Soviet Invasion of Afghanistan*; *Communist Power and Sub-Saharan Africa*; *The United States and the Republic of Korea*; and *Communism in Central America and the Caribbean*. All fourteen of them were published between 1977 and 1982.

Due to such publications, I was invited to join the editorial boards of *Current History, Mediterranean Quarterly, Orbis,* and *Strategic Review*. I am still an active member for the second and third of these academic journals. The last one, of course, is no longer being published.

One of the senior colleagues at Hoover was Franz Lassner, who had received his Ph.D. in history from Georgetown University. He served as director of archives and did outstanding work in accumulating such primary source materials as diaries and papers of distinguished American and foreign personalities. His office was on the tenth floor of the Tower, one elevator floor below mine.

One day, Franz came up the two flights of stack stairs to discuss a new job possibility. He showed me a letter offering him a substantial salary increase as well as the vice presidency at a college of textile technology in Philadelphia. He asked me for advice. This sounded like a familiar situation. I told Franz about my experience at Emory, pointing out that it might not be possible later for him to move from a relatively unknown school into the Ivy League. Of course, the decision had to be his. I warned him, however, not to be surprised if Dr. Campbell were simply to congratulate him without offering to match the salary.

That is in fact exactly what happened. A few years later, the college in Pennsylvania went bankrupt and Franz was without a job. He telephoned me about his predicament. By coincidence, I had just been approached by Vice President Thomas Sawyer at Freedoms Foundation in Valley Forge to recommend a director for its programs. I called back and gave him Dr. Lassner's name. Not only was Franz hired, but the family did not have to move, since Philadelphia was an easy commute to the Freedoms Foundation campus. And Mrs. Margo Lassner was delighted at this turn of events. Franz remained there from 1977 to 1991.

It was Dr. Lassner who subsequently invited me to direct a one-week summer program for high school teachers at Valley Forge. It was called "Problems in World Politics," and I had to find speakers from academia and the U.S. government. My bright assistant was Corliss A. Tacosa, who has since received a Ph.D. degree from Old Dominion University.

I enjoyed this brief "vacation" and asked that the honorarium be sent to the Hoover Institution. From the beginning, it had been my habit to direct all such checks (including those from articles and speaking engagements) to Hoover. It is an arrangement that works out well for both of us.

In addition to my administrative activities, I also became involved with the fundraising efforts that helped the Institution to expand. The truly prodigious efforts, of course, were those of Dr. Campbell.[2] Among the supporters I was able to cultivate was the Cowell Foundation in San Francisco. It had three trustees, two of whom always supported Stanford University with major gifts (the Cowell Health Center on campus reflects their generosity). The third trustee especially admired the Federal Bureau of Investigation. One of our assistant directors, Allan Belmont, happened to have been a former special agent and assistant director at the FBI. He and I paid frequent visits to the Foundation and impressed on this trustee the value of contributions to the archives. With his interest and support, we acquired grants of $200,000 each year for special acquisitions.

Then, unexpectedly, the Foundation announced it would cease operation because funds were running out. I suggested to our trustee friend that an official letter be sent to Dr. Campbell, inviting Hoover to apply for a terminal grant. This way, the university administration would not be able to exclude us from applying. All such applications had to be channeled through Stanford.

When the time came, instructions from the university limited the Hoover Institution proposal to one page, which would be ranked eighth (at the bottom) in terms of Stanford priorities. I prepared the application, typed single-spaced on one sheet of paper. It requested a terminal grant of $2 million, which would allow the special acquisitions fund to continue over a ten-year period.

At least two of the three Cowell trustees must have been sympathetic toward the Hoover Institution, because we received a check for $2 million. When I took it across the hall to the director's office and presented it to Dr. Campbell, he broke into a smile from ear to ear.

Other fundraising activities involved visits with the director to the Scaife Family Foundation in Pittsburgh. There I met Dan McMichael, who currently directs the Sarah Scaife Foundation. Richard Scaife had also always been generous toward the Hoover Institution.

---

2. See his book, *The Competition of Ideas: How My Colleagues and I Built the Hoover Institution* (Ottawa, Illinois: Jameson Books, 2001), 409 pp. The handwritten dedication reads: "To Richard Staar, one of the builders."

Sometimes, of course, our benefactors found us. One day, an elderly gentleman came to the circulation desk on the street floor of the Hoover Tower. By coincidence, Professor Sworakowski (who spoke fluent Russian in addition to Polish, German, French, and Romanian) happened to be there. The visitor introduced himself as John Bittson. He explained that he was born Ivan Bidzhan and had to flee his native land before the Bolsheviks could arrest him.

Dr. Campbell requested me to work with this gentleman along with Associate Director Richard Burress. We made many joint visits to San Diego, where Mr. Bittson resided. This future donor came up to the Hoover Institution on several occasions because of his interest in our Russian archival materials.

After several years had elapsed, Mr. Bittson passed away, leaving his entire estate of two million dollars to the Hoover Institution. This was a most welcome addition to the endowment. A large plaque hangs on the wall of the third floor in the Herbert Hoover Memorial Building, adjacent to the Tower. It presents a biographic sketch of this former Socialist Revolutionary Party activist, whom War Commissar Leon Trotsky had ordered to be shot on sight.

Yet another successful fundraising activity involved the annual application for $200,000 from the U.S. Government under Title VIII of the Education Act. Each year I prepared a proposal for this funding to support fellowships for post-doctoral research at the Hoover Institution dealing with Eastern Europe and the Soviet Union. In addition to the formal written application, I made oral presentations before the selection committee in Washington, D.C. This lasted twelve years and brought in a total of $2.4 million. We were able to support 147 young scholars in residence for either one summer or a full academic year. Ms. Deborah Ventura did outstanding administrative work on managing this program, which involved about twelve visting fellows per year.

Two former program participants serve as examples of noteworthy contributors to these research efforts. One special volume by a Title VIII fellow, Professor R. Judson Mitchell from the University of New Orleans, *Getting to the Top in the USSR: Cyclical Patterns in the Leadership Succession Process*, was published in 1990 by Hoover Institution Press. The author had contributed annual profiles on the Communist Party of the Soviet Union for our *Yearbook on International Communist Affairs* and was well qualified to write such an outstanding study.

Another such scholar, Professor Ewa M. Thompson from Rice University, produced an exceptional volume entitled *Imperial Knowledge: Russian Literature and Colonialism* (Westport, Conn.: Greenwood Press, 2000). Her work traces and analyzes the systematic tsarist and Soviet policy of enrichment through plundering of conquered peoples on the periphery of the Russian heartland.

Copies of the books which resulted from the grants under the Title VIII program (Public Law 98-164, 97 Stat. 1047–50) would be mailed to the Assistant Secretary of State for Intelligence and Research (INR). This person presided over the annual selection committee meetings, which I always attended. The constantly growing library of valuable writings helped secure a stable niche for the Hoover Institution under this program.

The Solzhenitsyn Visits

One of the memorable events at Hoover during this time involved the two research visits by famed Soviet dissident and author Alexander Solzhenitsyn. He was invited to become a Distinguished Visiting Scholar by Dr. Campbell as soon as we learned that he had been expelled from the USSR. In the meantime, this Nobel laureate moved to Switzerland from Germany without responding to our invitation. About a year later, however, a telephone message was received in Dr. Campbell's office announcing that the Solzhenitsyns would be arriving at San Francisco airport from Alaska two days later.

Jadwiga and I were at the gate to greet the couple and drive them to our home. Here we had a drink of Russian vodka and a light meal. We offered them the hospitality of a small, detached house on our property. However, I had also reserved accommodations at the faculty club in case they decided not to stay with us. They made the latter choice. Solzhenitsyn mentioned these quarters in the second volume of his memoirs, complaining about the loud music and noise from the campus. Apparently, he was prevented from falling asleep until early the next morning.[3]

At 9:00 a.m., both Solzhenitsyns arrived at the conference room on the eleventh floor of the Hoover Tower. Since the archives were located only one floor below, materials selected from collection registers could be

---

3. Aleksandr Solzhenitsyn, "Ocherki izgnaniia (1974–1978)," *Novyi mir* (Moscow), no. 11, November 1998, p. 125.

brought up rather expeditiously. I had warned our distinguished guest (who wanted anonymity) that he should not walk on the campus in the evening; some student was bound to recognize him and take a photograph. He disregarded my suggestion, and his picture appeared in the *Stanford Daily* a few days later.

We soon became deluged with mail and telephone calls to the extent that hardly any work could be done. Finally, with Dr. Campbell's approval, I suggested that Solzhenitsyn appear in front of the Tower, where he would make a brief statement to the press and other media. He agreed.

Dr. Campbell introduced Solzhenitsyn, who spoke about his research project and why he had come to Hoover. I stood next to him as interpreter. At one point, he stated that "after each rain, the sun will shine again." If translated literally, it would have sounded awkward, so I said, "Every cloud has a silver lining." Solzhenitsyn must have understood some English, because he raised his eyebrows and looked back toward the Tower entrance. One of our Russian-speaking research assistants, Constantine V. Galskoy, was standing there. This man nodded his head and said, "*Eto pravel'no*" ("That was correct"). Solzhenitsyn, understandably, hated the thought of being misquoted.

We then retreated via the front entrance into the Tower, through the basement, and out the back door. Jadwiga was waiting there with her car. Solzhenitsyn had indicated an interest in visiting the place where Father Junipero Serra, the famous Roman Catholic missionary, had established a school for Indian children on the outskirts of today's city of Carmel. Jadwiga drove us down there and back. Our guest talked knowledgeably about the expansion of the Russian Orthodox Church into Alaska, along the coast of Canada, and into northern California at Fort Ross.

In the following days, I remained at Solzhenitsyn's beck and call on the other side of the eleventh floor. He asked me to screen his mail as well as to take all telephone calls. "Traffic" along both of these channels to contact him increased in volume after the so-called "Meet the Press" event in front of the tower.

One call even came from Hollywood. The person on the telephone was a certain Warren Beatty. Not having understood the last name, I asked him to spell it. I had never heard of this man, who told me that he was the greatest movie director in town. That did not impress me, although I did remember a Clyde "Bring them back alive!" Beatty who used to catch wild animals in Africa and take them to the United States.

The Beatty on the telephone asked whether I had seen the movies "Shampoo" or "Bonnie and Clyde." When receiving negative answers, he said, "You don't go to movies, do you?" Beatty wanted to use Solzhenitsyn as an adviser for the next one of his movies, called "Reds," based on John Reed's *Ten Days that Shook the World*. Frankly, I never even brought the matter to our guest's attention.

In the last conversation we had on the eighth day of his first stay, I told Solzhenitsyn about the volume of mail (always giving him the letters in Russian without opening them) as well as most telephone calls. Among the latter was one from the AFL/CIO with an invitation to speak in Washington, D.C. He did not show any interest in this project at all.

Then, unexpectedly, that weekend Solzhenitsyn did call me again at home to ask whether I still had the AFL/CIO telephone number. I told him that it was at the office and I would be pleased to pick it up and deliver it to his room at the faculty club. On my way back with the telephone number, I found that the Solzhenitsyns ("Mr. and Mrs. Smith") had checked out earlier that day. Later in the evening, he called me again, and I gave him the information.

I believe that Solzhenitsyn always kept in mind the possibility that the KGB might attempt to assassinate him. That seemed to be the only explanation for his behavior. He certainly had ample justification to be extremely careful and keep his movements secret. There were several examples of prominent Russian emigrés being murdered by the Soviet secret police. That Stanford and Hoover appeared secure and serene meant nothing, of course.

Later on, Solzhenitzyn made a second visit, this time alone. In part, perhaps, it was because he had become an honorary fellow of the Hoover Institution. During this visit, the Nobel laureate also accepted the American Friendship Medal from the Freedoms Foundation at Valley Forge, Pennsylvania. It was awarded to him in the de Basily Room of the Hoover Tower building on 1 June 1976. The Freedoms Foundation also published his "Words on Freedom" in the form of an attractive brochure.

After two months on the Stanford campus, Solzhenitsyn disappeared again without prior notice, just as he had done the first time. When he and his wife finally settled in Vermont, we began receiving requests for articles and books that Solzhenitsyn could not find at either Harvard or the New York Public Library. Xeroxes from the articles were sent by regular mail, whereas books were registered and insured. The latter were always returned the same way.

In his first letter, Solzhenitsyn asked that some 1,114 pages be xeroxed from the journal *Krasnyi Arkhiv*, covering events in Russia during 1901–1908. Such requests were handled expeditiously by Ronald Bulatoff, a Russian-speaking archival specialist. Soon a second letter for more materials from *KA* followed. Next, we were asked for xeroxes from *Zaria* (Berlin), published during 1922 and 1923. Between 22 July 1976 and 19 June 1981, Solzhenitsyn and I exchanged more than fifty letters concerning materials at Hoover as well as other matters.

We soon learned that our honorary fellow had begun collecting private archives from Russian emigrés throughout the United States and Western Europe. When we heard about these activities, I wrote to Solzhenitsyn on 19 November 1976, suggesting that, after using them, he place these materials in the Hoover Institution archives as a repository. They could then become available to the hundreds of visiting scholars who came each year from the United States and many foreign countries. Solzhenitsyn acknowledged my suggestion, although he never sent us any of these unique materials. We assume that he took them to Moscow, instead.

On 11 June 1977, I wrote to ask whether our honorary fellow would give the keynote address at a conference on "Human Rights in the Soviet Union" to be held either the following spring or fall. A list of possible participants was enclosed for his approval. Solzhenitsyn replied two months later, refusing our invitation. The last correspondence is dated 19 June 1981, when I informed Solzhenitsyn that we had offered his protégé Mikhail S. Bernstam a research grant for 1981–82. Dr. Bernstam was still a research fellow at the Hoover Institution in 2002, although our correspondence with Solzhenitsyn stopped even before the couple returned to Russia. He still remains an honorary fellow of ours, together with Ronald Reagan and Margaret Thatcher.

Academic Freedom at Stanford

One of the professors in the English department had established himself as leader of a "Maoist" organization. He would hold rallies and urge students to go out at night and "do their own thing." Unfortunately, this was interpreted as a call to destroy what they could. One of these student mobs burned down the ROTC building on campus. Another time, they broke into the computer center, where considerable damage was done to this "symbol of capitalism." On yet another occasion, the main university library was invaded and its card catalog vandalized by pouring red ink (symbolizing blood) on the sections labeled "war," "revolution," and "peace."

The scruffy faculty member in question, although encouraging (without specifically calling for) the students to engage in destruction and vandalism, never actually participated in person. He held a tenured position and apparently thought that this status would afford him unlimited "freedom of speech."

At one point, a hostile group also attempted to occupy our Tower building. That structure, of course, is the location of the famed library and unique archival collections. Although the Hoover Institution was "independent within the framework of Stanford University," it also became a target for such protesters during the late 1960s. Ironically, of course, the mission of Hoover has always been the preservation of materials on war and revolution for the sake of building peace. When the radicalized students approached the Tower entrance one evening, they were met on the steps by about half a dozen Hoover "veterans" (Ed Bacciocco, Al Belmont, Pete Duignan, Lewis Gann, George Marotta, Paul Ryan, and myself). The anticipated showdown did not take place, and several hundred of these deluded youngsters finally turned around and left.

Despite his tenured status, the pseudo-Maoist faculty member and leader of the radical movement was tried by a group of his university peers. The accused had the courtroom decorated with a Chinese communist flag and a portrait of Mao Tse-tung as well as two bodyguards shouldering unloaded rifles. None of this intimidated or impressed the professorial judges, who recommended that the man be fired. This recommendation was carried out by the president of Stanford University, Dr. Richard W. Lyman.

More Peaceful Pursuits

As mentioned already, one of my responsibilities at Hoover involved the International Studies research program. The idea of a monograph series came to mind, to provide a publishing outlet for in-house scholars, visiting academicians, and others. Hoover Press made a marvelous contribution to this effort, because it published first-class books, especially under its executive director, Mrs. Patricia Baker.

The publications committee, chaired by Richard T. Burress, decided on distribution of research grants among worldwide applicants. Even if they already had publishers, many of the latter agreed to co-publication with Hoover Press. Dr. Burress, an attorney by training, provided balance to the proceedings in our committee. He had served in senior positions at the White House and knew how to calm down the—at times—heated intellectual discussions during our meetings.

One of the professors in the political science department, Jan F. Triska, had been using my book on *Communist Regimes in Eastern Europe* (1967) as a text. Before leaving on a sabbatical, he asked me whether I would be willing to teach that course in his absence. Having so many other commitments, I regretfully had to refuse. Other opportunities would present themselves, of this I remained certain at that time. Another invitation was soon forthcoming.

One of my other colleagues at Stanford, retired Professor Claude Buss, had been teaching in the National Security Affairs Department at the Naval Postgraduate School in Monterey, California. He invited me to give a guest lecture, and I ended up agreeing to offer a graduate seminar. This meant driving down each Sunday evening, checking into the Bachelor Officers' Quarters, meeting the students on Mondays and Wednesdays, and then driving back the evening of the second day. My four-day work schedule at the Hoover Institution consequently had to be concentrated within the remaining part of the week, which now included Saturdays and Sundays. I did this for only one semester, although it had been a most enjoyable exercise.

In this connection, I also became a Board of Visitors member at the U.S. Army's Defense Language Institute in Monterey. The work here called for examining the curriculum and making recommendations. The students lived in specialized dormitories, organized by language, and could converse after school hours. I had never encountered such an outstanding foreign language program, which turned out interpreters and interrogators *par excellence*.

A noteworthy overseas trip I made with Jadwiga at this time took us to Taipei, where I lectured at the Chinese Staff College on 4 September 1970. Each sentence was translated slowly, so that a one-hour presentation lasted four hours. No questions were asked. The escort officer slipped me an envelope "as a token of appreciation" on the way back to the hotel.

Upon inspection, the contents proved to be a single $1,000 bill (New Taiwan dollars, at an exchange rate of NT$40 to US$1). Jadwiga and I went shopping for a summer suit which would cost that amount. When I put these clothes on back in California, however, thread at the seams began to break. It dawned on me finally that these clothes were probably sold to undertakers, whose customers only needed to wear them once.

"Love Affair" with the Marine Corps

One of my graduate students in the political science department at Emory University, LTC H. M. Thomason, USMCR, had introduced me to the director of the 6th Marine Corps Reserve and Recruitment District (MCRRD) in Atlanta, Georgia. This contact with Colonel A. A. Vandegrift, USMC, resulted in a recommendation to Marine Corps Headquarters that I receive a direct commission as a reserve officer. I had two mobilization occupational specialties: (1) primary, as an intelligence officer and (2) secondary, as a foreign language officer.

The commissioning ceremony took place at 6th District headquarters on 27 December 1960. I immediately joined a volunteer training unit that drilled at Georgia Institute of Technology. Apart from being a member of VTU 6-4 (staff), first under Brigadier General George E. Tomlinson (followed by Colonel James H. Finch), I also taught a course in international relations to Air Force ROTC cadets at Emory University, beginning with the spring of 1961. This was done on a *pro bono* basis.

My next set of orders directed me to report at Marine Corps Schools in Quantico, Virginia. Here, I attended Phase I of the Junior Course during the last two weeks of July 1961. The following summer, new orders sent me to Camp Lejeune, N.C. That same year, in the fall, I was asked to become liaison for 6th MCRRD to assist the officer-selection officer (in Atlanta) on the campus of Emory University.

During the last two weeks of June 1963, new orders took me to the U.S. Navy Amphibious Base in Little Creek, Virginia. During 1963–64, I taught at the Naval War College in Newport, R.I., and received an associate duty without pay assignment at the Naval Officers' School, USMC Reserve Training Center, Fields Point, Providence, R.I. Toward the end of that academic year, orders came to augment the 6th Staff Group from Atlanta, then under Colonel James R. Harper, Jr., during the last two weeks of May 1964 at air-sea-land maneuvers which included a battalion of regular marines as the "aggressor." I served as intelligence officer (S-2) in these war games for the Atlanta reserve unit.

En route from Newport back to Atlanta, I stopped for three weeks of active duty in August at the USMC Educational Center in Quantico,

Virginia. During that period, I prepared a study for the Ed Center director on establishing a civilian academic chair of military history, to be attached to the Command and Staff College. This recommendation, based on my report dated 27 August 1964, was subsequently implemented.

During the latter part of June and early July 1965, active duty for training orders took me back to Little Creek, Virginia, and its amphibious warfare base. That same summer, I attended a course on strategic intelligence at the Defense Intelligence School in Washington, D.C.

While teaching at the National War College (1967–69), I belonged to VTU 4-52, which was a civil affairs unit. That first summer, I also attended the U.S. Army Civil Affairs School at Fort Gordon, Georgia, during the last two weeks of June 1968.

After moving to California, I commenced a full ten-year affiliation with the USMC Command and Staff College (C&SC) at Quantico, Virginia, where I served on the adjunct faculty. This involved commuting from San Francisco to Dulles airport about once each month to offer graduate-level seminars for field-grade student officers. Brigadier General Harold Chase, USMCR, directed this program. In addition, my regular two weeks on active duty took place each summer.

Apart from the foregoing, I joined VTU 12-3 at Naval Air Station, Moffett Field, here in the San Francisco Bay Area. My unit was commanded by Colonel John Roscoe, USMCR. This talented officer conceived of and implemented a computerized system that identified and coded the talents of reserve officers who could be tapped for service with the Development Command at Quantico. My last reserve affiliation involved the U.S. Navy Reserve Politico-Military Affairs Company 11-1 on Treasure Island, California, commanded by Captain Bruce Handler, USNR.

In addition to the above, I prepared three other studies (apart from the one recommending establishment of a civilian chair) for C&SC at Quantico. These were: (1) assessment in 1971 of the evaluation systems at the Basic School, Amphibious Warfare School, and Command and Staff College; (2) a study in 1973 of library assets in support of the C&SC curriculum; and (3) evaluation in 1974 of the guest lecture program at C&SC.

Active duty for training in Quantico during the last two weeks in May 1981 ended my two-decade–long love affair with the Marine Corps. It had been a great experience and, hopefully, I did my country more good than harm! Regrettably, my forthcoming presidential appointment to the U.S.

conventional arms control delegation in Vienna precluded any further USMC Reserve activities.

Almost twenty-one years after being commissioned, on 25 September 1981, I received the Presidential Legion of Merit "for meritorious conduct in the performance of outstanding services." This is a ribbon I wear on my lapel with pride. The then Commandant of the Marine Corps, General Paul X. Kelley, also presented me with a full-sized USMC flag, which stood behind my desk in Vienna next to the flag of the United States.

Several of my colleagues at the Hoover Institution had served in the U.S. Marine Corps as well. Among the most illustrious were the previously mentioned Richard T. Burress, who fought as a first lieutenant and platoon leader during the World War II invasion of Okinawa. Another senior colleague, George P. Shultz, attained the rank of captain in that same war. The latter is a Distinguished Fellow at the Hoover Institution, a retired professor at the Stanford Graduate School of Business, and, of course, the former U.S. Secretary of State under President Ronald Reagan.

CHAPTER 4

THE 1980–81 TRANSITION

A new direction in my life began during preparations for the 1980 presidential campaign of then California governor, Ronald W. Reagan. Together with several colleagues from the Hoover Institution, we had the privilege of briefing the future candidate both at his Sacramento office and also in a conference room on the 11th floor of our Tower building on the Stanford University campus.

On one of the latter occasions, the governor's aide, Peter D. Hannaford, requested a copy of my notes. Some of the ideas I had presented during the briefing later made their way into a Reagan speech, entitled "United States Foreign Policy and World Realities." He delivered it to members of the Foreign Policy Association in New York City. I found this exciting and happily accepted an invitation to speak at an all-day seminar in southern California, where Governor Reagan gave the luncheon address.

My name appeared on the list of foreign and defense policy advisors, released on 22 April 1980, and subsequently among the seven members of a working group on policy towards the Soviet Union and Eastern Europe. When Reagan was elected President, I was then invited to join the transition team. We were given office space in a government-leased building on "M" Street, N.W., in Washington, D.C.

Years earlier I had joined the Cosmos Club, a private social organization for men in government as well as the arts and sciences. Its building is centrally located, only a few blocks from Dupont Circle. It was a convenient place for me to stay. Every day at 6:30 a.m., without having had even a cup of coffee, I literally ran along Massachusetts Avenue to the intersection with Connecticut Avenue and then down to "M" Street. Despite the winter chill at such an early hour, we held daily meetings (including weekends). They were chaired by Edwin Meese III and began punctually at 7:00 a.m. A former deputy U.S. district attorney for Alameda County, California, our chairman later served with distinction in two cabinet-rank positions, as Counselor to the President (1981–85) and then as U.S. Attorney General (1985–88). He was also a member of the National Security Council.

In his memoirs, Meese explains that "with all the policy planning and research going on, someone had to keep track of the whole process, so I created the Office of Policy Coordination (OPC) and placed Darrell Trent in charge."[1] It was Darrell who had invited me to become associate director for national security affairs at OPC. He himself later received appointment as Deputy Secretary of Transportation.

Planning for the Future

Through former contacts and good fortune, we assembled a group of about twelve professionals for my unit, culled from Capitol Hill (congressional staffers), universities, and experts with federal government agencies. All of us from academia worked *pro bono*, meaning that we were paid neither salaries nor reimbursed for travel, meals, and lodging. This did not seem to bother anybody, and the *esprit de corps* remained high.

These activities took up seven days of each week and often did not end until late in the evening. At times, it was close to midnight before we could assemble and distribute copies of position papers for the next 7:00 a.m. meeting. One day, we were invited to brief the president-elect at Blair House about our activities. When Ed Meese mentioned the time our staff meetings began, Governor Reagan asked why so early. Ed replied that this way nobody could claim any prior commitment.

We had been given a complex, yet necessary assignment. Our task was to discover issues that should be resolved in the national security field during a certain time frame. We would then identify the decision-making level (presidential, executive agency, congress) to which it should be directed and suggest possible courses of action. The format of each position paper we would submit included a brief background discussion as well as analysis of the pros and cons regarding different policy options. We were

---

1. Edwin Meese III, *With Reagan: The Inside Story* (Washington, D.C.: Regnery Gateway, 1992), p. 59.

to make no recommendations, however; this step would be taken by those in charge at the executive level.

Our work focused on most of the central issues of the day. We wrote up and discussed such diverse topics as relations between Cuba and the Organization of American States, the grain embargo, Iran and U.S. Claims Commission legislation, the situation in Namibia, reorganization of the Departments of State and Defense, current levels of plutonium production, enhanced radiation warheads, MX basing and location, the new manned bomber, the impending law of the sea conference, status of the *Nimitz* aircraft carrier, the development of a possible "Marshall Plan" for Central America and the Caribbean, a "third" approach to foreign aid, nuclear nonproliferation measures and treaties, international communications policy, the illegal immigration of Haitians, PLO participation in multilateral agencies, U.S. export competitiveness, American policy toward the International Monetary Fund/International Bank for Reconstruction and Development, foreign investments in the U.S., and arms control strategy.[2] We covered other subjects as well.

Richard V. Allen, who became President Reagan's first national security adviser, had taught political science at the Georgia Institute of Technology while I served on the faculty at Emory University. During the transition, he asked me to join his group. I felt obligated to complete the work assigned by Ed Meese, however, and declined this opportunity.

Before returning to California, I prepared strong letters of recommendation, addressed to the director of presidential personnel (E. Pendleton James), for those on our team who were interested in obtaining political appointments. Several thousand such possibilities are listed in *U.S. Government Policy and Supporting Positions*. These are printed for use of the Senate Committee on Governmental Affairs every four years, regardless of which political party wins the White House. I did not send a memo to presidential personnel on my own behalf; while I had been honored to serve with the policy transition team, I was not convinced that such intense work would be in my own—and, of course, my family's—best interests.

At the end of January 1981, it was a relief to be back on the 11th floor of the Tower and to resume my position as principal associate director (and acting director in the absence of the director) at the Hoover Institution. I

---

2. See Robert E. McCarthy, *Log of Meetings, 1980–81*, in the Hoover Institution archives.

could continue publication of articles and books as well as participate in scholarly conferences. Nonetheless, returning to the routine of administrative work and research could never be as exciting as the transition had been. No rose is ever without its thorns!

Call from the White House

Then, one day, the telephone rang. An associate director from the Office of Presidential Personnel, who was in charge of tracking ambassadorial appointments, was calling to inquire about my interest in being considered for chief of mission at the Mutual and Balanced Forces Reduction talks in Vienna, Austria. This appointment carried a Class I designation, the highest among four such ambassadorial ranks in the U.S. Foreign Service.

Even though no offer actually had been made, it was incumbent upon me to request leave-of-absence for public service in case I were to be selected. The director of the Hoover Institution, Dr. W. Glenn Campbell, did not seem too enthusiastic about my request, however, saying that the Institution already was "lean at the top." I pointed out that, after twelve years as principal associate director, I needed a "sabbatical"; besides, such an opportunity comes along only once in a lifetime. He reluctantly agreed with me.

I discussed the possibility with Jadwiga that same evening. The next morning, I called back to say that I would be delighted to become part of the candidate pool. Early in May 1981, the U.S. Marine Corps sent me orders for two weeks of summer active duty at the Command and Staff College in Quantico, Virginia. It was there that the summons for my new "tour of duty" reached me from Washington, D.C.

Changing into civilian clothes, I drove into the city for the appointment with Eugene V. Rostow, the director of the U.S. Arms Control and Disarmament Agency. We had a most amiable conversation. Rostow, former dean of the law school at Yale University and deputy secretary of state in the Carter Administration, told me about several of the other leading candidates for the ambassadorship. My name was among the top three.

The formal selection took place within the confines of a small group of six individuals that included Wendy Borcherdt (associate director of presidential personnel), who chaired the meetings; Richard V. Allen (national security advisor); William P. Clark, Jr. (deputy secretary of state); Richard T. Kennedy (undersecretary of state for management); E. Pendleton James (director of presidential personnel); and Michael K. Deaver (deputy chief of staff to the President), who reportedly did not attend many of these meetings.

During late June, on a Thursday afternoon, the telephone rang in my Tower office. A military-sounding voice told me that the President of the United States (who was at the "Western White House" in Santa Barbara, California) would like to speak with me. The conversation was brief and to the point. President Reagan invited me to become his ambassador to the Mutual and Balanced Forces Reduction negotiations and said that I should expect security people to contact me shortly.

The following Monday morning, a special agent from the FBI sat in my office and explained the paperwork involved. The fact that I held a "secret" clearance with the Marine Corps and even "top secret" with the U.S. Department of Defense meant nothing; the background check and investigation for a presidential appointment would be very thorough and could take six to eight weeks. The forms I needed to fill out were indeed long and required detailed information going back several decades. Each address, every school attended, all positions held and names of supervisors, membership in all organizations as well as financial disclosure documents—virtually every detail about my life—had to be supplied.

Finally, the U.S. "top secret" and the NATO "cosmic" clearances came through. After these preliminaries, it was time for the most comprehensive "oral exam" I would ever undergo: the confirmation hearings before the seventeen-member Senate Foreign Relations Committee in Washington, D.C. In preparation for these, I moved back to the Cosmos Club. The diplomat whom I would succeed, a career foreign service officer named Jonathan Dean, allowed me to study his voluminous reports from Vienna, and officials at the U.S. Arms Control and Disarmament Agency (ACDA) were also most helpful in providing me with current information.

Prior to the hearings, I had requested appointments with each member of the Senate Committee on Foreign Relations. In addition to becoming acquainted, I wanted to give them the opportunity to discuss their concerns and priorities with me, if they chose to, before the very public and politically charged hearings. In one instance, the Department of State secretary assigned to me was told that Senator Alan Cranston had no time for such a meeting; when informed that I was a resident of California, however, he found the time.

Before these face-to-face sessions, I had studied biographic sketches of the pertinent U.S. senators which were published in the *Congressional Directory*. In one case, I learned that Senator Claiborne Pell from Rhode Island had served as the young foreign service officer who opened the American consulate in Bratislava after the end of World War II. Having written a book on East Central Europe, I took the opportunity to talk with the senator about Czechoslovakia.

These meetings proved most beneficial. As I had hoped, they gave me the opportunity to discuss my ideas about arms reduction in a relaxed atmosphere and learn something about the men who would decide whether or not to recommend approval of my appointment to the full United States Senate.

The White House officially announced my nomination to head the U.S. delegation at the MBFR negotiations on 11 September 1981. The commission had been signed on that date by President Ronald W. Reagan and Secretary of State Alexander M. Haig, Jr.

Twenty days after the presidential news release, I appeared before the Committee on Foreign Relations. I thought I was prepared for everything. However, when the chairman first asked me to present a prepared statement, I was momentarily taken aback. Nobody, either at the Department of State or at ACDA, had informed me about this requirement.

Confirmation Hearings

Having taught political science over a period of ten years at Emory University, with two stints as professor at two war colleges, I felt comfortable giving an impromptu presentation on the "state-of-play" at the Vienna talks. Under these circumstances, it was concentrated on the historical and political aspects of the situation. This was probably the best introduction I could have made to the committee. I then talked about what might be done to break the current deadlock between West and East.

The senators listened with interest. Then came the questions. They were all important and demonstrated that the senators had done their homework. In addition to those put to me at the hearing, eighteen other questions were to be answered in writing. The questions and answers below are taken verbatim from the transcript, provided to me by ACDA.

1st Question: Now that the Reagan Administration has been in power for nine months, what can you tell us about its views on arms control?

Answer: As you know, this Administration has been seriously concerned over the deterioration of the U.S. position vis-à-vis the Soviet Union during the past ten years. The Soviets chose, for a variety of reasons, to make the "decade of détente" also the decade of what is probably the most intensive arms buildup the world has ever seen. We neglected our defenses in a number of important areas during that same period of time. What has resulted is an imbalance which is not only dangerous militarily but damaging to the objectives of a serious arms control and arms reduction policy. This Administration proceeds from the assumption that a state of balance [in terms of manpower and equipment] provides the best platform for successful disarmament negotiations and that the Soviets will never negotiate seriously until they are convinced of our earnestness of purpose in restoring and maintaining that balance.

2nd Question: In particular, can you tell us anything about the Administration's views on arms control in Europe or on conventional arms control?

Answer: President Reagan's determination to rectify the errors of past years and to restore the balance between the free West and the states of the Warsaw Pact is part and parcel of a consistent policy which also envisions serious efforts at arms reduction. If it is our responsibility in NATO to ensure that our strength is sufficient to meet any challenge from the Warsaw Pact, we also owe it to our people over the long term to explore every reasonable opportunity to lighten this burden of armaments which we have been bearing for so long. This must be done in a spirit of absolute realism, however, which leaves no room for wishful thinking about what the Soviet intentions might be.

3rd Question: We understand that the Administration is doing a review of arms control and, in the framework of that review, is looking at MBFR. What are the results? What options were considered?

Answer: The Administration's review of the MBFR talks, as a part of its overall review of arms control policy, has not yet been completed. Obviously, there is a wide range of options. Obviously, too, these various options will have to be considered not only from the standpoint of United States concerns but, since it is a multilateral negotiation, from the standpoint of the interests and perception of our Allies.

Rather than trying to describe in detail the various options that are under consideration—what would be in any case inappropriate—I would like to say a word about my own view of the underlying central elements in the MBFR talks. The two most important areas, it seems to me, are those of data—or, to use a somewhat broader and more comprehensible term, information—and verification. It goes without saying that these two areas are very closely related. Whether we go for modest reductions or significant ones, whether we focus on the near term or on the long run, we cannot proceed, it seems to me, without agreement by both sides as to numbers of troops, organizational structure, location, etc. Any effort to patch together an agreement, however limited in nature, which attempted to ignore this fundamental problem would not only be questionable in military and security terms; it would encourage the Soviets to persist in a secretive, obstructive, uncooperative approach to the concrete aspects of arms control which has been damaging not only to MBFR but to the whole range of arms control negotiations in which we and the Russians have been engaged.

Clearly, we can never be convinced that the Soviets have changed their ways and started to provide complete and accurate information without an adequate program of verification. This means, in the area of troops and conventional weapons just as in the area of nuclear weaponry, that national technical means, as valuable and impressive as they are, will not suffice. Some form of cooperative measures will have to be found which permits us to satisfy ourselves beyond a shadow of a doubt that the numbers are as they have been stated and that the agreed reductions have in fact been carried out. This goes very much against the Soviet grain. But it is evidence of the seriousness with which this Administration approaches arms control matters.

4th Question: With our defense program increasing, and the continued heavy commitment to Europe, why are we pursuing MBFR negotiations? Is there anything in the present MBFR negotiating program or any of the options under consideration which interferes with defense programs for Central Europe?

Answer: Arms control, including MBFR, cannot be the sole answer to our national security. It does not provide a substitute for national defense. In fact, it is this Administration's conviction—and one which I share—that only a strong U.S. and Western defense posture and the demonstrated determination by the U.S. and the West to maintain a strong defense can provide the basis for successful arms control negotiations with the Soviets.

Even if an MBFR agreement were in force, improvements to NATO's defenses would still be necessary. There would still be the need for a strong U.S. commitment to the Alliance.

MBFR, as presently constituted, concerns only manpower. Thus, an MBFR agreement, as currently envisaged, would prevent only an increase in manpower.

5th Question: Why did you take this job, and what do you expect to accomplish with it?

Answer: I believe that the MBFR talks have proven useful in a number of ways even without a reduction agreement. They have established a carefully defined forum for conventional arms control in which the Soviets and their allies have been forced to encounter, if not face up to, some of the concrete problems of arms control relating to numbers, definitions, verification, etc. In addition, the Vienna forum has a certain instructive potential for the public view of these matters, particularly in Western Europe. I am not convinced that we have exploited this potential as well and as consistently as we might have done; ideally, it seems to me, the MBFR talks could be used to illustrate rather vividly the Soviet unwillingness to come to terms with the vast imbalance which has been created in the Central European area, and which goes far beyond any legitimate defense needs that the countries of the Warsaw Pact might have.

6th Question: We understand that one of the stumbling blocks on MBFR has been Eastern unwillingness and particularly Soviet unwillingness to come clean about how many Soviet soldiers there are in Eastern Europe. Can we break this deadlock and, if so, how?

Answer: I would not like to speculate on the motivations of the East in tabling its manpower data. I will say that we and our Allies are confident of the figures we have on Eastern forces, and we have made our views clear to the East. We have sought to investigate the possibility that Eastern figures are based on definitions that do not include all elements we count under air and ground military manpower. So far, however, we have identified no significant difference in the definitional approaches of the two sides. It would be our intention, nevertheless, to continue to try to resolve the data dispute with the East in a constructive way.

7th Question: We understand that another stumbling block has been on-site inspection. The USSR has accepted on-site inspection, at least in principle, in other forums. Why haven't they accepted it in MBFR?

Answer: It is true that the East has indicated it has problems with the Western inspection proposal, but the East has not given a comprehensive and constructive response to our proposals for associated measures. We therefore do not consider that the negative Eastern reaction on inspection represents its definitive position.

Our inspection proposal is certainly more comprehensive and far-reaching than the on-site inspection scheme the Soviets have accepted—I believe you are referring to the Peaceful Nuclear Explosion Treaty—and it will require a greater compromise of their tradition of secrecy for them to accept the measure in MBFR.

In any case, we consider the matter to be still under discussion.

8th Question: What advantage would there be in negotiating an MBFR agreement? Is the present negotiating program the one we should be following?

Answer: We are reviewing the entire question of the Western negotiating program. Because that review is not complete, I do not feel that I should get into the details of the options we are considering.

Generally, however, we believe that, if we can achieve an agreement which (1) creates a stable conventional balance at lower levels of forces, (2) contributes to confidence among the neighboring Central European states, and (3) is supported by an adequate program of verification based on accurate information on opposing military forces, this would be beneficial for all of Europe.

9th Question: How do the Allies feel about pursuing MBFR? Do they all have the same attitude?

Answer: One of the advantages of the MBFR negotiations, even though they have not as yet resulted in troop reductions, has been the process of Alliance consultations on the talks throughout their eight-year history. Alliance cohesion that has been the result of working out a unified Alliance position on all aspects of the Western negotiating program has had benefits far beyond the talks themselves. Once the negotiating positions have been worked out in Brussels, the members of the Alliance participating in the talks have always strongly supported the Western position.

All of our Allies agreed that MBFR is a valuable channel of communication between East and West on security issues, and all support the objective of a more stable balance at lower levels of forces.

10th Question: How does MBFR relate to other arms control negotiations in prospect for Europe? For instance, to TNF [Theater Nuclear Forces] modernization and arms control or the French CDE [Conference on Disarmament in Europe] proposal?

Answer: As you know, in December 1979 the NATO foreign ministers announced a coordinated program of force modernization and arms control. At that time, we decided to focus on manpower reductions in MBFR and therefore dropped our previous proposals for "Option III" armament reductions. This decision was made in part because, under NATO intermediate-range nuclear force (INF) modernization plans, the Pershing I's were to be replaced in coming years with the Pershing II's, which are included in the INF arms control negotiations which NATO has proposed. Moreover, as part of the NATO program, the U.S. announced, and completed in 1980, the unilateral withdrawal of 1,000 tactical nuclear warheads from Europe. Thus, two of the three elements of the Western nuclear reduction offer in MBFR were being treated elsewhere. This approach was intended to simplify the negotiating problem of reaching a Phase I agreement in MBFR.

The proposal for a Conference on Disarmament in Europe (CDE) is being discussed in the context of the Conference on Security and Cooperation in Europe (CSCE), which is an all-European forum plus Canada and the United States. We have made clear that we envisage the mandate for a Conference on Disarmament in Europe as limited to confidence building measures (CBMs). MBFR, on the other hand, covers a specific part of Central Europe and it involves negotiations on arms reductions. Although within the MBFR context we are discussing associated measures for the purpose of verifying compliance with the arms reduction aspects of MBFR and for confidence building, we believe that MBFR and a conference on European security should be distinct and should not interfere with each other.

11th Question: We note that, for budgetary reasons, the U.K. Government recently decided to make cuts in the British Army of the Rhine, and the Bonn government is cutting back the number of its troops participating in exercises. Is there a danger that these governments also may cut their forces unilaterally without trying to do so in the context of an MBFR agreement?

Answer: As is generally known, one of the reasons the NATO Alliance was first interested in MBFR was to prevent, or to eliminate the need for, unilateral U.S. withdrawals from Central Europe. In fact, one of the side benefits of MBFR is that it has been an important factor in the decisions of all Allied governments *not* to reduce their forces unilaterally. It is our belief that decisions concerning Alliance force levels should be made with the Alliance in mind and in the light of NATO's balance with the Warsaw Pact.

I see no evidence that either the United Kingdom or the Federal Republic of Germany is planning to reduce their forces unilaterally below the commitments they have made. Both have strongly affirmed their support of MBFR.

12th Question: How does the Administration square its policy of beefing up our forces in Central Europe with the Western position in MBFR calling for troop reductions? If an agreement were reached in

MBFR, would the Administration be willing to reduce and limit U.S. forces in Central Europe?

Answer: We believe the negotiations will be most successful if the Soviets and their allies are convinced of Western steadfastness in restoring and maintaining the balance in Central Europe. Although we will, of course, be ready to explore every opportunity to create a more stable balance through negotiated reductions, we do not intend to be caught short by neglecting our Alliance defense responsibilities while waiting for the East to adopt a forthcoming approach in MBFR. If an agreement were reached in MBFR, it would be because we and our Allies had determined it would be in the West's security interest, and in that case, we would be willing to reduce and limit our forces.

13th Question: If NATO nations increase defense spending by three percent annually, how would this affect the chances of successfully concluding an MBFR agreement?

Answer: Since such increases in defense spending and NATO's long-term defense program for force improvements do not necessarily involve significant increases in air and ground manpower, no direct impact on the Western MBFR proposal has been identified. More broadly, however, such programs demonstrate Western resolve in responding to Eastern force improvements. In this sense, NATO is negotiating from ever increasing strength.

14th Question: Is it true that MBFR might constrain U.S. reinforcement of forces already stationed there in a crisis?

Answer: Under our proposal, both the U.S. and USSR as well as the Eastern and Western forces in the area as a whole, would be constrained under MBFR limitations from increasing their total collective manpower in Europe except for agreed exceptions (for example, to permit normal exercises). Our response to a crisis would depend on many factors, including whether the East had violated the agreement. However, we believe the provisions of a properly designed MBFR agreement would help and not hinder Alliance decision-making as well as effective Alliance response in a crisis.

15th Question: Would an MBFR agreement affect our ability to use European bases as staging areas for Rapid Deployment Joint Task Force [RDJTF] elements en route to trouble spots in the Middle East or elsewhere?

Answer: No. It is our position that RDJTF elements, or indeed any forces transiting the area of reductions en route elsewhere, are not subject to MBFR residual ceilings because they do not augment forces stationed there.

16th Question: It seems that vastly increased Eastern firepower, not manpower, is the key threat to the Alliance in Central Europe. If so, why do we need to continue the MBFR negotiations?

Answer: That is a reasonable concern. One of the original objectives of MBFR was to alter the size and offensive orientation of Warsaw Pact forces through the withdrawal from Central Europe of large numbers of Soviet troops and tanks in units and reductions of non-Soviet Warsaw Pact manpower. But this negotiating effort met with little success. It was therefore decided in 1979 to shift the Western focus to a first agreement of limited manpower reductions in order to start the MBFR process. This approach was combined with a significant package of associated measures to enhance warning, and inspire confidence as well as to verify reductions. Measures of this type would clearly enhance the military value of a Phase I agreement.

Nevertheless, we are concerned about enhancing the military value of an MBFR agreement, and this concern is a major element in the Administration's ongoing review of MBFR policy.

17th Question: Would an MBFR agreement, if one existed, provide useful additional leverage in the Polish crisis to discourage the Soviets from intervening militarily? If so, why has the Administration not supported an MBFR agreement actively?

Answer: An MBFR agreement along the lines the West has been proposing throughout the negotiations would involve a limitation on the number of troops the Soviets could deploy in Central Europe, i.e., in the entire area of the [East] German Democratic Republic, Czechoslovakia, and Poland. The introduction of additional Soviet troops, unless otherwise specifically provided for, would be a violation of the agreement. To this extent, that is, to the extent that Soviet intervention in Poland would involve abrogation of an MBFR agreement (if one were in effect), there would presumably be an inhibition on Soviet actions. But we must be realistic: this would be only an inhibition; it would not prevent a Soviet decision to intervene. We do not think it would be wise to seek or to justify an MBFR agreement solely (or primarily) because of the hope that it might be a deterrent to Soviet actions in Poland.

18th Question: Why have Administration officials avoided even mentioning MBFR, the only actual arms control negotiation currently underway with the Soviets, in their public statements on arms control?

Answer: I suspect you would have to ask the individual officials. However, as you know, the focus in arms control at the moment is, and rightly so, on START and INF. The fact that MBFR (and other arms control subjects, such as those treated by the Committee on Disarmament in Geneva) has not received public attention does not imply a lack of interest on the part of the Administration. It probably simply reflects a lack of "newsworthy" progress in MBFR.

Briefings Prior to Departure

Jadwiga and I did not wait for the Senate Committee on Foreign Relations and Senate votes before heading back to California. The news of my confirmation reached us a few days later. We then packed our personal effects, did not take either a car or any furniture, and arranged for the rental of our condominium on the Stanford campus. These accommodations were welcomed by a visiting professor from Oslo, and the second year by an academic couple from Paris. The Department of State had invited both of us to three days of in-depth briefings, during 25–27 August 1981 (i.e., *before* confirmation hearings), for newly appointed ambassadors-designate and their spouses. This represented an encouraging "vote of confidence."

Chaired by Shirley Temple Black, former ambassador to Ghana and later chief of mission in Czechoslovakia, these sessions were packed with information. Participants heard reports from top-ranking officials: the director-general of the foreign service, under secretaries for management and political affairs, regional and functional assistant secretaries of state, the acting director of intelligence and research, the deputy inspector-general, the U.S. ambassador to the People's Republic of China, and the acting director of the Office for Combating Terrorism, among others.

Some of these presentations were not relevant to the MBFR negotiation process, e.g., the work of our ambassador to Mainland China or communications and administrative resources of an embassy. Our mission would be highly specialized and rather small in comparison with the bilateral ones accredited to another country. Nonetheless, the remainder of the program was most interesting and indeed outstanding.

Six of the thirteen ambassadors-designate were political appointees, and all appeared to have excellent qualifications. This included knowledge of pertinent foreign languages or experience in-country. Thomas Aranda, Jr. (Mexico), for example, spoke fluent Spanish; John E. Dolibois

(Luxembourg) had been born in that country; David B. Funderburk (Romania) had studied in Bucharest on a Fulbright Fellowship; David Charles Miller, Jr. (Tanzania) had lived three years in Nigeria; Langhorne A. Motley (Brazil) had been born and raised in that country, being bilingual in Portuguese and Spanish; I, of course, spoke German, Polish, and Russian.

The group compared favorably with the seven career foreign service officers who also took part in these briefings before being posted overseas. Unfortunately, the general impression seemed to be that career FSOs were mostly well qualified for *any* position, whereas political appointees for unspecified reasons were not as well qualified. This perception certainly was inaccurate with regard to our group. Forty-two percent of President Kennedy's appointments had been political in the foreign service, compared with 41 percent for President Reagan.[3]

The Foreign Service Institute at the Department of State also offered foreign language classes as well as two-week area studies programs for those being posted overseas. We did not avail ourselves of either opportunity, because they were unnecessary from our point of view and would have meant delaying the departure for Vienna. The new round of MBFR talks would resume in September.

Useful publications were distributed at the seminar, such as *Diplomatic Social Usage*. It told me that "Ambassadors of the United States retain the title of *The Honorable* for life." I realized, of course, that this distinction had no applicability in academia. And yet, it gave me a warm feeling.

---

3. *Washington Post*, 16 August 1983.

CHAPTER 5

BALANCE OF POWER

President Reagan's national security adviser, Richard V. Allen, addressed a distinguished audience at the Metropolitan Club in Washington, D.C.[1] His talk presented a most authoritative analysis of presidential policies vis-à-vis the USSR, from his perspective as an insider who undoubtedly had helped shape the outlook of the President even before he took office.

The policy of the previous administration had been to acquiesce to the imposition of communism throughout Eastern Europe, as well as Soviet "national liberation" wars in the Third World. Considerable "looking the other way" was required, in order for the United States to maintain an atmosphere of détente with Moscow. According to Allen, President Reagan rejected this conventional wisdom of the day. Even before his inauguration, Governor Reagan had developed a tougher strategy in regard to the Kremlin.

The gist of this strategy is revealed in the declassified National Security Decision Directive (NSDD) 75, entitled "U.S. Relations with the USSR." As described by Richard Allen, it stated that the United States would no longer be content merely to shape and influence Soviet behavior, but would set out to change the Soviet system itself, and literally "roll back" Soviet advances and conquests outside its borders.

To use Allen's words, this approach indeed represented "a sea change in U.S. policy."

---

1. Richard V. Allen, "The Man Who Changed the Game Plan," *The National Interest*, no. 44 (summer 1996), pp. 60–65.

Ronald Reagan introduced a breath of fresh air and realism into presidential public statements. When he said that communists would "lie, cheat, and steal," Moscow paid attention. When he declared that the doctrine of Mutual Assured Destruction (MAD) made hostages of the American people, the Kremlin listened.

President Reagan continued "to speak the truth about them [the Soviets] for a change, rather than hiding reality behind the niceties of diplomacy."[2] I would remember the president's words of wisdom during my tour at MBFR in Vienna.

Implementation of NSDD

By mid-1981, the new administration in Washington took steps to demonstrate its new resolve. It began to deploy the B-1 bomber, started expansion of the navy toward a goal of 600 ships, moved to perfect the MX and cruise missiles, and substantially increased funding for military research and development. The Soviet economy could not hope to match such a buildup. In addition, the USSR would soon be cut off from access to advanced technology. Through the efforts of the Central Intelligence Agency and the Pentagon, the technology embargo would extend to other NATO members as well.[3]

Finally, in a move to put pressure on the Soviet economy, Saudi Arabia cooperated with the United States by increasing oil production from two million to nine million barrels per year. The result was a surplus on the world market and a decline of prices from $30 to $12 per barrel. The Soviets began to lose approximately $10 billion per year in income from the export of their own oil. Moscow, thus, had much less money with which to produce expensive weapons systems.

Between 1981 and 1985, President Reagan had to deal with four successive Soviet leaders—Leonid I. Brezhnev, Iurii V. Andropov, Konstantin U. Chernenko, and Mikhail S. Gorbachev—or an average of one per year. The first change in leadership came on 10 November 1982, and the last on 10 March 1985. It seemed like a lost cause to handle in rapid

---

2. Quoted by Stephen F. Knott, "Reagan's Critics," *The National Interest*, no. 44 (summer 1996), p. 69.

3. Richard F. Staar, "The High Tech Transfer Offensive of the Soviet Union," *Strategic Review*, vol. 17, no. 2, spring 1989, pp. 32–39.

succession so many different individuals; furthermore, the first three were arguably senile or on life support systems before they died. Consequently, the identities of the real decision makers for the regime—and their priorities—were also part of the subterfuge that characterized the era.

A survey of international views and policies for calendar year 1981 suggests that the Kremlin leadership had a lot on its agenda. In addition to political uncertainty at home, it was attempting to solve the crisis regarding the Solidarity movement in Poland as well as maintain gains in the Third World achieved during the previous two decades.[4]

By the use of proxies, the USSR had made extraordinary progress in both Africa and Asia (see Table 3). The attempt to exert control as well as influence culminated in the ten-year (1979–1989) unsuccessful attempt by 100,000 Soviet troops to subjugate Afghanistan. In addition, there was an unprecedented peacetime expansion of both nuclear and conventional armaments. Deployment by Moscow of the SS-20 triple-headed intermediate-range nuclear missiles reached a total of about 160 launchers already installed by mid-1980 and one per week added thereafter. They were targeted against West European members of NATO as well as U.S. forces stationed in that region.

The Soviet Union also held a three-to-one advantage over the United States in highly accurate intercontinental ballistic missiles, developed and deployed during the previous decade. When the U.S. Congress refused to support deployment of the MX missile, President Reagan decided to explore construction of a defensive system. Thus was born the Strategic Defense Initiative (SDI), for which research has been done both on sea-based and land-based counterparts.[5]

---

4. R. Judson Mitchell, "Union of Soviet Socialist Republics," *1982 Yearbook on International Communist Affairs* (Stanford, Calif.: Hoover Institution Press, 1982), pp. 479–84.

5. See Martin Anderson, *An Insurance Missile Defense* (Stanford, Calif.: Hoover Institution Press, 1986), p. 12.

Table 3
Movements with a "Socialist" Orientation in Third World Countries

Country	Name of Movement
Afghanistan (1978)	People's Democratic Party of Afghanistan*
Algeria	National Liberation Front (FLN)
Angola (1976)	Movement for People's Liberation of Angola— Labor Party
Bahrain	National Liberation Front*
Benin (1981?)	People's Revolutionary Party of Benin*
Burkina-Faso	National Council of the Revolution (CNR)
Burundi	Union for National Progress (UPRONA)
Cape Verde	African Party for Independence of Cape Verde (PAICV)
Chad	National Democratic Union*
Congo/Brazzaville (1981)	Congolese Workers' Party* (PCT)
Ethiopia (1978)	Workers' Party of Ethiopia*
Ghana	Provisional National Defense Council
Grenada	Maurice Bishop Patriotic Movement*
Guinea	Democratic Party of Guinea (PDG)†
Guinea/Bissau	African Party for Independence of Guinea (PAIGC)
Madagascar	Congress Party for Independence of Madagascar (AKFM)
Mali	Democratic Union of the Mali People (UDPM)
Mozambique (1977)	Mozambique Liberation Front* (FRELIMO)
Nicaragua (1980?)	Sandinista National Liberation Front (FSLN)
São Tome and Principe	Movement for the Liberation of São Tome and Principe
Seychelles	Seychelles People's Progressive Front
South Korea	National Democratic Front of South Korea*
South Yemen (1979)	Yemen Socialist Party*
Suriname	National Democratic Party*
Syria (1980)	Arab Socialist Resurrectionist (Ba'th) Party
Tanzania	Revolutionary Party of Tanzania (CCM)
Zambia	United National Independence Party
Zimbabwe	Zimbabwe African National Union–Patriotic Front*

Notes: * Called vanguard parties by Soviet writers.
† The PDG was dissolved after the April 1984 military coup.

Source: A. M. Prokhorov (ed.), *Ezhegodnik bol'shoi sovetskoi entsiklopedii, 1981* (Moscow: *Sovetskaia entsiklopediia*, 1981), p. 212.

✧ ✧ ✧ ✧

At his first press conference, President Reagan accused Soviet leaders of resorting even to crimes to pursue their objectives. While quite verifiably true, this was not at all what the Soviets wanted to hear. Secretary of State Alexander M. Haig, Jr., in a similar setting, described the USSR as the primary supporter of international terrorism. In response, toward the end of February 1981, Leonid Brezhnev addressed the 26th CPSU Congress with an eight-point "peace proposal." Designed for propaganda purposes, it was picked up and disseminated around the world through international communist front organizations.

Ronald Reagan's NSDD 75, quoted above, provided a clear picture of new American policies toward the USSR. Our objectives would fall within specific lines:

1. To contain and reverse over time Soviet expansionism by competing effectively on a sustained basis with the Soviet Union in all international arenas ...

2. To promote ... the process of change in the Soviet Union toward a more pluralistic political and economic system in which the power of the privileged ruling elite is gradually reduced ...

3. To engage the Soviet Union in negotiations to attempt to reach agreements which protect and enhance U.S. interests ...

NSDD 75, dated 17 January 1983, had been directed toward Brezhnev's successors. It stated that "unacceptable [Soviet] behavior will incur costs that would outweigh any gains ... " and that "this message will be conveyed clearly during the succession period." On the other hand, "genuine restraint in their behavior would create the possibility of an East-West relationship that might bring important benefits for the Soviet Union."

The paragraph concerning arms control stated that American proposals would be "consistent with necessary force modernization plans and will seek to achieve balanced, significant, and verifiable reductions to equal levels of comparable armaments." Meanwhile, under military strategy, it concluded that "the U.S. must modernize its forces—both nuclear and conventional—so that Soviet leaders perceive that the U.S. is determined never to accept a second place or a deteriorating military posture."

Case Study: Poland

For all its apparent might, however, Soviet authority was starting to unravel in Eastern Europe. It all started in August 1981 with strikes at major industrial plants around Warsaw and a spill-over at Gdańsk on the Baltic coast, where about 140 enterprises stopped work. The leader of the Solidarity independence movement was a 37-year-old electrician, Lech Wałęsa.[6] His would become a household name around the world.

Table 4
World Socialist System, 1989

**Socialist Commonwealth of Nations
(Council for Mutual Economic Assistance Members)**

Country	Year Joined
Bulgaria	1949
Cuba	1972
Czechoslovakia*	1949
East Germany†	1950
Hungary*	1949
Cambodia	(observer)
Laos	(observer)
Mongolia	1962
Poland*	1949
Romania	1949
Soviet Union	1949
Vietnam	1978

---

6. See Aleksei Danilov, "Mezh dvukh ognei," *Nezavisimoe voennoe obozrenie*, no. 12 (27 March–2 April 1998), p. 7; see also Table on the "World Socialist System."

Other Communist-Ruled States

Albania
China
North Korea
Yugoslavia   (associate member)

* Since 1989, these East–Central European governments had been reconstituted without communist participation. After renaming themselves "socialist," however, some of the former communist parties have made political advances.

† Absorbed by the Federal Republic of Germany in October 1990.

Source: *Pravda*, 23 September 1989, p. 5.

✧ ✧ ✧ ✧

A measure of Soviet control was reasserted when General Wojciech Jaruzelski became prime minister of Poland in February 1981. Then, on 1 October, he was "elected" first secretary of the ruling Polish United Workers' [Communist] Party. The general had grown up as a teenager in the USSR, after the Hitler-Stalin pact allocated eastern Poland to the Soviet Union in 1939. His family soon found itself among the approximately 1,600,000 middle-class Poles deported to Siberia or Central Asia. As a young officer in the newly formed "Kościuszko" division, after the German invasion of the USSR in June 1941, Jaruzelski chose to remain with that pro-Soviet group rather than join Polish troops in England. He, thus, returned to Poland with the Red Army.

According to the below-cited Russian source, a meeting of the CPSU Politburo in Moscow on 29 October 1981 decided unanimously that restoration of order in Poland should be handled by the Polish communists themselves. The Soviets did not want a repeat of Czechoslovakia (1968), where the Red Army once again imposed its will on an "ally." A recently published book by the former archivist of the Russian Federation sheds light on the Soviet decision not to invade Poland. It cites primary source materials, including transcripts from hitherto secret CPSU Politburo meetings. Iurii V. Andropov, as KGB chairman and *de facto* Soviet leader in place of the ailing Brezhnev, told his colleagues on the Politburo that the line would be maintained "not to introduce our troops into Poland" for the purpose of smashing the Solidarity movement of industrial workers against the communist regime in Warsaw.[7]

At a subsequent working session of the Politburo on 10 December 1981, Andropov repeated the foregoing, based on the fear that the West would invoke economic sanctions against the USSR. "We should manifest care for our country, strengthening the Soviet Union. This is our main concern."[8]

After USSR leaders had repeatedly refused to invade Poland, General Wojciech Jaruzelski sent them the following message: "During the night of 12–13 December 1981, martial law will be proclaimed throughout all territories of the Polish People's Republic. Full responsibility for this measure is assumed by myself." Little did the Soviet comrades know that this step represented the beginning of the end for communist rule over all of Eastern Europe and that, within nine years, the Soviet Union would disintegrate.

During the night of 6–7 November, Colonel Ryszard Kukliński disappeared from his general staff office in Warsaw, where he had been involved with developing plans for introduction of martial law in Poland, and succeeded in escaping to the West. His subsequent report on the situation received CIA distribution to only five individuals: President Reagan, Vice President George Bush, Secretary of State Alexander Haig, Defense Secretary Caspar Weinberger, and National Security Adviser Richard Allen.

The United States government, in the person of President Reagan, played a major role during the ensuing events throughout Poland. The President signed a classified National Security Decision Directive in early 1982 for the purpose of destabilizing the Polish communist regime. Its implementation supported the Solidarity movement, with the assistance of Pope John Paul II in the Vatican and the Roman Catholic church in Poland. Funds for Solidarity "came from the CIA, the National Endowment for Democracy, secret Vatican bank accounts, and Western trade unions."[9]

As the West offered such support, the KGB tried to defuse tensions with a new kind of publicity campaign. With Andropov's actual ascen-

---

7. See Rudolf G. Pikhoia, *Sovetskii Soiuz: Istoriia vlasti, 1945–1991* (Moscow: Izdatel'stvo AGS, 1998), p. 407.

8. Ibid., p. 411.

9. Knott, *op. cit.*, p. 71.

dancy, media in the United States began to publish reports that he shared Western values. Behind this disinformation campaign stood the KGB, which worked hard to create a new image of the party-state chief. Thus, Andropov secretly listened to jazz, read Susan Sontag novels, and drank Scotch whiskey. In actual fact, he never indulged in any of these things. However, he did inherit more power than any Soviet leader since Stalin.[10] KGB disinformation, nevertheless, was accepted as being the truth by the mass media and even some policy-makers in the West. The extent of fabrication is evident, given that Andropov lasted only fifteen months, part of this time on a life-support system.

Back in Poland, however, secret communications equipment and printing presses resulted in distribution of hundreds of different newsletters as well as underground newspapers. Government radio programs were interrupted by slogans calling for resistance and support of the banned Solidarity movement, operating underground. The movement peaked in 1987. At this point, with Mikhail S. Gorbachev at the helm in the USSR and "new thinking" about alliances in place, Jaruzelski was forced to begin negotiations with the Church and subsequently with Lech Wałęsa. Eventually, in 1990, Wałęsa would become the first popularly elected president of Poland.

Years later, Jaruzelski testified at Warsaw on 19 April 2000 during the repeat trial of twenty-two communist-era riot policemen. They had shot and killed nine coal miners shortly after introduction of martial law in December 1981. Jaruzelski justified his decision to introduce martial law by saying that it was a "lesser evil" and that it had saved Poland from intervention by Warsaw Pact allies which meant, of course, the Soviet Union.[11] This contradicts the known decision in Moscow not to intervene that had been communicated to Jaruzelski, as mentioned in the foregoing. Then, on 5 September 2001, Jaruzelski's own trial commenced in Warsaw regarding his responsibility as defense minister for the killing of unarmed shipyard workers who were demonstrating against food-price increases. This trial continues.

The eventual fall of the Iron Curtain and the collapse of the USSR was almost a decade away, however, when the talks in Vienna were taking

---

10. Pikhoia, op. cit., p. 415.

11. The article entitled "Wojciech Jaruzelski revisiting Polish history," *The Economist* (London), 26 August 2000, p. 42, repeated the same false claim.

place. At that time, it would have been foolhardy to expect the Soviets to be forthcoming at MBFR, when their world empire seemed to be threatened by forces they themselves unwittingly had unleashed. It was this atmosphere that would continue to affect and even overshadow negotiations in Vienna.[12]

The situation can be summarized by quoting from a document, recently declassified, which had been produced by the U.S. intelligence community in 1982. These key judgments appeared as National Intelligence Estimate (NIE) 11-4-82, entitled "The Soviet Challenge to U.S. Security Interests." It begins by stating that Moscow's relationship with the United States was fundamentally adversarial, based on its ideology and view of geopolitics. The constant increase in military power and capabilities represented the basis for extension of the Kremlin's "global presence and influence at the expense of the United States and the West." It further asserts that "sustained expansion and modernization of Soviet general purpose forces ... demonstrate Moscow's intention of dominating the regional military balance in Central Europe . . . ."[13]

Dark Shadow of the Warsaw Pact

The postwar military alliance known as the "Warsaw Pact" or the Warsaw Treaty Organization came into being in the capital of Poland on 14 May 1955. It represented a legal justification for continued stationing of Soviet troops throughout East-Central Europe. In addition, between 1956 and 1968, bilateral status-of-forces agreements were signed by the USSR successively with Poland, East Germany, Romania, Hungary, and Czechoslovakia. Later, it would provide the "counterbalance" to NATO in the West.

The Austrian State Treaty of 15 May 1955 had obligated the USSR to withdraw its troops from Hungary and Romania within forty days. It did so only from the latter country some three years later in June 1958. Troops

---

12. See also Peter Schweizer (ed.), *The Fall of the Berlin Wall: Reassessing the Causes and Consequences of the End of the Cold War* (Stanford, Calif.: Hoover Institution Press, 2000), especially his chapter on pp. 1–47.

13. See Donald P. Steury (ed.), *Intentions and Capabilities: Estimates on Soviet Strategic Forces, 1950–1983* (Washington, D.C.: CIA Center for the Study of Intelligence, 1996), pp. 475–81.

remained in the former. Assertions of socialist brotherhood to the contrary notwithstanding, the WTO relationship clearly represented that of master and client states.[14]

With its occupation forces throughout the region, Moscow-imposed governments were "elected" and administered by satellite communist party organizations. This arrangement was tolerated for more than a decade, as these countries began their postwar reconstruction.

Three events alerted Soviet leaders to the fact that citizens of these satellite states did not willingly support their puppet rulers. In October 1956, the Hungarian revolution would have swept away a hated communist regime, had not the Soviet army reoccupied the country in force. Then, in 1968, when the local communist party leader, Alexander Dubček, in neighboring Czechoslovakia attempted to "put a human face" on his regime, Soviet troops invaded that country. Only in Poland did the strikes during July 1980 lead to martial law, invoked by the local communist regime without Soviet intervention.

During the early 1980s, however, Soviet troops were still garrisoned in four of the Warsaw Pact member states:

1. the Northern Group of Forces, with headquarters at Legnica, Lower Silesia in Poland;

2 the Southern Group of Forces at Tököl near Budapest, Hungary;

3. the Central Group of Forces at Milovice, Czechoslovakia; and

4. the Group of Forces in the so-called German Democratic Republic (GDR) at Zossen-Wünsdorf near East Berlin.

Figures for these Soviet troops comprised respectively two, four, five, and nineteen divisions. An approximate ratio of one-to-one between armored and motorized rifle divisions prevailed, with a considerably heavier concentration of USSR firepower in its own divisions than existed within each of the satellite armed forces.

---

14. Malcolm Mackintosh, "The Evolution of the Warsaw Pact," *Delphi Papers*, no. 58 (London, June 1969), p. 25.

In the GDR, Soviet occupation troops outnumbered those of the East Germans by a ratio of almost 3½ to 1. This was a significant standing army to maintain in an allied country! In addition, Soviet soldiers were equipped with ground-to-ground guided missiles and a capability of delivering nuclear warheads at targets up to 185 miles away. It is doubtful that the USSR would have allowed its East German "allies" to assume control over such weapons of mass destruction.

Five Soviet divisions continued to be stationed in Czechoslovakia after the 1968 invasion. They also were there to protect the uranium mines at Jáchymov, Teplice, and Príbram as well as those located in nearby East Germany, just south of Aue. Total output of this strategic materiél went directly to the USSR for production of nuclear warheads.

In Hungary, the ratio of Soviet to indigenous forces totaled two to one in armored divisions and three to one in aircraft ever since the abortive October 1956 revolution. USSR troops also ensured delivery of uranium from the mines at Pécs.

East-Central Europe represented a source of other strategic raw materials, such as bauxite from Czechoslovakia; basic chemicals, rare metals, and bismuth from East Germany; metallic sodium from Poland; as well as cadmium, molybdenum, titanium, and graphite from throughout the region.

During more than thirty years, from 1956 into 1988, developments among Warsaw Treaty Organization members pointed in one direction: preparation for a war against NATO in which tactical nuclear weapons could be used. At the same time, there were clearly plans to keep open the "conventional option," as well.

USSR military doctrine of the 1980s painted a chilling picture of a possible conflict in Central Europe. Under one scenario, beginning with Soviet strategic nuclear strikes, ground operations would be launched simultaneously by massive armored and motorized rifle divisions in conjunction with airborne units on a large scale. Such movements, at speeds of up to 75 kilometers per day, would be supported by battlefield nuclear weapons, unless the conflict remained strictly conventional.[15] Needless to say, the sphere of operations would be the territory of the WTO "allies," all to be sacrificed in case of Soviet military action.

---

15. See Harriet Fast Scott and William F. Scott, *The Armed Forces of the USSR*, 3rd rev. ed., Boulder, Colo.: Westview Press, 1984, 455 pp.

NATO and Its Priorities

The North Atlantic Treaty Organization, on the other hand, traces its origins back to 1949, during the height of the Cold War. At that time, the Soviets had consolidated their control over almost all territories that were occupied by the Red Army in Eastern Europe as a result of World War II. Only Yugoslavia under Josip Broz-Tito remained independent. Neighboring Albania, with its rabid communist leader, Enver Hoxha, also remained independent from and outside of the Soviet bloc. Later Hoxha would go so far as to court and ally Tirana with distant Beijing rather than deal with the Soviets.

NATO came into being on 4 April 1949 during the Soviet blockade of Berlin. For the United States, this represented a sharp departure from traditional avoidance of "entangling alliances" during a time of peace. The need to maintain such an alliance was made clear by the invasion of South Korea in June 1950. That the USSR might attack Western Europe could not be ignored. These developments led to NATO becoming "the central and single most effective multi-national security organization in Europe."[16]

Stepping into a situation with such strong military overtones, I was pleased to know that my superior at "Foggy Bottom" (Alexander M. Haig, Jr.) held the military rank of a general. It was a privilege to meet him at the Department of State after approval of my nomination by the Senate of the United States and before departure for Vienna.

I felt immediately comfortable with this man, who had been vice chief of staff for the U.S. Army and later Supreme Allied Commander, Europe (SACEUR). He served as U.S. Secretary of State during an eighteen-month period.[17] I took it as a good sign, too, that Secretary Haig's executive assistant, Colonel Sherwood D. Goldberg, had been graduated from Dickinson College.

Prior to arrival in Vienna, I realized that Soviet leaders took their world outlook seriously. They had achieved short-term victories during the 1980s throughout Latin America, which they portrayed as a "continent in upheaval." Nikita S. Khrushchev himself had coined the term *revolutionary*

---

16. David S. Yost, *NATO Transformed* (Washington, D.C.: U.S. Institute of Peace Press, 1998), p. 27.
17. Alexander M. Haig, Jr., *Caveat: Realism, Reagan, and Foreign Policy* (New York: Macmillan Publishing Company, 1984), 367 pp.

democracy as the basis for supporting Third World leaders of lower middle-class origins who were not proletarians. More than 34,000 students from the Third World were enrolled in academic, technical, and military training courses at Soviet colleges and universities.[18]

Unknown to me at this time was the fact that Soviet leaders had read a Hoover Institution volume, as later mentioned by Secretary Shultz in his memoirs. He discusses a meeting at the Kremlin with Mikhail S. Gorbachev, who picked up a book from the table next to him. It was *The United States in the 1980s*, a collection of policy essays by scholars of the Hoover Institution at Stanford University. "I know all about your ideas," he said. In this, he was right on target; Ronald Reagan had looked to the Hoover Institution for help in his administration.[19]

In my contribution to this book, I had discussed the USSR's succession problem, its foreign propaganda, espionage, foreign trade, military strategy, and its relations with the Third World. I predicted that Brezhnev's death would be followed by disorientation in Moscow and recommended that a strong American president should place relations with the USSR on a genuine *quid pro quo* basis. Among the points I made—that perhaps caught some of Gorbachev's attention—were the following:[20]

- Soviet propaganda themes should be systematically exposed by the Voice of America, Radio Free Europe, and Radio Liberty. The amount of accurate information from reliable Western sources should be increased for listeners behind the Iron Curtain.

- USSR espionage could be reduced by limiting the number of Soviet "diplomats" in the United States. During September 1971, Britain had expelled 105 USSR embassy, trade union, Aeroflot, and *Narodnyi Bank* personnel (about one-fifth of those in London). The same occurred in Canada, albeit on a more limited basis, during spring 1979.

---

18. Richard F. Staar, *Foreign Policies of the Soviet Union* (Stanford, Calif.: Hoover Institution Press, 1991), pp. 18–19.

19. George P. Shultz, *Turmoil and Triumph: My Years as Secretary of State* (New York: Charles Scribner's Sons, 1993), p. 589.

20. Richard F. Staar, "The Soviet Union," in Peter Duignan and Alvin Rabushka, eds., *The United States in the 1980s* (Stanford, Calif.: Hoover Institution Press, 1980), pp. 735–755; at 752–55.

- In foreign trade, helping Moscow solve its economic problems by shipments of grain and advanced technology had traditionally proved counterproductive. Such trade should be curtailed and the USSR forced to pay with gold, petroleum, and other raw materials needed in the United States.

- START-II would not restrict the USSR from attempts to attain strategic superiority over the United States (the same applies to East-West talks on reduction of forces in Central Europe). Therefore, tough Soviet bargaining must be reciprocated.

- In the Third World, the Kremlin was gaining footholds located near maritime "choke points." The Sino-Soviet conflict could be exploited, with the U.S. supporting the PRC in blocking further expansion of the USSR.

- More powerful than oil are the huge agricultural surpluses in the United States. During 1978–1979 alone, some $13.5 billion worth of these products were sold to other countries. The United States might consider establishing a "Grain Board," which would purchase all such surpluses and, thus, control their sale to other countries.

This was the situation as we were about to depart for Vienna. I took the oath of office from Professor Eugene Rostow, director of ACDA, in Washington, D.C., with Jadwiga holding the bible.

Chapter 6

The Vienna Talks

It was now time to put ideas and words into action. After our plane had landed at Schwechat airport on the outskirts of Vienna, we were met by career foreign service and military officers assigned to the American MBFR delegation. The former Chief of Mission had already returned to Washington for reassignment before our arrival. Still tired from the long flight, we were to face a long line of diplomats from all nineteen government delegations (twelve NATO and seven Warsaw Pact) that same evening. This first reception at our residence in 1981 must have cost a fortune. Jadwiga, in the aftermath, decided to eliminate hard liquor and expensive hotel-catered canapés in the future. Instead, our guests received California wine and European cheese with crackers and fruit. As time went by, many confided that they were deeply relieved to have a change from the heavy fare at other official cocktail parties.

The following day, I was introduced to my new "routine." This was essentially the official schedule until Jadwiga and I returned home in 1983. The format of endless meetings had been firmly established over the previous eight years of "negotiations." The American mission to MBFR, comprising thirty-two individuals, included four representatives from the armed forces: a retired lieutenant general, a lieutenant colonel, and two majors (one of the last being an aide to the three-star officer). Upon our departure, the number had dropped to twenty-nine, suggesting the difficulty of cutting staff. It became possible, however, to trim the annual budget from $1.2 million down to about $900,000 in response to the mandate for all government operations under the new administration. Let me add that the savings did not all come from the wine and cheese!

By contrast, the other eleven Western delegations were much smaller: there were only two representatives from Luxembourg and twelve or thirteen each from the Federal Republic of Germany and the United Kingdom. The size of our American support staff must have been the envy of both West and East. Of course, the U.S. delegation did function as secretariat for the NATO side too, which required a larger number of clerical personnel just to manage the voluminous flow of memoranda and reports.

During the week, every Monday and Wednesday, the twelve Western delegations would hold meetings halfway across town from the U.S. mission. This comprised the so-called Ad Hoc Group. These meetings usually lasted all day, with a break for lunch. The so-called informal meetings, on Tuesdays, were attended on a rotation basis by two delegations from each side (with U.S. and USSR representatives at all sessions). They were shorter and broke up for a late lunch. Every Thursday, a formal meeting took place in the Redutensaal at the Hofburg Palace. All delegations attended it, which usually culminated with a press conference. This hall was where the Congress of Vienna, which ended the Napoleonic wars of the nineteenth century, had held its deliberations. As time went on, I often thought of Nicolson's book about these peace talks; they had lasted almost ten years.[1] World War II, of course, had ended more than thirty-five years before our current talks, yet we too were still trying to resolve issues born of that conflict. Finally, on Friday mornings, heads of the three largest Western delegations (U.S., U.K., and Federal Republic of Germany) would arrive for a trilateral meeting in the American delegation headquarters at Obersteinergasse 11. This group would then head out for an informal luncheon at a local restaurant in the vicinity.

Such a schedule hardly left one time for reflection. In addition, it seemed that the less we accomplished, the more paperwork we produced. Nonetheless, we never missed a deadline, even if this meant over-time by the staff. There was a genuine *esprit de corps* here, and many worked on even without compensation. Members of the career foreign service and support personnel, for the most part, were superb. And, as these things go, Vienna did not appear on the list of hardship posts. There was one unique difficulty, however. An atmospheric phenomenon known as the *Foehn*,

---

1. Harold Nicolson, *The Congress of Vienna: A Study in Allied Unity, 1812–1822* (New York: Harcourt Brace Jovanovich, 1946), 312 pp.

which can occur at any time of the year (day or night), brings with it a low pressure system, which can result in excruciatingly painful headaches. Jadwiga was one of those who found herself literally "under the weather."

MBFR chiefs of mission from other NATO member states, although all career diplomats, accepted me, the lone political appointee. (See list of U.S. representatives.) We established a good rapport and enjoyed the company of the British, West German, Greek, Italian and Turkish ambassadors and their wives. Initial courtesy calls on all chiefs of mission from both sides proved to be a lengthy procedure, yet it also turned into a fascinating study of character.

On one occasion, Ambassador Baron Willem J. De Vos van Steenwijk from the Netherlands asked whether he could offer anything with coffee, meaning brandy, of course. I requested a cigar. He replied that he did not smoke and found something else to occupy me. Later, this gracious gentleman sent me a box of American "Dutchmasters" by special messenger. Jadwiga and I also became friendly with Ambassador A. Murray Simons, who had been posted to MBFR from Canada. His demeanor and distinguished British accent suggested that he belonged to the upper class in England. His beautiful wife, Jill, and two young sons added luster to the family.

The most aristocratic of my colleagues, however, were the ambassador from Italy, Fausto Bacchetti, and wife Amata. They both had the bearing and manners of the nobility. The ambassador later contacted me for certain research materials, copies of which were sent from the Hoover Institution archives for a book on which he had been working. In turn, the diplomat representing the Federal Republic of Germany, Walter Boss, looked the most distinguished of all the Westerners with his white hair. He spoke fluent English, no doubt as a result of practice with his charming American-born wife, Annie. Boss was later sent by the *Auswärtiges Amt* to be the FRG's chief of mission in Tokyo.

✧ ✧ ✧ ✧

Table 5: U.S. Ambassadors to MBFR and CFE

1.	Stanley Resor	1973–1978
2.	Jonathan Dean*	1978–1981
3.	Richard F. Staar	1981–1983
4.	Morton Abramowitz*	1983–1985
5.	Robert D. Blackwill	1985–1987
6.	Stephen J. Ledogar*	1987–1989
7.	H. James Woolsey, Jr.	1989–1990

Notes: * Career foreign service officers.

(Names and dates have been pieced together from the press. ACDA officials never responded to several requests for this information, even after the author had made a personal visit to that agency.)

✧ ✧ ✧ ✧

The ambassador from Greece, Constantin G. Politis, expressed some concern about how long he would remain at Vienna because of unsettled politics in Athens. As things turned out, he and his lively wife, Lia, actually stayed at MBFR longer than we did.

Finally, His Excellency Ecmel Barutçu from Turkey seemed to be the most "Americanized" among all West European chiefs of mission. He spoke English fluently with an American accent. His predecessor, also accredited to the government of Austria as well as to MBFR, had been assassinated in Vienna, possibly by an Armenian terrorist. Since that time, Ambassador Barutçu came to our meetings with an armed guard who doubled as his chauffeur. We visited him and his wonderful wife, Günseli, several years later in Istanbul. Their daughter was educated at an American university.

On the other side, the Warsaw Pact representatives took their lead from USSR Ambassador Valerian V. Mikhailov, who physically resembled former Soviet leader Nikita S. Khrushchëv. During the 65th anniversary celebration of the "Great Socialist October Revolution," held on 7 November 1982 at the bilateral embassy, Mikhailov attempted to have me drink vodka with him as a toast to their "Fourth of July." It was hard to imagine why, exactly, he put me on the spot this way. My diplomatic excuse for not drinking was medication (which frankly I was not taking). It was a tense evening: the U.K., West German, and U.S. chiefs of mission had received instructions from their respective capitals to attend for fifteen minutes only and then leave together as a protest against the threat of the possibly impending Soviet military occupation of Poland. All of us did so.

Another time, on a "cultural" occasion, Jadwiga had a pleasant conversation in German with Hella Wieland, M.D., the wife of the East German ambassador. Their good-natured exchange was abruptly broken off by a stocky woman who approached Dr. Wieland and told her in Russian to stop "cultivating" my wife. We later learned that the Wieland children were not permitted to live in Vienna, apparently being "held hostage" back in the GDR to prevent their parents from defecting to the West. Such was the personal cost of having to represent a government with little regard for even its most accomplished citizens.

Relations with the chief of mission from Poland, Stanisław Przygodzki, also seemed to be developing well. He always sat next to Jadwiga at the weekly press conference. They spoke to each other in Polish, and, finally, the ambassador received permission from his Ministry of Foreign Affairs to invite us for dinner. This was an invitation we were both ambivalent about. On the one hand, it promised to be a fascinating evening and would certainly evoke in us a certain nostalgia. On the other hand, the tense situation in a country that would be forever in our hearts filled us with some trepidation as well. The invitation was "postponed" indefinitely, however, on 13 December 1981, when the communist regime in Warsaw proclaimed martial law and the struggle with Solidarity became worldwide news.

At a later date, Ambassador Przygodzki was permitted to marry another Polish foreign service officer. He and his bride probably expected to receive assignments back at the foreign affairs ministry in Warsaw. This did not happen. He remained at MBFR in Vienna, and she was sent to the Polish embassy in Lisbon.

We had some edgy social interaction with the Soviet side, as well. The youthful and athletic political officer at the Soviet mission, Evgenii G. Kutovoy, proposed that we play doubles in tennis. His partner would be the young Bulgarian ambassador, who was not a strong player. Kutovoy suggested that I invite the then-Canadian chief of mission, David C. Reece, to be my partner and that we use a court belonging to the Russians at a vacation resort south of Vienna. This resort was formerly a hotel that had been commandeered by the Red Army at the end of World War II.

When we arrived there on the appointed evening, to our surprise, we found that the indoor court had a waxed and polished hardwood surface. Instead of bouncing, the balls skidded out of bounds. This is not usually how the game is played! The Russians, however, obviously felt comfortable on their court and played far better than we could. In addition, Ambassador Shopov, the Bulgarian, did not appear. To replace him, Kutovoy had recruited another Russian, who was clearly ready to keep us on the run.

Needless to say, we lost the first and only set by a score of 6 to 1. Ambassador Reece refused to continue. He sat down and watched me play singles, individually with each of the Russians. Kutovoy, I'm delighted to report, did not present any problems. His partner, however, was much tougher, although the result, 7 to 5, still favored me. It is safe to say, of course, that our interaction was not really much of a confidence-building measure!

I invited both of our opponents to a return match at a resort north of Vienna, called "Happy Land." These courts, also indoors, had a standard clay surface. My new partner was a foreign service officer and head of our political section, Leo J. Reddy. He had played varsity tennis at Georgetown University and did not mind at all a little challenge. The Russians were defeated soundly in two sets and refused to play a third one. A promise to contact us for a return match was soon forgotten.

Our initial residence in Vienna, "inherited" from our predecessors, belonged to an Austrian family temporarily living in Spain. When the owners notified us that they would soon return to Hungerberg Strasse 14, Jadwiga began searching for another home. In the meanwhile, we moved to a hotel in one of the suburbs. The administrative officer soon found a new residence for us at Steinfeld Gasse 1. It overlooked Grinzing and its historic church. It was here that Beethoven found out he was deaf when he realized he could see but no longer hear the sound of the swinging bells.

Since we had not shipped our car from California, we decided to purchase a new German-built automobile from a dealer in Munich. At the end of the tour, we could resell it at no profit to somebody connected with the American delegation. In addition to a 10 percent discount for diplomats, the 40 percent in "luxury" taxes was refunded after we had crossed the border from Germany into Austria and mailed the stamped export certificate to our BMW dealer. This car allowed us to spend our second Christmas at the Igls winter resort in the Austrian Alps, where the Winter Olympics had once been held. We also made a few week-end trips throughout the *Waldviertel* region near Vienna (the name refers to the fact that one-fourth of the country had once been covered by forests).

Security Considerations

As mentioned previously, we had been briefed by experts from the Office for Combating Terrorism at the Department of State on what to expect during our overseas assignment. However, it was only several years later that the U.S. Congress passed the Omnibus Diplomatic Security and Anti-Terrorism Act (1986). Perhaps for this reason, we had been given no specific training in personal defense, hostage survival, and defensive driving. Such instruction, even if never used, would have given us a little more peace of mind.

On the other hand, during our assignment in Vienna, I was offered items such as a bulletproof vest and a special blanket with which the driver would cover me in case we were stopped by terrorists. Since the driver happened to be an Austrian national, I placed myself in his position and concluded that he would probably forget the blanket and think of his own safety first. And while I like to think I would have shared it with him, I decided nonetheless to refuse the offer of the bulletproof blanket.

The vest appeared useful, however, especially since an American military officer (Lt. Col. Charles A. Ray) had been shot and killed by a terrorist in broad daylight on a street in Paris. However, I wore my vest only one time several months later en route to a briefing at U.S. European Command (Eucom) headquarters in Stuttgart. I took it off after General W. Y. Smith, USAF, told me that neither he nor any of his officers wore such protection, and I never put it on again. Neither did I carry a pistol, although offered one by the Department of State in Washington, D.C.

Our visit to Eucom took place during 11–13 June 1982. The USAF executive jet picked us up at Vienna airport for the flight to Stuttgart, Germany. From there, a helicopter made the trip to the Patch Barracks helipad, where we were met and taken by limousine to our VIP quarters.

Several ladies looked after Jadwiga, who had been invited to a program of her own. The luncheon in my honor was served in the commander-in-chief's mess hall. Seven flag officers, four colonels, one USN captain, plus the civilian political advisor ate with us. Two hours of briefings and discussion followed in the Headquarters conference room. After a tour of the command center, a full hour was spent with the political advisor.

A formal dinner commenced at 19:30 in the deputy commander-in-chief's quarters. It included a high-ranking German government official from Baden-Württemberg, the political advisor, a future U.S. secretary of defense (William J. Perry), who then served as consultant to the Air Force Secretary, the civilian chief of plans and analyses, a U.S. Army major general, and a USN captain. Their wives attended as well. Professor Perry subsequently joined the faculty in the Stanford School of Engineering and held a joint appointment as Senior Fellow at the Hoover Institution.

The following morning, we were flown on a UH-1 helicopter to the 2d Armored Cavalry Regiment at Goff, right at the border with East Germany. After being briefed on the facility and its activities, we boarded the helicopter for a flight along the border trace. We also received comprehensive briefings about the military situation on both sides of the border.

Early in the afternoon, we returned to Stuttgart and were flown back to Vienna on the same executive jet that had brought us to Germany. When we were airborne, I thought to myself: what a wonderful experience. But was it really worth the expense? It was not as though the enormity of the situation had previously been unknown to those present.

In some respects, security measures seemed to be left over from the aforementioned Congress of Vienna. In many ways, the obvious was simply overlooked. The automobiles in our motor pool were old American limousines, dating back about ten years. They had armored plating on the sides. Terrorists, of course, would shoot through the windshield or the side windows. Furthermore, all diplomatic license plates were coded in Vienna to indicate the foreign country of origin. It would not have been difficult to establish that we were Americans, even though we flew no flags. I felt obliged to point this out to my Department of State superiors. They concurred with the recommendations, and the limousines were replaced with much smaller European-made rental cars that had regular plates like those used by Austrian citizens.

Security for our office building, located halfway across the city from the bilateral American embassy, remained in the hands of a U.S. Marine Corps detachment of specially trained enlisted personnel. We appreciated their presence greatly. Jadwiga and I attended the 10 November 1981 USMC birthday ball at the Hilton Hotel, where the master of ceremonies introduced me as the oldest marine present. Every young marine in dress blues then kissed Jadwiga on the cheek as we passed along the receiving line. We made a point of inviting all guards not on duty, together with other members of the U.S. delegation, to Valentine's Day and July 4th parties at our residence. I also attended a dining-in ceremony where the USMC detachment was housed.

These young marines performed exemplary services, guarding the office building day and night. Their security checks were exhaustive: they determined whether safes were locked and examined desk drawers for classified materials after office hours. Armed with a .45 caliber pistol, the guard on duty behind the entrance to the building would not have been saved from a bazooka fired from the outside through the wooden door. I recommended to Washington that the sentry be enclosed in a bullet-proof pillbox as protection from such a potential assault. This was finally done about one year after we had returned to the States.

Our residence itself would have been difficult to protect, however. It was surrounded by a large garden and a low metal fence that easily could have been vaulted. The Austrian government offered to assign two uniformed police officers who would patrol the street on a 24-hour basis, i.e., six men per day and night. That, of course, would have indicated to anyone interested that someone of importance lived there. We expressed our gratitude for the offer and declined. The Regional Security Officer (RSO) from our bilateral embassy recommended that we purchase a Doberman or a German police dog and let him run loose in the garden day and night. Any terrorist could have killed the animal by throwing a piece of poisoned meat across the fence, so we also declined that kind of protection.

Finally, the RSO decided to install a heavy door to our bedroom on the second floor which could be bolted with a steel bar from the inside. That might have saved us from danger on the outside, although ultimately how would we escape? The RSO "solved" that problem by providing us with a rope ladder which we would lower through the window and then climb down into the garden. Jadwiga was reluctant to lower herself into the waiting arms of a terrorist, so again we found ourselves without a real solution.

Actually, at one point there was some danger of an assassination attempt. The Department of State had sent cables to all U.S. ambassadors in London, Paris, Rome, Bonn and Vienna with information (presumably from intelligence sources) that some of us may have been targeted by a certain unnamed terrorist organization. We remained in Vienna, although we could have taken the first plane back to the States. Very fortunately, nothing happened.

Jadwiga and I used to walk or ride our bikes to the office on Sunday mornings, pick up the weekend newspapers, and then return by a different route. We never did anything that would suggest a pattern. Even with tennis, which I played several times each week throughout the year (on indoor courts during the winter), I would vary the times and places as well as partners. We had agreed that if I were held for ransom, Jadwiga would respond by offering the kidnappers money to keep me!

It would be only after sixteen years had passed, with terrorist attacks against American embassies in Kenya as well as Tanzania, that the House of Representatives voted $1.4 billion for increased security of such installations.[2] The United States has over 14,000 personnel stationed overseas at 252 diplomatic posts in 160 foreign countries. The Department of State employs 38 percent, the Pentagon 37 percent, and other agencies the remainder.[3] While this is a sizable group to look after, in every respect it is well worth the cost.

The Negotiations

Having officially commenced on 30 October 1973, the MBFR talks were almost eight years old when we arrived in Vienna. Their agreed-upon purpose involved reduction of conventional ground and air forces of opposing military alliances in Central Europe. These were stationed in

- Belgium, Netherlands, Luxembourg, Federal Republic of Germany in the West;

- Czechoslovakia, the German Democratic Republic, and Poland in the East.

However, the talks themselves involved all members of NATO (except France) as well as all of those from the Warsaw Treaty Organization (WTO).

Reduction to lower and equal levels would have accomplished a number of important goals. It would have introduced stability by eliminating the significant preponderance of WTO forces and reduced the

---

2. *New York Times*, 22 July 1999.
3. Ibid., 7 November 1999.

possibility of a surprise attack from the East. "Equality" would ensure that a conflict would not escalate from conventional to nuclear weapons. A treaty that established limits, measures, verification, and contingency responses would also result in both sides being able to cut back safely on defense expenditures.

According to carefully compiled Western data, the Warsaw Pact armies in Central Europe had deployed 57 divisions that totaled 960,000 ground force personnel (including 475,000 Soviet troops). By comparison, NATO disposed of 25 divisions in the reduction area, or 750,000 men; 200,000 of these were American. The East disputed these figures, admitting only to 800,000 general force troops, or merely 50,000 more than the West.

In addition to data, Western proposals took into account the fact that U.S. forces would be withdrawn 3,500 miles from Central Europe compared to a Soviet move of between 360 and 420 miles from East Germany, Czechoslovakia, Hungary, and Poland. In addition, one-third of the Federal Republic of Germany's population and one-fourth of its industry were concentrated within 60 miles of the border with the communist-ruled (East) German Democratic Republic. That the Soviets could move more quickly and decisively was something that would remain a grave concern.

Only a few weeks after the talks had originally opened in September 1973, NATO proposed that both sides strive for parity by reducing troop levels to 700,000 men on each side. Two years later, the West offered to remove 54 aircraft (F-4's) capable of delivering nuclear weapons, 36 Pershing I intermediate-range missiles, and 1,000 battlefield nuclear warheads. In return, a Soviet tank army of five divisions would be withdrawn. The WTO and Moscow rejected both of these proposals.

Toward the end of 1979, NATO offered a more modest proposal: it suggested the withdrawal of 13,000 U.S. and 30,000 Soviet troops and sought to introduce a comprehensive set of "associated measures" that would include mutual inspections to verify the withdrawals. The Warsaw Pact turned down this proposal also, because it would have admitted that the East had 170,000 more ground forces in Central Europe than did the West. Incidentally, the Soviets and their allied negotiators adopted our terminology by using the words "East" and "West."

A review of the U.S. defense posture during 1981 had led to intensive consultations with our allies at NATO headquarters in Brussels. This resulted in a comprehensive Western proposal, submitted to the other side at the Hofburg Palace during our last formal session before the summer break in July 1982.[4]

After almost nine years of unproductive talks, we finally had a document that would represent the basis for a treaty. Or so we thought! The draft envisaged a commitment by each side to reduce to a common collective ceiling of 900,000 total ground and air force manpower, with 700,000 to be allocated to ground forces. In other words, decades after peace was declared in Europe, with no territory or other claims actively being disputed, we were trying to bring the numbers of would-be combatants, poised to face off, down to fewer than a million on each side. It was a sobering state of affairs.

Such a reduction in stages was to be fully verified. The West's associated (that is, confidence-building and verification) measures, first offered in 1979, now became an integral part of the draft treaty. The first stage of reductions, i.e., only 13,000 and 30,000 ground troops respectively, also reflected the earlier proposal mentioned above. The major difference from previous efforts by NATO centered on the fact of a single agreement being in place rather than two separate ones. This eliminated the so-called linkage issue from negotiations. However, there still remained two major problems to be resolved: the question of agreed-upon data and of associated measures.

The substantial differences regarding figures on Warsaw Pact manpower in the reduction area represented the central unresolved issue in the Vienna talks. The overall discrepancy amounted to 170,000, which did not include air forces in the East. If the latter were added, the total came to approximately 210,000 men. The unspoken reason for this difference was the political purpose served by these troops in Eastern territory. Whereas NATO troops were in Western Europe for defense, WTO troops were also in the East to impose Soviet economic and political hegemony in the region. To admit that almost a quarter million more men were "needed" in the East would spotlight the nature of their role there. In addition, to say that for every four or five NATO troops, WTO needed six would not make the Soviet military seem truly "equal."

---

4. James L. George, "The New MBFR Treaty Proposal: An American Perspective," *NATO Review*, vol. 30, no. 5 (1982), pp. 8–11, provides a summary analysis.

Without agreement on the size of forces, before their reduction and limitation, a treaty would be unverifiable, unworkable, and unenforceable. It would be militarily useless and politically unacceptable. Lacking prior agreed data, NATO representatives explained repeatedly that it would be impossible to ascertain precise residual levels. In other words, without a proper initial head count (and agreement on what constituted a head), there would be no final, non-controversial tally at the end. Furthermore, there could be no mutual understanding of what would constitute a violation of the treaty or what might be an entirely appropriate movement of troops (for training, for instance). However, the East remained unwilling to discuss these matters.

The Eastern position on associated measures remained the second and only other remaining obstacle at the Vienna talks. It had been agreed at the inception of MBFR talks in 1973, however, that such measures comprised an integral part of the subject matter for these negotiations. The Western package included the following seven measures:

1. Notification in advance of all out-of-garrison activity by one or more division-size units, the single exception being that alert activities needed to be announced only at the time they commenced.

2. The right of both sides to observe such pre-notified activities, measures (1) and (2) to cover the territory of all European participants and a considerable part of the USSR.

3. Major movements of ground forces of all direct participants into the reduction area from the outside would also be pre-notified.

4. An annual quota of inspections by both sides in the area of reductions from the ground, air, or both.

5. Permanent exit/entry points to monitor military movements, with observers for duration of the treaty, i.e., a period of fifteen years.

6. Exchange of information on forces to be withdrawn as well as on personnel strength and troop organization in the reduction area.

7. Prohibition on interference with national technical means of verification, meaning reconnaissance satellites.

From the WTO perspective, the above was not in their best interests. They wanted to proceed as they thought necessary without Western input, curtailment, or badgering. And they already had good intelligence sources for NATO activities: western governments and news media were quite accurately and publicly debating NATO deployment, expenses, objectives, political support, and so on!

In the midst of these negotiations in Vienna, on 13 December 1981, the population of Warsaw awakened to the sound of tanks and armored personnel carriers. Streets were being patrolled by police and military units. On that day, during early morning hours, the so-called Military Council of National Salvation (headed by General Wojciech Jaruzelski) proclaimed martial law. That military junta governed Poland until July 1983.

Thousands of Solidarity members were jailed. Mail was censored, telephones tapped, and all newspapers (except communist ones) were banned. Universities were closed. Strikes along the Baltic coast, in plants and at coal mines were suppressed by force. During this period, about 750,000 Polish citizens emigrated.

Although martial law lasted officially only until mid-1983, the general perception in the West was that it continued *de facto* until 1989. In that year, the political and economic situation of the USSR was undergoing "new thinking." Solidarity assumed power in a peaceful transition. The change took place gradually, without force being applied by the communists. The military junta in Poland decided to accept the inevitable: semi-free elections and, ultimately, a transfer of power to Solidarity.[5] At the time of the MBFR talks, however, Poland was still held by force, and the USSR, economically revived by its oil sales after the Western energy crisis of the 1970s, had the will and wealth to keep Eastern Europe in the socialist fold.

Ambassador Valerian V. Mikhailov, head of the USSR delegation, spoke briefly after the West had presented its draft treaty at the formal session on 15 July 1982. He stated only that "this is a step in the right direction." We took this to mean that the East would accept our draft as the basis for serious negotiations after the summer recess. The U.S. delegation worked during that "vacation" period to prepare for the September resumption of talks.

---

5. See Jan Maksymiak, "Poland 20 Years After," in RFE/RL, *Newsline*, vol. 5, no. 235, part II (13 December 2001), pp. 11–12.

When negotiations resumed, the East objected to several fundamental aspects of the associated measures package: (1) geographic extension of the first two measures listed above; (2) the existence of exit/entry points for the treaty's duration; and (3) on-site inspection. All of the "measures" could be accomplished, according to Soviet party and government leader Leonid I. Brezhnev,[6] by "national technical means." Although he died one year later at the age of seventy-five, his words continued to be used at the talks.

Warsaw Pact representatives began to repeat the argument that their "official" data were sufficient for an agreement. They criticized the West's package of associated measures as being too extensive and too intrusive. NATO was also condemned for failing to address separate air force ceilings and reduction of weapons systems. It seemed to be a case of damned if we did, damned if we didn't.

Ultimately, it took a name change, from MBFR (1973–1989) to CFE, or Conference on [Armed] Forces in Europe, as well as the near-collapse of the Soviet empire, before the treaty we had hoped for was finally achieved. This treaty, which signified the formal resolution of the worst of the Cold War, was signed in Paris on 19 November 1990. An adaptation agreement followed almost exactly six years later, when representatives of thirty governments (now including the former Soviet republics which had become independent) signed a new treaty. Changes that had added eleven new signatories also reflected expansion of NATO with addition of three new members (Poland, Hungary, and the Czech Republic) as well as disintegration of the Warsaw Pact on 1 April 1991.

The December 1996 treaty, signed at the Istanbul summit, represented "a complete restructuring" of the CFE document. The former two group limits (Warsaw Pact and NATO) were then replaced with "national ceilings." Each signatory was allocated specific numbers for the five categories of treaty-limited equipment (TLE). Any increase in these levels had to be accompanied by corresponding reductions in the level of the same weapons category held by a former ally.

This treaty did indeed change the military situation of Europe. For instance, Greece and Turkey increased their attack helicopter forces by thirty-five and twenty-seven aircraft respectively. Kazakhstan, with no entitlement under the 1990 treaty, received 385 TLE units from Russia. By

---

6. Quoted in *Der Spiegel*, 2 November 1981, p. 58.

contrast, NATO ended up some 15,876 TLE short of the new limits. The United States took a 60 percent reduction, from 13,088 to 7,582 TLE units.

In comparison, Moscow revealed on 1 July 1999 that it had exceeded smaller zone limits by 260 tanks, some 1,500 armored combat vehicles, and 200 artillery pieces prior to its second invasion of Chechnya. The final act of CFE had obligated Russia to withdraw *all* TLE from Moldova (the former Soviet republic of Moldavia) by the end of 2001 as well as to reduce holdings in Georgia to the levels in Moldova by the end of calendar year 2000.

All thirty treaty signatories had to ratify the adaptation agreement before it could become effective. In the case of Russia, that country insists that a large envisaged occupation force be permitted throughout Chechnya, which may extend Moscow's non-compliance for some years to come. Foreign Minister Igor Ivanov indicated that ratification of the treaty will not represent a high priority for Russia. Another government official suggested that the process may take many years' time.[7]

One should finally mention that the November 1990 CFE Treaty had been violated by the USSR even before that document was signed. Between mid-1988 and the end of 1990, the Soviets moved more than half of their TLE in the first three categories from Central Europe to east of the Ural Mountains, i.e., beyond the area specified by treaty for reductions (Atlantic to the Urals). This was admitted openly by the USSR defense minister in an article published by the armed forces daily newspaper. See Table 6.

✧ ✧ ✧ ✧

---

7. See Wade Boese and Christopher Fischer, "Pragmatism in Practice: CFE," *Jane's Intelligence Review*, vol. 12, no. 2 (February 2000), pp. 14–19.

Table 6
Soviet CFE-Limited Equipment in East-Central Europe

Category	Mid-1988	End of 1990	Moved Beyond Urals
Battle tanks	41,500	21,000	20,500
Armored combat vehicles	45,000	29,600	19,300
Artillery systems	50,300	14,000	28,400
Combat aircraft	11,000	5,150 est.	5,850 est.
Attack helicopters	2,900 est.	1,500 est.	400 est.
TOTALS	150,700 est.	71,250 est.	74,450 est.

Sources: Marshal D. T. Iazov, "Vysokii rubezh istorii," *Krasnaia zvezda*, 29 November 1990, p. 3 for all figures in the first three categories; Alan Riding, "Arms Pact to Codify Europe's New Power Balance," *New York Times*, 18 November 1990, pp. 1, 18; U.S. Congressional Budget Office, *Budgetary and Military Effects of a Treaty Limiting Conventional Forces in Europe* (Washington, D.C.: GPO, September 1990), p. 8.

✧ ✧ ✧ ✧

A further instance of subterfuge involved a pre-November 1990 transfer of three Soviet armored divisions, with their heavy main battle tanks, from the ground forces command to coastal defense under the navy. By changing their designation, these divisions would not be counted in the reduction process. According to the U.S. Arms Control and Disarmament Agency, these three divisions had a total of 815 tanks, some 972 armored combat vehicles, and 846 artillery pieces, for a total of 2,631 heavy weapons systems that would be excluded from the CFE count. The latter, of course, covers only ground forces equipment.

CFE Verification

The greatly expanded treaty area, between the Atlantic Ocean and the Ural Mountains, would appear to have magnified the problem of inspections. However, the CFE treaty provided for verification that the tens of thousands of pieces of treaty-limited equipment (TLE) would be destroyed or withdrawn from the expanded area. The former Warsaw Pact member states had about 1,500 declared military bases and depots compared with some 1,900 in NATO countries.

A verification regime included the following elements, which went into effect ten days after the last treaty ratification had been received:[8]

1. Intensive inspections of baseline data during the past 120 days;

2. Monitoring of destruction and other forms of reduction during a three-year period;

3. Repeated inspections of new baseline data during 120 days after reductions;

4. Compliance inspections at declared and undeclared sites for unlimited duration of the treaty.

The above seems to have been unprecedented in East-West relations. However, verification is a responsibility of each signatory to the treaty. Monitoring by military surveillance satellites was restricted to the United States and the then USSR. A major deficiency of the CFE treaty involved lack of applicability and, hence, of monitoring the military production of signatory states. In any event, large parts of the Soviet Union remained outside the CFE zone; the peculiar delineation probably had to be accepted by the West in order to have the treaty signed.

Inspection visits commenced as soon as the treaty had come into force. Phase 1 included some seven hundred inspections for all signatories plus one hundred on a "challenge basis" during the reduction phase. The latter meant that either side could demand an inspection at any time. The numbers were to be reduced to four hundred and sixty respectively. It had been anticipated that most of these inspections would take place in the Soviet Union itself.[9]

---

8. Henny van der Graaf, "New Verification Regimes in Europe," in Jürgen Altmann *et al.* (eds.), *Verification at Vienna* (Frankfurt am Main: Peace Research Institute, 1992), p. 46.

9. Ibid., p. 50.

CFE Compliance

At the end of June 1991, the United States and USSR held talks to resolve the problems of transfer and designation change to circumvent initial treaty data counts. The bilateral nature of these talks was criticized by other NATO members.

Also of concern was the fact that arms sales of TLE took place by the then Soviet Union and by some of its former East European "allies" to any country that would purchase them. Many such customers were located in the Middle East. Bulgaria, Czechoslovakia, and Hungary, in addition to the USSR, participated in these sales of tanks plus other heavy equipment.[10] As the Gulf War showed, the weapons sold to the Middle East were not necessarily first-rate.

Within months of the bilateral talks, the collapse of the Soviet Union and restored independence of the East European countries resulted in a completely new situation. Henceforth, the latter became independent actors. Russia, within a smaller territory, permitted the compliance aspect of CFE to become stronger.

Although the number of new states (including former USSR republics) could have made verification much more difficult, the reverse actually occurred. When Poland, the Czech Republic, and Hungary became members of NATO in March 1999, the door had been opened for other former Soviet satellite states to attempt the same. In effect, Russia had been moved back to more or less historic tsarist borders. With the loss of the three Baltic states, the three others in the Trans-Caucasus, the four Central Asian republics, Ukraine, and Belarus, it seemed that many, if not all, of these countries would strive for acceptance into European organizations.

As a result, verification procedures included the following tasks with respect to monitoring:[11]

1. Removal of manpower as well as removal or destruction of surplus TLE, including more than 100,000 units of the latter plus several times that many troops on both sides;

---

[10] Ibid., p. 82.
[11] Richard Kokoski and Sergei Koulik, (eds.), *Verification of Conventional Arms Control in Europe* (Boulder, Colo.: Westview Press, 1990), p. 4.

2. Monitoring of weapons, many small and mobile;

3. Movement of manpower and weapons both into and out of reduction zones;

4. Production facilities located within the region, regarding agreed levels of armaments.

View from the East

According to a 1991 study on security in Europe, sponsored by an institute at the Russian-American University in Moscow, some of the most difficult problems at the talks were never resolved. For example, the West refused to discuss guided missiles on naval vessels as well as strike aircraft on carriers; Moscow considered this to be a form of Western "cheating." In addition, the United States had rejected the Soviet proposal that confidence-building measures on land also be applied to naval weapons.[12]

This Russian source acknowledges that in December 1990 the strategic situation in Europe had changed fundamentally. The desperate need for Western loans and investments, the end of the Warsaw Pact and CMEA, and the looming push for independence in the Soviet republics put extraordinary pressures on Gorbachev's policy makers. According to its Russian authors, the treaty "could become a substantial step toward slowing down the arms race, ending the Cold War, and normalizing the situation in Europe." The CFE reductions would take place within the framework of "reasonable sufficiency for defense." The same study asserted that the treaty would be more important for the former USSR, because it would lead to stabilization of conditions in the region based on contractual obligations by all signatories. When further negotiations would resume, the USSR should bring up the concept of reduction in naval armaments (see Table 7) as well as tactical nuclear weapons.[13]

On 23 October 2001, Russia announced that it would be in compliance with CFE treaty limitations by the end of 2001. Compliance required the

---

12. V. N. Starodubov and V. M. Tatarnikov, *Dogovor ob obychnykh vooruzhënnykh silakh v Evrope* (Moscow: Rossiisko-Amerikanskii Universitet, 1991), p. 5.

13. Ibid., pp. 8–10.

removal of certain equipment from the troubled Trans-Dniester region (the pro-Russian part of Moldova). This did not take place, however: allegedly, the local population had "prevented" removal of the weapons. On 31 January 2002, Russia's first deputy foreign minister, Viacheslav Trubnikov, declared that Moscow does not envisage withdrawing its military contingent from the Trans-Dniester Republic, after all, and expects an agreement to continue the *status quo*.[14]

Table 7
Naval Armaments, *USSR* vs. *NATO*

Categories of Weapons	USSR	NATO	Ratio
Aircraft carriers	2	15	1:7.5
Landing craft (above 1,200 tons)	24	84	1:3.5
Ships with guided missiles	23	274	1:11.9
Naval aircraft	692	1,630	1:2.4

Source: Starodubov and Tatarnikov, *Dogovor ob obychnykh vooruzhënnykh silakh v Evrope* (Moscow: Rossiisko-Amerikanskii Universitet, 1991), p. 7.

Note: For an update on the above figures, see the International Institute for Strategic Studies, *The Military Balance, 2001–2002* (London: Oxford University Press, 2002), pp. 48–79, 113–114.

---

[14] Cited in RFE/RL, *Newsline*, vol. 6, no. 21 (1 February 2002), part II, p. 9.

CHAPTER 7

DECISION-MAKING AND NEGOTIATIONS

With the help of historians, political scientists, and the press, Westerners gained a fairly good understanding about how U.S. government policymakers came to their decisions. The same could not be said vis-à-vis our main adversaries. We knew, of course, that delegations to MBFR from Eastern Europe implemented without question all directives that came from Moscow via the Soviet delegation. In fact, they had little choice in the matter. The latter even prepared the formal presentations, given by a satellite representative, when it came to the East's turn for speeches at plenary sessions on Thursdays in the Hofburg Palace. Talk about a captive audience!

The extent of this control was not really even concealed. One memorable occasion took place when the Bulgarian delegate's name appeared on the agenda. Ambassador Lubomir Shopov had received a copy of "his" speech in the Russian language from a messenger—in public view of all attendees just as the meeting was about to begin. Of course, Shopov did not have a chance to read the text in advance. Despite five years at the diplomatic academy in Moscow and a fluency in the Russian language, he stumbled over the text on several occasions which obviously embarrassed him.

I witnessed one exception to this rule. At another plenary session, Ambassador Octavian Groza from Romania (a political appointee who had successfully supervised construction of a huge hydroelectric dam on the Danube River) was scheduled to address the nineteen delegations. The four official languages for these negotiations were English, French, German, and

Russian. We wondered which one Groza would use. His background did not include any study in the USSR. He ended up speaking French and, from the look on Ambassador Mikhailov's face, we knew that the text had not been submitted to the Soviet delegation for advance approval. Such a talk could only be given once!

It was well known that the ultimate levers of power in the Soviet decision-making process had always been centered within the CPSU Political Bureau. This was the heart of the Soviet establishment. At one point in time during the MBFR talks in Vienna, that ruling body numbered an even dozen men. They included the following (see Table 8):

Table 8
CPSU Political Bureau (1982)

Name	Other Position
Andropov, Iurii V.	CPSU General Secretary
Aliev, Geidar A.	First Deputy Prime Minister
Chernenko, Konstantin U.	Secretary, Organization Affairs
Gorbachëv, Mikhail S.	Secretary, Agriculture
Grishin, Viktor V.	First Secretary, Moscow city
Gromyko, Andrei A.	Foreign Minister
Kunaev, Dinmukhamed A.	First Secretary, Kazakhstan
Pelshe, Arvid T.	Chairman, CPSU Control Commission
Romanov, Grigorii V.	First Secretary, Leningrad
Shcherbitskii, Vladimir V.	First Secretary, Ukraine
Tikhonov, Nikolai A.	Chairman, Council of Ministers
Ustinov, Dmitrii F.	Defense Minister

Source: R. Judson Mitchell, "Union of Soviet Socialist Republics," *1983 Yearbook on International Communist Affairs* (Stanford, Calif.: Hoover Institution Press, 1983), p. 336.

✧ ✧ ✧ ✧

The Arms Control Commission of the Politburo, however, which made all important decisions regarding arms control, had been formed back in November 1969. It consisted of five individuals. After the USSR Academy of Sciences chairman, Mstislav V. Keldysh, was "retired" the following year, these men continued their work through the early 1980s (see Table 9):

Table 9
Arms Control Commission of the
CPSU Political Bureau

Ustinov, Dmitrii F.	CPSU Central Committee Secretary for Defense Affairs
Akhromeev, Sergei F.	First Deputy Chief, General Staff
Gromyko, Andrei A.	Foreign Affairs Minister
Andropov, Iurii V.	KGB chairman until November 1982, when he succeeded Brezhnev as CPSU Secretary General
Smirnov, Leonid V.	Deputy Prime Minister and chairman, Military-Industrial Commission

Sources: Aleksandr G. Savel'yev and Nikolay N. Detinov, *The Big Five: Arms Control Decision-Making in the Soviet Union* (Westport, Conn.: Praeger, 1995), pp. 183–194. See also Oleg A. Grinevsky, "Disarmament: The Road to Conversion," in Vlad E. Genin, general editor, *The Anatomy of Russian Defense Conversion* (Walnut Creek, California: Vega Press, 2001), pp. 158–207.

✧ ✧ ✧ ✧

According to a former Soviet ambassador to MBFR[1], the above "Big Five" reported regularly to the CPSU Political Bureau on the status of negotiations and on proposals to be offered by the East at these talks in Vienna. Such proposals actually originated with experts in the foreign affairs and defense ministries, who were responsible for political and technical aspects respectively. Foreign Minister Gromyko and Secretary for

---

1. See Oleg A. Grinevskii, *Tainy sovetskoi diplomatii* (Moscow: Vagrius, 2000), p. 336.

Defense Ustinov supervised this work and had unlimited access to every source of information.

After proposals had been vetted through the above two party/government agencies, they would be placed on the agenda for a "Big Five" meeting. If Gromyko and Ustinov agreed, none of the other three members would voice opposition to the proposal. A "Note to the Central Committee" would then be submitted to the Politburo. Most often, it simply received approval. The work of subordinate foreign affairs and defense experts, thus, became institutionalized in the form of a "Small Five" committee.

When the civilian Ustinov became defense minister in 1976, his successor as defense secretary of the CPSU Central Committee, Iakov P. Riabov, was not made a member of the "Big Five." The group then was reduced to a "Big Four," with Ustinov, Andropov, Gromyko, and Smirnov as members. Whether this made the Commission more efficient is unknown.

Ustinov, representing not only the CPSU Central Committee but also the defense ministry, had two main objectives: to strengthen the armed forces and to weaken the United States. Commission member Andropov, however, reportedly did not play a significant role here, although intelligence and propaganda were of special interest to the KGB. Instead, Gromyko, already a "grand old man" of the Party, had the task of supervising ideology and propaganda. Finally, Smirnov represented the military-industrial complex and, thus, would always support Ustinov as his *alter ego* on the Commission. In short, two members dealt with real defense issues, and two dealt with how these would play out. It was not a group open to innovative solutions or departure from past positions.

The existence of this inner group was revealed to me in the course of a strange experience. Early one evening in 1982, prior to a reception at our residence, an uninvited member of the Soviet delegation appeared on the doorstep and rang the bell. Ushered in, this man asked to speak with me, and I met him in a private study. He obviously had been drinking. We had long suspected him of being a KGB officer under delegation cover.

This man told me in Russian that the "Group of Four" consisted of the names above and that they had decided against signing an MBFR treaty. This was the first time that I had heard about such a high-powered decision-making center in Moscow. A report on the same was sent to Washington by cable that very evening. Thus, it was more than eight years into the treaty negotiation process before we knew who was truly "calling the shots" for the Soviet side. The incident embodies how difficult it was to make progress in the talks.

The next question was, who really provided the Commission with its facts and figures? Among the "feeder" research groups that influenced the course of policy was the Institute of the USA and Canada (ISKAN, or *Institut Soedinënnykh Shtatov Ameriki i Kanady*), directed by Georgii A. Arbatov. There had long been speculations by "Kremlin-watchers" in academia that this center in Moscow was the site of much arms control policy work. Galina Orionova, who had worked for several years at ISKAN and defected in London, revealed that this research institute did not have any such input and was being used only to influence the United States by means of disinformation.[2]

On one occasion, I had the opportunity to deliver a lecture (at the invitation of Dr. Arbatov), entitled "Superpower-Ally Relations: East and West," in mid-April 1973 at ISKAN. I addressed the Institute's department heads, who were seated around a long table, along with the younger staff of researchers in bleachers at the end of the room. The presentation compared the U.S. and NATO with the USSR and Warsaw Pact. I spoke just as I would have to a Western academic audience.

My lecture started with a review of Soviet military doctrine, which had been based upon mobilization of all forces for victory between 1941 and 1945. This doctrine had remained unchanged even after the development of nuclear weapons. I then pointed out that, following the Cuban missile crisis in October 1962 and Khrushchev's ouster two years later, a reconsideration of military doctrine took place. The reformulation involved a complex pattern of targeting the United States with ICBMs which carried nuclear warheads. In addition, between 1966 and 1970, the defense budget, including research and development, doubled, according to the Soviets' own figures.

I then moved on to the subject of superpower-ally relations. As in any political science lecture, I commenced with a discussion of traditional alliances in which smaller members may resent actions of the superpower. The example I gave, however, was not one that netted me a positive reception: I pointed out that in the August 1968 occupation of Czechoslova-

---

2. See Barbara L. Dash, *A Defector Reports: The Institute of the USA and Canada* (Falls Church, Va.: Delphic Associates, May 1982), which includes biographic data on ISKAN "scholars."

kia, Romania had refused to participate and, indeed, publicly condemned the Warsaw Pact invasion.

In contrast, I went on, the United States attitude toward NATO centered on the belief that only a mutuality of interest could cement such an alliance. Even control over U.S. nuclear weapons in Western Europe since 1964 had been within the purview of a special NATO Planning Group, which was by no means a "figurehead" organization.

During the discussion period, only one question was asked: why did the United States build a base on the tiny island of Diego Garcia? In response, I stated that the base had nothing to do with the topic. However, after a disclaimer about any connection with the White House or the Pentagon, I did remark that the Indian Ocean represented an ideal location from which American nuclear-powered submarines could fire their SLBMs and hit every conceivable target of any significance on the Soviet Eurasian landmass. Silence and no further questions.

Despite spending two full weeks in Moscow with Jadwiga, and having been assured that I would be invited back to continue the discussion, there was no approach by ISKAN to return then or at any future time.

With the policymaking groups in mind, i.e., the institutes and universities informing the Arms Control Commission of the Politburo, there was a certain stability in the overall way things got done. Nonetheless, the changes in who headed the Politburo itself had broader implications. It soon became obvious to the U.S. delegation members in Vienna that the succession problem in the Soviet Union would inevitably affect the policy decision-making process. At the end of the 26th CPSU Congress on 3 March 1981, all members of the Political Bureau were reelected unanimously. However, with Brezhnev's death on 10 November 1982, the demise of his successor, Andropov, fifteen months later, and the death of Chernenko a little more than one year after that, both sides at the talks were biding their time. Finally, a younger man, Mikhail S. Gorbachëv, was chosen Secretary General at a Central Committee plenum on 11 March 1985. In effect, the "interregnum" had lasted almost exactly four years.

The day that Brezhnev's death was announced by TASS, that is, early on the morning of Thursday, 11 November 1982, I had been scheduled to take my turn and chair the weekly plenary MBFR session in the Redutensaal of the Hofburg royal palace. As customary, when a chief-of-state died from one of the negotiating countries, it was incumbent on that day's chairman to make the announcement and then ask for a minute of silence. My mind already was giving some thought as to what policies

Brezhnev's successor might follow, and I suspect that the respectful "silence" was a time of quiet anxiety for many in the room.

The outside world now knows that Andropov, even more than his predecessor, seemed to have been mesmerized by a distorted view of U.S. intentions. For instance, he continued seeking information on "Operation Ryan," the Soviet code name and acronym for a surprise nuclear missile attack (*raketno-iadernoe napadenie*) against the Soviet Union by the United States. This permanent operational assignment to collect data on the nonexistent U.S. plan lasted from 1981 to 1984 and has since been discussed in a published book.[3] One of the co-authors had served as KGB station chief in London prior to his defection. Original Russian-language messages, translated into English, from the Moscow Center are reproduced in this extraordinary volume. Had these appeared in a novel, critics would have made clear their disbelief.

An enclosure to a February 1983 directive, addressed to Soviet espionage chiefs in NATO capitals, assigned targets for information on Operation Ryan. Spies were to scour political, economic, and military sectors as well as civil defense and the local intelligence services, for "the plans." The Center's anxieties had peaked when President Reagan described the Soviet leadership as the "focus of evil in the modern world" on 8 March 1982. Only two weeks later the U.S. Strategic Defense Initiative was announced. SDI was clearly explained as building a shield in space, with laser-based technologies to destroy attacking missiles during mid-flight. Did this represent a signal, preparing the American people for war? The Soviets decided not to take any chances.

Their contingency plan included infiltration by sabotage teams armed with suitcase-size nuclear, bacteriological, and chemical weapons. These would be stockpiled by KGB agents in advance at various out-of-the-way locations throughout the United States. (Lt. General Aleksandr I. Lebed' revealed during an interview in 1997 that "perhaps 100, perhaps 500" of these portable bombs had been in the custody of the GRU, or Chief Intelligence Directorate."[4] As former Russian Security Council Secretary,

---

3. Christopher Andrew and Oleg Gordievsky, *Comrade Kriuchkov's Instructions: Soviet Files on KGB Foreign Operations, 1975–1988* (Stanford, Calif.: Stanford University Press, 1993), p. 240.

4. Konstantin Eggert, "General Lebed' nameren naiti iadernye chemodanchiki," *Izvestiia*, 7 October 1997, p. 1.

between June and October 1996, Lebed' had access to the contents of truly chilling archival materials.) In addition, an increase of Soviet disinformation activities was taking place, just as Andropov himself denounced the alleged "military psychosis" in the United States.

Andropov's death on 9 February 1984 did not change the underlying mind-set, and the hunt for Operation Ryan continued. However, the two leading military alarmists soon left the scene: the chief of the General Staff, Marshal Nikolai V. Ogarkov, was posted outside of Moscow, and the defense minister, Marshal Dmitrii K. Ustinov, died in December 1984.

Even though fear of a surprise nuclear attack had receded at Moscow Center, suspicions regarding the "Main Adversary" (*glavnyi protivnik*)—as the United States was called—remained. As KGB chief, Vladimir I. Kriuchkov fully let slip the dogs of disinformation. The all-out campaign included documents forged by Service "A" (in charge of active measures). Examples of these are the following:

- a booklet distorting two hundred years of America's history, issued by a fictitious Danish organization;

- a "document" about an alleged CIA plot to supply South Africa with nuclear weapons;

- alleged U.S. National Security Council plans to intervene in Poland

- the "CIA- and Zionism-originated" tribunal on Afghanistan in Paris;

- the slogan, "Reagan Means War."[5]

In February 1985, the Moscow Center came up with a new theme: "U.S. strategy strives for military superiority over the Soviet Union." Henceforth, top-priority information would be sought on:

- military implications of space shuttle construction;

- the anti-satellite (ASAT) program, and;

---

5. See Vladimir Malevannyi, "Uroki operatsii 'Rian,'" *Nezavisimoe voennoe obozrenie*, no. 40 (26 October–1 November 2001), p. 7.

- the Strategic Defense Initiative (SDI).

In April 1985, the military attaché in London told his GRU (military intelligence) officers that Moscow believed SDI eventually would intercept 90 percent of all Soviet ICBMs. He saw little chance for Moscow's efforts to keep pace with the United States. The Kremlin seemed to have faith that U.S. technology would achieve miracles to Soviet detriment. Under these circumstances, the chances of the East and West finding common ground for an arms reduction treaty were nonexistent.

Good Defenses Make Good Neighbors

The American side also operated its decision-making process through an inter-agency system. It included representatives from the Department of State, the U.S. Arms Control and Disarmament Agency, the Department of Defense, the Central Intelligence Agency, and the National Security Advisor's Office in the White House. To make matters even more complicated, the Department of State had both geographic and functional bureaus, as did the Pentagon.

Inter-agency meetings were attended by the Chief of Mission to MBFR, whenever he came to Washington, D.C. This usually coincided with the end of a negotiating round in Vienna. The ambassador was also summoned back for a special event, such as attending a meeting with President Reagan at the White House. On one occasion, together with U.S. ambassadors to the Strategic Arms Reduction Talks, or START (Lt. Gen. Edward L. Rowny [U.S. Army]) and the Intermediate-Range Ballistic Missile, or INF negotiations (Paul Nitze), we briefed the President privately in the Oval Office. The three of us then held a joint press conference in the White House briefing room. In mid-1982, we did not yet have much progress to report.

As a rule, policy items of real importance had to be vetted through the inter-agency process to receive White House approval. That is exactly what happened with our draft treaty proposal. After an eight-year period without either side having previously submitted a full-length draft document for discussion, we had a breakthrough of sorts. This was finally accomplished in July 1982 through NATO, after having been approved by all twelve member governments represented at the talks in Vienna. Ambassador Valerian V. Mikhailov of the Soviet Union, when accepting the proposal which he obviously had not yet read, stated that "this is a step in the right direction."

Ultimately, however, it was more of a misstep. After the summer break and an opportunity to study the draft agreement, it finally seemed to us that West and East could sit down and begin to negotiate in earnest. Unfortunately the Soviet delegation, as well as its six WTO allies, instead commenced an organized campaign of destructive criticism of the proposal. This lasted a full year. Then, just before the following summer break, at a press conference, on 21 July 1983, the Czechoslovak spokesman for the East announced that his side had rejected our draft treaty and would not accept it even as a basis for negotiation.

A former Soviet ambassador to the MBFR talks has a plausible explanation for this strange behavior. In his book,[6] he covers only the period of 1,001 days when Nikita S. Khrushchëv held power, yet the underlying reasoning was still in effect more than a decade later.

It was clear to the West that Moscow did not want to negotiate an equitable treaty at that time. The problem was that the WTO required negotiations for propaganda purposes more than it needed a treaty to make the peace. Indeed, another seven and one-half years were to go by before an agreement would be reached in November 1990 by the renamed conference on Conventional Forces in Europe (CFE). By then, the USSR itself was showing signs that it would end up in the "dustbin of history," to quote Lenin's prediction about the West.

Negotiating Tactics

In every respect, the "communist" perspective obviously differed from that shared by Western delegates. As noted already, whatever Moscow decided had to be implemented by WTO without discussion by its delegate to MBFR, Ambassador Mikhailov. Flexibility, mutual respect, and genuine partnership among allies remained absent under such a system. Hence, the protracted nature of talks like the ones in Vienna or Geneva on arms control. Secrecy was all-pervasive in the Eastern delegations, which frequently did not know what the rapid changes in Moscow leadership might portend for the talks at Vienna.

---

6. Oleg A. Grinevskii, *Tysiacha i odin den' Nikity Sergeevicha* (Moscow: Vagrius, 1998), 368 pp.

From the very beginning, Soviet negotiators were advised to "ask for more than they [the West] will want to give. . . ." This did not reflect the standard "creation" of bargaining chips for negotiations, however. The Soviet tactic was extreme and rigid. The principle simply stated that "what's mine is mine, and what's yours is negotiable," according to Foreign Minister Andrei Gromyko.[7] This phase was called "prepositioning."

In order to prepare for the talks, the Soviets relied on espionage to gain information concerning Western plans. They were certainly efficient in intelligence gathering even at a low level. When we arrived in Vienna, for instance, I sent copies of my one-page biographic sketch to all Western delegation heads and omitted doing so for the East. There was no need to do otherwise: the Western delegates would need one, whereas Moscow had already circulated my vita, and probably excerpts from many of my publications about the Soviet bloc, as well.

Clandestine information gathering was well funded, but money that might have been used, Western-style, for developing productive relationships was in short supply. Ambassador and Mrs. Mikhailov did try to cultivate us with invitations to dinner and brunches. From time to time he took me and the U.S. political section head to a local *Bierstube*, where the prices were low. When reciprocating, I always invited my Soviet counterpart to a place such as the restaurant at the Hilton Hotel. Through an intermediary, Mikhailov finally requested that I not ask him to "expensive" restaurants because his entertainment funds were extremely limited.

We never became friends, although both of us maintained guardedly warm relations. Each bilateral meeting took place in the company of our respective political or military advisers. Thus, there could never be a "walk in the woods," like the one Ambassadors Paul Nitze and Yulii Kvitsinskii took outside of Geneva during the INF negotiations on 16 July 1982.[8]

Another tactic in the negotiating process as practiced by the Soviets was "reactive response." Here, they waited for the West to reveal its position before doing so themselves. In general, this negotiating approach is designed to give the other side little sense of the tactician's priorities and

---

7. Quoted by Jerrold L. Schecter, *Russian Negotiating Behavior* (Washington, D.C.: U.S. Institute of Peace Press, 1998), p. 64.

8. See U.S. Congress, Committee on Foreign Affairs, *Soviet Diplomacy and Negotiating Behavior, 1979–88* (Washington, D.C.: U.S. Government Printing Office, August 1988), pp. 177–181.

often characterizes "bad faith bargaining." During the CFE talks, for example, the East insisted on hearing the Western proposal before explaining how it would reposition its forces.[9] The Soviet stance at that time remained aggressive, with maximum demands being tabled at the outset.

As mentioned in the foregoing, prepared instructions on how to proceed were transmitted to the Soviet delegation in Vienna and could not be altered in any way. A former Russian career diplomat summarized how such instructions were prepared in Moscow: "The draft is the first step; then, of course, the Ministry of Defense, the KGB, and other interested ministries have to approve. Next, the Politburo blessed it, and finally the formal instructions were issued."[10]

In practice, this meant that Soviet/WTO representatives served more as spokesmen than as active negotiators. Toward the end of a negotiating round, the talks would stall and remain at an impasse until they returned from Moscow with new instructions.

Negotiating with a hidden agenda represented another tactic used by the Soviet side. In addition, they often began with a general statement that could be accepted readily in principle by all present. The West would find itself agreeing to Soviet statements that had excellent propaganda value but served little real purpose. Everyone would support "world peace" and "reduced hostility," of course, but it looked especially good for them to have such words come out of Soviet mouths.

Purposefully vague language was aimed at undermining Western demands for specific information. As a result, there was little real getting down to business. Such delay tactics are often used to provoke an adversary into making premature compromises, just for the purpose of getting talks "moving." The Eastern side was well aware that public pressure in the West was a powerful influence on the talks. WTO, on the other hand, could afford to wait. This applied to all arms reduction talks, including MBFR, as well as INF and START.

Russian standard operating procedures included not only arguing and stalling[11] but also other kinds of pressure tactics. During one of the Thursday plenary sessions in 1982, Ambassador Mikhailov launched a

---

9. Schechter, *op. cit.*, p. 69.
10. Ibid., p. 72.
11. Ibid., pp. 82–84.

bitter attack against the United States for its decision to install intermediate-range ballistic missiles in Western Europe that could reach the Soviet Union. Everybody around the table knew that the USSR already two years earlier had deployed 160 nuclear-tipped SS-20 IRBMs pointed at NATO targets, with two being added per month thereafter. The U.S. decision had been controversial, however, and the subject of bitter demonstrations by West Europeans who felt "caught between irrational superpowers." In this way, the Soviet ambassador was able to recast, briefly, the argument. It is probably safe to say that the Eastern "allies" cringed at his announcement.

Fortunately for our group, the U.S. delegation during 1981–83 never became the target of "abuse, intimidation, and ridicule," as apparently occurred in other venues (and, perhaps, at other times also in Vienna). Our Soviet counterparts were persistent and intransigent during my tenure at MBFR, determined to force us into concessions and compromise. However, they were always professional and cordial enough at day's end.[12]

Russian-style negotiations—as well as entertainment—seemed to include a fair amount of alcohol. Although none of the principals or delegation heads ever became inebriated, the American and Russian military advisers at MBFR (ours held a two-star rank, i.e., a retired major general, whereas his opposite was two ranks lower as a colonel) consumed almost a fifth of bourbon at a reception in our residence one afternoon. This did not seem to have affected either one of them, however. The role of "toasting" and "vodka diplomacy" was certainly part of the competitive spirit in place there. The strongest drinks I ever took at a cocktail party were Campari with soda or one glass of wine with dinner. Hard liquor never appealed to me, although there was plenty of that at receptions and on other occasions. And if I had ever downed a glass of vodka, I might have found myself inundated with bottles of the stuff by observant WTO wellwishers!

At a certain point, even good food and drink can become a bit oppressive. Ambassadors should be warned they need excellent digestion. Once, the chargé d'affaires at the U.S. embassy in Vienna asked Jadwiga and me to stand at the beginning of a receiving line during the traditional 4th of July reception. This we did, of course, in the absence of the bilateral ambassador. What surprised us were the refreshments they offered: hot

---

12. Ibid., pp. 85–90.

dogs and Coca Cola. The deputy chief of mission explained that he had run out of entertainment funds! He did not need to apologize to us!

Obviously, there was no need for "back channel diplomacy" at MBFR. That could only be practiced by an administration in Washington, D.C., that wished to pursue such an unorthodox and dangerous course. It had been used to almost disastrous effect by the Kennedy brothers through Colonel Georgii Bolshakov, a Soviet military intelligence officer who headed the TASS bureau in Washington, D.C., as cover. He deceived the U.S. president through the latter's brother about "defensive weapons" in Cuba until U-2 photographs later proved otherwise.[13] The stakes obviously were much lower in Vienna.

Arms Control and Disarmament Agency

Established by an act of Congress in September 1961, the rationale for ACDA and its separate bureaucracy had been based upon

1. the need for a unique agency that would attract talent, offer new policies, and propose the means to implement them;

2. the desire to provide a clear voice on arms control in the U.S. government; and

3. introduction of an autonomous channel of information to the President.

Unfortunately, ACDA directors rarely had direct personal access to the President. Much depended upon how the new agency's head could establish good relations with the Secretaries of State and Defense as well as the National Security Advisor. No ACDA director had ever been a statutory member of the National Security Council, and this disadvantage was carried over into the Reagan administration.

ACDA received an additional assignment among its responsibilities under the 1976 Arms Control Export Act, which required the agency to

---

13. See interview with a lieutenant general (aviation), "Voinu udalos' predotvratit," *Krasnaia zvezda* (21 September 2000, p. 3) for a Russian admission that nuclear-tipped missiles in Cuba had indeed been pointed at targets in the United States.

evaluate prospective arms sales in terms of established legislative criteria. Sometimes approval for sales was recommended, contingent upon provisos which reportedly had little effect on other government agencies.

An amendment to the original legislation establishing ACDA required an annual report to be submitted. It was to discuss the impact of certain U.S. weapons programs on arms control policy as well as negotiations. In general attempts to satisfy both of these requirements reportedly had been futile,[14] perhaps because of the agency's inferior status vis-à-vis the other government "players."

Although ACDA maintained representatives on more than twenty interagency policy-making committees, it did not chair any of these. The key ones, involving arms control, were headed by officials from either the Department of State or the Department of Defense. They always outranked the ACDA members.

However, the law did mandate that the ACDA director attend NSC meetings "involving weapons procurement, arms sales, consideration of the defense budget, and all arms control and disarmament matters."[15] The original 1961 legislation had established grade levels for the ACDA director, his deputy, and the assistant directors one step below those in comparable positions at the departments of state and defense. On 10 August 1983, President Reagan announced that he would request Congress to upgrade the above positions to the same levels as their counterparts in other government agencies.

Despite the foregoing, in the course of the first two years of the Republican administration, the ACDA budget was reduced by some 30 percent. Personnel cuts affected about one-fourth of the agency, down to an authorized level of 154 individuals. The research budget, mostly contracted to organizations outside the government, went down from $6 million to only $1 million.[16]

---

14. Barry M. Blechman and Janne E. Nolan, "Reorganizing for More Effective Arms Negotiations," *Foreign Affairs*, vol. 61, no. 5 (summer 1983), pp. 1159–1164.

15. Quoted by Charles R. Gellner, and Lynn F. Rusten, "The United States Arms Control and Disarmament Agency," *Arms Control* (Washington, D.C.), vol. 5, no. 2 (September 1984), pp. 144–145.

16. Lawrence Weiler, "The ACDA Scandal," *Arms Control Today*, vol. 13, no. 6 (July 1983), pp. 1–3 and 7–8, at p. 3.

Not affected by the above developments, the MBFR delegation in Vienna remained fully staffed and perhaps even overstaffed. Yet one of the foreign service officers attempted to convince me that each FSO must have his or her own secretary! The rationale presented revolved around the argument that we should have this "surge capacity" just in case there were to be a sudden breakthrough at the talks, resulting in a treaty. Such reasoning, I could not buy!

My own relations with the ACDA director, Professor Eugene Rostow, were most cordial. He had been sworn in on 30 June 1981 and resigned on the same day that I did. This man brought prestige and distinction with him each time that he came to Vienna.

When Professor Rostow addressed our Thursday meeting at the Hofburg Palace, he spoke with such authority and enthusiasm that I felt proud to be on the same team. No visitor from the United States or from any other country could match the impression made by this scholar and dedicated public servant.

The other outstanding individual from ACDA was Dr. James L. George, assistant director for multilateral affairs from 30 March 1982 and acting director after Rostow's resignation, between 13 January and 13 April 1983. Jim and his deputy, Dr. Jack Tierney, visited Vienna on several occasions. Both of them became my good friends.

During one of the Vienna visits, Rostow stayed as an honored guest in the quarters assigned to us. Every morning (this was winter), he had bananas at breakfast, which were required for his health. It took a little doing to procure them, but we were delighted to oblige. The second time, however, Rostow did not accept our invitation but instead occupied a small room at the hotel where President John F. Kennedy had stayed during his summit meeting with Nikita S. Khrushchev. The size of his room certainly suggested that the ACDA director had made a point of saving money for the U.S. government.

The problem of budgets was no small matter. The total annual budget for ACDA had dropped from $18,500,000 (1981) to $16,768,000 (1982), and then to $16,006,000 (1983). This did not really affect the MBFR delegation in Vienna, as we had been instructed to reduce our annual expenditures by one-fourth. I am happy to say that we accomplished this without any layoffs. However, the decision to cut our budget was resented. One of the career foreign service officers, a little miffed, told me that a single modern jet fighter cost more than our previous annual expenditures.

With due reflection on the usefulness of both budgeted items, my response to him was, "So what?" This, of course, ended the conversation.[17]

The professional staff members at ACDA in Washington, D.C., provided the solid expertise and institutional memory required for the delegation to operate successfully. In addition to brief visits by the George/Tierney team, as well as Director Rostow, the agency rotated two of its staff members to Vienna on longer details. Headed by a senior ACDA official, the small group included an analyst as well as a secretary. Telephone and cables provided for near-instant communications between Vienna and Washington, D.C.

It should be mentioned that a secure telephone line on which the messages were scrambled as well as coded cables were available to the ambassador. The MBFR delegation had two code clerks, who rotated on duty. They would encode and also decode messages between Vienna and Washington, D.C.

The overwhelming majority of the U.S. delegation, foreign service officers and staff as well as representatives from the Department of Defense and ACDA, were dedicated and hardworking individuals. They came to the office on weekends, when necessary, without additional compensation. Special acknowledgment should be made of the USMC detachment that guarded the building, day and night, as discussed in the previous chapter.

---

17. ACDA budget figures for 1978 through 1984 appear in Gellner and Rusten, *op. cit.*, p. 141.

CHAPTER 8

PUBLIC DIPLOMACY

Although a presidential National Security Decision Directive (NSDD 77) on this subject was not issued until 14 January 1983, it was obvious to all of us much earlier that an active public relations campaign was needed to counter Soviet propaganda in the arms control arena.[1] Nothing like this had ever been pursued within the MBFR context before. Yet it was absolutely crucial at this point.

All aspects of official public affairs were coordinated by a United States Information Agency (USIA) officer at the bilateral embassy for all three missions (that is, MBFR and the U.S. Mission to International Organizations in Vienna, which was headed by Ambassador Roger Kirk). The public affairs officer (PAO), however, was preoccupied with bilateral American-Austrian programs. Given the importance of the MBFR negotiations, the large number of journalists from around the world stationed in or on assignment to Vienna, and the intense Warsaw Pact (especially Soviet) propaganda activity, our delegation required a full-time senior PAO officer.

It happened by chance that I met Charles Z. Wick, the USIA director, who was attending an international function in the Austrian capital. Mr. Wick accepted my invitation to visit our delegation offices. Here we were able to convince him that one of his PAO's should be assigned on a full-time basis to direct our efforts in the field of public diplomacy. Not too long thereafter, he assigned Dr. John Karch, then on the faculty of the

---

1. Full text of the directive appears in R. F. Staar, ed., *Public Diplomacy: USA versus USSR*, 1986, pp. 297–299.

National War College, to be PAO for the delegation. A career USIA officer, Dr. Karch had served in both Eastern Europe and the USSR—an ideal person for our new position. He brought with him a profound knowledge of the region and spoke several foreign languages, in addition to having expertise with the tools of public diplomacy. His wife Loretta was a charming and gracious presence, as well.

Several years earlier, Dr. Karch had been sent by the U.S. Information Agency, to interview me in Atlanta. While he was there, I asked that he present a lecture to my International Relations class about the work of his agency. He did so, with great enthusiasm and erudition. I was understandably pleased that so accomplished and congenial a person was now going to join "our team."

In his new position, Dr. Karch spoke for all Western delegations at the weekly news briefings that followed the closed plenary sessions. In effect, he was acting as NATO spokesman. In addition to his time reporting to the chief of the U.S. mission, the other Western delegations at MBFR, and to NATO headquarters in Brussels, he also joined the international journalists' club in Vienna. He and his wife became actively involved with numerous NATO, Warsaw Pact, and international media activities. The positive reporting by the media on the Western position at MBFR was in no small measure due to Dr. Karch's deliberate efforts. Subsequently, USIA assigned him to serve simultaneously as public affairs counselor at the bilateral U.S. embassy in Vienna. Truly he had an unlimited capacity for hard work!

As part of my own PR and intelligence campaign, I wrote articles and granted interviews on a regular basis. During calendar year 1982, articles of mine were published by the *San Francisco Chronicle* on 16 July, *Christian Science Monitor* on 22 July, and *Vital Speeches of the Day* on 15 September. Interviews at the MBFR office in Vienna were also given to Don Cook (*Los Angeles Times*), John Tagliabue (*New York Times*), Hal Piper (*Baltimore Sun*), Herbert Feichtlbauer (*Die Furche*), Bill Rademaekers (*Time*), and Wacław H. Bniński (*Voice of America*). In addition, we held two press conferences in our delegation building with foreign journalists stationed in Austria. Among them were *Izvestiia* and *Pravda* correspondents. Austrian television invited ambassadors to MBFR from both West and East Germany as well as the U.S. and USSR for a joint live TV interview. Only the Russian representative had to rely on an interpreter; the rest of us spoke German.

In addition, many visitors dropped by to see us. They included a group from the National War College (several of them kindly remembered the two years I had taught there as a visiting civilian professor); Dr. Robert Marschik, who held ministerial rank at the Austrian foreign office; Drs. John P. Hardt and Richard F. Kaufman from the Congressional Research Service and the Joint Economic Committee of Congress, respectively; U.S. Congressmen William Carney (New York), Robert K. Dornan (California), and Clement J. Zablocki (Wisconsin); as well as U.S. Senator Orrin G. Hatch (Utah). We also welcomed some 28 members from the Commonwealth Club of California; and about the same number of alumni from Stanford University on separate occasions.

Italy, Germany, Scandinavia

Then there were speaking engagements in other foreign countries. A distinguished history professor, David M. Kennedy, invited me to lecture at the Stanford overseas campus in Florence. Since Jadwiga had studied in Italy for several years and spoke the language fluently, we accepted the invitation. The campus was located in a beautiful villa, and we had a most enjoyable "working vacation" there.

The alert Dr. Karch seized upon the opportunity to set up a schedule for me which included interviews for television and the press. I would also make presentations before government officials, military officers, and other prominent personalities. Sitting in the front row at one of these events in the U.S. consulate auditorium was an elegantly dressed man in a custom-tailored silk suit. Later I learned that this individual was the mayor of Florence—and politically, if not sartorially, a communist.

An unclassified dispatch from the U.S. consulate in Florence, dated 2 December 1981, described the two-hour session before this high-level invited audience as having had a special impact. "The clarity and persuasiveness of the message, the vigorous delivery, and the stimulating Q and A [question and answer period] made this one of the best, most productive programs."

The event was covered by half a dozen newspapers, including one in Israel, as well as by local television. The USIS cable concluded that "Ambassador Staar's program was a brilliant success."

Official visits to NATO headquarters at Brussels took place twice a year, during March and November, in the company of two other MBFR ambassadors from the western alliance. On one occasion, I stayed with the deputy chief of our mission to NATO, Stephen J. Ledogar, a career foreign service officer who had been a Department of State fellow at the Hoover Institution during 1972–1973. He became the last ambassador to MBFR as well as the first at the follow-on CFE talks. His hospitality "saved" the government expenses for my hotel room and meals.

Several conferences in the Federal Republic of Germany provided a welcome break from MBFR routine. The Friedrich Ebert Foundation at Bonn, the German-Atlantic Association, as well as the annual *Wehrkunde* politico-military deliberations, also in Munich, gave me an opportunity to converse with opinion-molders and policy-makers from both sides of the ocean. I accepted an invitation to participate in the February 1982 *Wehrkunde* meeting, since six of my articles had appeared previously in that organization's monthly magazine. The keynote address was delivered by our own Secretary of the Navy, John F. Lehman, Jr., who expertly elucidated U.S. defense policies. I had met him previously during the transition in Washington, D.C.

The most extensive and intensive exercise in public diplomacy involved the tour of Scandinavia, which lasted ten days, from 21 through 31 October 1982. Jadwiga and I started in Oslo, where U.S. Ambassador Mark E. Austad gave us his official residence (he had left to accompany the King of Norway to the United States). One of the memorable meetings there involved a future prime minister, Gro Harlem Brundtland, whose husband had invited me to address his research center. She is now director of the World Health Organization, having degrees in both medicine and public health.

The two-day program in Oslo opened with a dinner for parliamentarians and media leaders. After my 15-minute presentation on the draft treaty, which NATO had submitted to the Warsaw Pact representatives the preceding July, I described the current talks in Vienna. Discussion continued through dinner and afterwards. The next day we met with Mrs. Brundtland and several other members of parliament for breakfast at the U.S. ambassador's residence.

During mid-morning, I briefed Under Secretary Eivinn Berg at the foreign ministry. This was followed by an hour-long session with nine reporters. After that, about twenty researchers as well as foreign and defense ministry officials listened to my talk during a two-hour seminar at the Norwegian Institute of Strategic Studies. Lunch followed with a smaller group of diplomats. My interview that afternoon on television reached an estimated two million viewers.

The work schedule in Stockholm (our second stop) began on Sunday, the day of our arrival. Jadwiga and I were guests of honor at a reception with members of parliament, the defense staff, foreign ministry, and the Institute for International Affairs, given by U.S. Ambassador and Mrs. Franklin S. Forsberg.

The following day's program included five groups, each of which required a different approach in the basic presentation. According to the USIS cable from Stockholm, "Ambassador Staar's ability to read his audiences' interests and to switch gears accordingly was most impressive." These groups included (1) the "country team" at the U.S. Embassy; (2) security specialist Lars Christiansson, editor of *Svenska Dagbladet* and his assistant; (3) a roundtable discussion with security and disarmament specialists at the Foreign Ministry; (4) senior researchers at the Institute for International Affairs; and (5) an evening buffet with Sweden's top editors and writers on defense and security. "A stand-up introductory speech followed by an active Q and A session must be counted among the most successful press events held at this post," stated an evaluation of the fifth above event (which was given without notes) in the USIS cable from Stockholm.

The final stop, at Helsinki, lasted three days. We were guests of Ambassador and Mrs. Keith F. Nyborg. Both were of Finnish extraction, and they spoke the language fluently. Only two hours after arrival, we had to give a press conference that was followed by a TV interview. The remaining time was similarly busy: The next day included a meeting with the Pugwash Committee of Professors at the University of Helsinki for two hours; then a talk and discussion period at the American Center before thirty Defense Force representatives, also lasting a total of two hours; and finally a dinner at the U.S. ambassador's residence. The following morning included a call on Foreign Minister Pär Stenbäck and, subsequently, a meeting with other officials of his ministry.

The USIS embassy cable stated that the audiences "welcomed Ambassador Staar's combination of historical perspective and grasp of current issues.... The effect of his statements was enhanced by Finnish news reports of Soviet President Brezhnev's bellicose speech to the military, calling for increased military spending."

Unfortunately, the Helsinki International Radio Service, having summarized the press conference on 26 October 1982, had quoted my prediction that an agreement could be reached in Vienna by the spring of 1983. This triggered a cable signed by Kenneth W. Dam, U.S. Deputy Secretary of State, requesting a full transcript from my press conference. In actual fact, a qualification had been omitted from the Radio Helsinki summary, namely that two problems remained to be solved before a treaty could be signed: agreements on the actual strength of forces deployed in the reduction area and verification procedures. A full official transcript confirmed the omission.

It should be noted that the standard 29-page, double-spaced text of my speech, on the basis of completely open sources, had been sent to Washington, D.C., for clearance on 15 June 1982. No changes or alterations were made by the executive secretary of the U.S. Arms Control and Disarmament Agency. This clearance did come up in connection with the visit to Helsinki, mentioned in the foregoing.

An abbreviated version (about ten double-spaced pages) served as the basis for an address I had delivered on 25 August 1982 before the Commonwealth Club in San Francisco, California.

After the tours of Italy and Scandinavia, invitations began coming to Dr. Karch for me to make other appearances during the remainder of 1983 and into 1984. The itineraries for these trips read like a "grand tour" of Europe: (1) Berne, Rome, Madrid and Paris, as well as (2) Berlin, Bonn, Frankfurt, Freiburg, Munich and Stuttgart. Unfortunately, these plans were never realized.

In effect, we had already been implementing what NSDD-77 (entitled "Management of Public Diplomacy Relative to National Security" and dated 14 January 1983) subsequently required U.S. foreign service officers to follow at their stations abroad. A special planning group (SPG) for this purpose was established under the National Security Council. It included the national security adviser as chairman and the following members (or their designated alternates): secretaries of state and defense, directors of the U.S. Information Agency and the Agency for International Development, as well as the assistant to the President for communications.

This SPG had responsibility for "planning, direction, coordination and monitoring the implementation of public diplomacy activities." It had been established to ensure that "a wide-ranging program of effective initiatives" would be developed and also implemented "to support national security policy objectives and decisions." In addition, four inter-agency standing committees were to be established for the purpose of better coordination.

In non-diplomatic talks, we were all to make a concerted effort to keep everyone up to date on U.S. policies and objectives.

Later, my successor at MBFR, a career foreign service officer, invited Dr. Karch into his office and told him—in no uncertain terms—that he would not participate in the kind of public affairs that had been planned for and implemented by me as his predecessor. He was obviously ignoring the specific National Security Decision Directive, cited in the foregoing. Strictly speaking, he had no choice but to implement it. Nonetheless, personal style and objectives played a considerable role in what got done and what went unattended.

In the Soviet Union, overall action strategies for propaganda were handled very straightforwardly. Plans would be approved and signed by the most senior secretary of the CPSU Central Committee and issued in the form of binding directives. The International Department within the party Secretariat was the hub for public diplomacy planning. As discussed in the previous chapter, research centers like the Institute for Study of the USA and Canada provided policy support studies for the CPSU Secretariat. This system continued to operate, rather effectively, until the USSR fell apart in 1991.[2]

The fact that the USSR was spending at least $3.5 billion per year for "public diplomacy" would suggest the high value Moscow attached to this kind of activity. It was truly a "sledgehammer and sickle" approach. According to an unclassified study by the U.S. Central Intelligence Agency, the Soviet Union had

> developed a world-wide network of assets second to none, consisting of an extensive shortwave radio system, broadcasting in many languages; two news agencies; the pro-Soviet communist parties; the international communist fronts; bilateral friendship societies and other quasi-official instrumentalities; a large corps of correspondents, many of them Soviet intelligence officers; the foreign clandestine propaganda assets of the KGB; and the intelligence services of Cuba and Moscow's East European allies.[3]

---

2. See Lisa Jameson, "Soviet Propaganda: On the Offensive in the 1980s," in Richard F. Staar (ed.), *Public Diplomacy: USA versus USSR* (Stanford, Calif.: Hoover Institution Press, 1986), pp. 18–45.

3. W. Glenn Campbell, "Foreword," in ibid., pp. ix–x; citing the CIA study from GAO report to Congress ID-79-28 (23 July 1979), p. 25.

By manipulation of the media and use of fronts, it was possible to add a veneer of authenticity to even preposterous stories the CPSU wanted to circulate. The United States could not hope to challenge the Soviet propaganda machine in place. With roots which dated back to before the 1917 seizure of power in Russia, its methods of promoting international communism were well-developed and widespread. Ultimately, decisive action had to be taken if the Soviet pen were not to prove just as mighty as its sword. Resource allocation increased substantially under the Reagan administration to counter this attack. Before that time, however, the Department of State and Congress had shown little interest in the problem.

Subsequently, the public diplomacy arm of the Department of State "made efforts to encourage State officials overseas to take a more active interest in public aspects of foreign relations. Although this does not appear to have had much general impact, there have been a number of cases in which small department or combined [with USIA] teams traveling in the field have worked with embassy staffs to bring specific topics to the attention of opinion leaders and the public."[4]

Along these lines, in a set of concluding remarks at the Hoover Institution conference in 1986 cited above, Ambassador Philip C. Habib suggested that a structure be added in Washington, D.C., that would deal with "gray or black types of Soviet activity in the field of [covert] public diplomacy." He and his colleagues had few successes and many failures in trying to respond to this Soviet challenge. The specialized group established by NSDD-77 had been incapable of viewing a problem "in an issue-by-issue manner on a regular seven-day-a-week basis." This could not be done by a committee.[5]

✧ ✧ ✧ ✧

---

4. Gifford D. Malone, "Functioning of Diplomatic Organs," in ibid., p. 136.
5. Habib, "Concluding Remarks," in ibid., pp. 285–86.

Soviet Foreign Propaganda

The Central Intelligence Agency estimated that during 1980 the USSR had spent more than $3.3 billion on foreign propaganda and covert action, as follows (see Table 10).

Table 10
Soviet Expenditures for Propaganda

Budget Item	Cost (in millions)
CPSU International Department	$100
TASS	550
Novosti (APN)	500
Pravda	250
Izvestiia	200
New Times and other periodicals	200
Moscow radio foreign service	700
Press sections in Soviet embassies	50
Clandestine radio stations	100
Communist international front organizations	63
Subsidies to foreign communist parties	50
KGB's Service "A"	50
Covert action operations by KGB foreign residencies	100
Support to national liberation fronts	200
Special campaigns (anti-NATO modernization)	200
Lobbying activities in the United States	5
TOTAL	$3,318

Notes: The estimate of more than $3.3 billion per year in Soviet expenditures for propaganda and covert action can be broken down as above if one counts only proportional costs of foreign as distinct from domestic propaganda and if other activities of the KGB are not considered. The indirect cost, borne by foreign communist organizations, is not included.

The annual Soviet budget for radio and television a few years ago totaled two billion rubles, according to the chairman of *Gosteleradio*, who revealed this over Moscow central television on 18 September 1987. Cited by Viktor Yasmann, *Radio Liberty Research* (Munich), RL 398/87 (8 October 1987): 1.

SOURCES: U.S. Congress, House, Permanent Select Committee on Intelligence, Subcommittee on Oversight, *Hearings on Soviet Covert Action: The Forgery Offensive*, 96th Cong., 2d sess. (Washington, D.C.: GPO, 1980), p. 60; Kathryn Johnson, "How Foreign Powers Play for Status in Washington," *U.S. News & World Report*, 17 June 1985, p. 39, on the $5,469,000 officially reported by lobbyists for the USSR during 1984.

✧ ✧ ✧ ✧

These activities were the stuff of spy novels. They included accusation and derogatory terminology, harassment, censorship, radio jamming, forgeries, and general disinformation as institutionalized tools of the party state. By their own later admissions, the Soviets used four major techniques of "persuasion": falsehood, omission, distortion, and suggestion. The examples below illustrate each of these:

1. Falsehood, in the TASS statements about the defensive nature of shooting down Korean Airlines Flight 007 (the USSR claimed that this civilian jet was a "spy plane" on a surveillance mission).

2. Omission, in the USSR response to American charges of seven arms control violations (Moscow made almost the same accusations about the United States, without any supporting evidence).

3. Distortion, exemplified by explaining détente in one way to client regimes and in another to elites in the West.

4. Suggestion, in which data were presented in a misleading way, so that invalid conclusions are drawn by target audiences.

The reader should keep in mind that I am not using the rhetoric of the time in the above descriptions. As numerous sources will attest, these "techniques" were intentionally malignant.

The importance attributed to propaganda activities can be seen from the fact that two central committee party organs supervised the overall effort:

the Ideology Commission (including a department with six sub-units) as well as the Foreign Propaganda Commission. It should be noted that the citizens of the USSR were subjected to this kind of ideological terrorism, as well. Twice each year, "official slogans" would be released (before May Day and prior to the 1917 Revolution anniversary in early November), which embodied the "politically correct" thinking of the time..

Where arms control was concerned, I would like to point out that three basic methods were applied to present Soviet foreign policy as being dedicated to peace:

1. "White" or overt psychological warfare, conducted by official organs (Moscow radio, TASS, and newspapers);

2. "Gray" from allegedly independent organizations and groups (Radio Peace and Progress or Soviet friendship societies), where the USSR role in a statement or publication was partly concealed; and

3. "Black," closely combined with terrorist and covert activities; announcements of this kind allegedly originated from within target countries (clandestine radio stations, forgeries, disinformation, where the Soviet hand is concealed), when in fact the source was simply reciting what it was told to say.

International communist front organizations played a key role in projecting unflattering images of the United States. Pretending not to follow the Moscow line, nevertheless, they were virtually controlled by the Soviet Union. See Table 11 for a listing of the most important fronts during the last ten Soviet years. These organizations continued their operations and received funding even as USSR President M. S. Gorbachev promoted his policies of "new political thinking," *glasnost'* ("openness"), and arms reductions (1985–1991).

Table 11: International Communist Front Organizations, 1990

	Year Founded	Claimed Membership	Headquarters	Number of Affiliates	Number of Countries	Soviet Support
Afro-Asian People's Solidarity Organization (AAPSO)	1957	no data	Cairo	87	—	$1,260,000
Christian Peace Conference (CPC)	1958	no data	Prague	—	ca. 80	210,000
International Association of Democratic Lawyers (IADL)	1946	25,000	Brussels	—	ca. 80	100,000
International Federation of Resistance Movements (IFRM)	1951	5,000,000	Vienna	78	27	125,000
International Institute for Peace (IIP)	1957	no data	Vienna	no data	no data	260,000
International Organization of Journalists (IOJ)	1946	ca 250,000	Prague	—	120-plus	515,000
International Union of Students (IUS)	1946	40,000,000	Prague	117	110	905,000
Women's International Democratic Federation (WIDF)	1945	200,000,000	East Berlin	142	124	390,000
World Federation of Democratic Youth (WFDY)	1945	150,000,000	Budapest	270	123	1,575,000
World Federation of Scientific Workers (WFSW)	1946	1,000,000	London	ca. 46	70-plus	1,575,000
World Federation of Trade Unions (WFTU)	1945	ca. 214,000,000	Prague	92	81	8,750,000
World Peace Council (WPC)	1950	no data	Helsinki	—	145-plus	49,380,000
TOTAL						$63,445,000

Sources: U.S. Congress, House, Permanent Select Committee on Intelligence, Subcommittee on Oversight, *Hearings on Soviet Covert Action: The Forgery Offensive*, 96th Cong., 2d sess. (Washington, D.C.: GPO, 1980), pp. 79–80, which also gives a breakdown of Soviet financial support (staff, salaries, administration, travel, publications, conferences, and in-house meetings); Wallace Spaulding, "International Communist Organizations," in *1990 Yearbook on International Communist Affairs* (Stanford, Calif.: Hoover Institution Press, 1990), p. 501.

❖ ❖ ❖ ❖

The CPSU International Department directed and provided coordination regarding how "information" was placed and revealed. All activities were in turn supervised by the front organization known as the World Peace Council. A full-time Soviet official sat in each one of the international headquarters maintained by the front organizations.

Directives for the World Peace Council were sent from the International Department in Moscow to the WPC headquarters in Helsinki, passing through the Soviet Peace Committee on the way. The latter group was headed by Genrikh A. Borovik, the brother-in-law of KGB chief V. A. Kriuchkov. Similar front organizations were likewise directed by 'corresponding" bodies in the USSR. Together, they comprised a worldwide Soviet propaganda network.

Not infrequently, support for their messages came from Western scholars and scientists, too, who unwittingly served their cause. For instance, "fact-finding" tours were regularly offered to distinguished foreign visitors. Many were reluctant to believe that their fellow experts "on the other side" would knowingly engage in intellectual dishonesty. They would accept certain "facts" at face value, then transmit the desired "hook" to colleagues back home. Friendship societies were often made to serve a similar purpose on the Soviet end. Here, political cynicism could be successfully exploited.

The most active international fronts during the early 1980s included the above-mentioned World Peace Council, the World Federation of Trade Unions, the World Federation of Democratic Youth, and the International Union of Students. Together they comprised the worldwide Soviet propaganda network. Not infrequently, support for certain perspectives came from apolitical Western scholars and scientists who served as unwitting instruments. The fronts would adopt a line (for instance, general disarmament or various "peace offensives") that paralleled and supported

USSR foreign policy initiatives. They sought to "spread Soviet propaganda themes and create a false impression of public support for the foreign policies of the Soviet Union,"[6] according to expert testimony before the U.S. Congress.

In addition, there existed specialized peace movements which attempted to influence arms reduction negotiations both in Geneva and in Vienna. The Pugwash movement of "scientists for peace, disarmament, and security" had been established on the initiative of Albert Einstein and Bertrand Russell in 1957. Only twenty-two participants attended the inaugural meeting, although it ultimately had branches in seventy-five countries. Toward the end of October 1982, as mentioned previously, I had the opportunity to address the Pugwash Committee of Professors at the University of Helsinki. This session lasted about two hours and may have convinced some of the participants that the United States had made a genuine commitment to achieve a treaty at the MBFR talks. Pugwash, with its emphasis on "fairness" and "balance" and the prestige of its membership, enjoyed considerable credibility. The mammoth injection of Soviet propaganda it received led many Western participants to feel that surely some of the Soviet claims must have had validity. We now know that there was never much to them.

Another (bilateral) specialized peace movement was launched in October 1960; its membership was restricted to Soviet and American public figures. Known as the Dartmouth Meetings, participants met on college campuses in the United States as well as overseas (for example, in Jûrmala, Latvia; Moscow; and Leningrad). While in the United States, participants were subject to U.S. Department of State restrictions. Georgii A. Arbatov, head of ISKAN, nonetheless gave TV and newspaper interviews; lectured before 1,000 people; and spoke to breakfast as well as luncheon groups.[7] He was warmly received for presenting "the other perspective."

International Physicians for Prevention of Nuclear War (IPPNW) was formed in December 1980. This creation coincided with Moscow's campaign to prevent the United States from deploying intermediate-range nuclear missiles in Western Europe. At its peak, IPPNW claimed 145,000 medical doctors as members (including 30,000 Soviets), from the USSR

---

6. See Permanent Select Committee on Intelligence, *Soviet Covert Action* (Washington, D.C.: GPO, 1980), p. 80.

7. *Washington Post*, 1 May 1983, p. B-7.

and forty-two foreign countries. The first conference, held in Virginia, announced its purpose as raising public awareness of the consequences of a nuclear war. Other meetings were held in Amsterdam, Montreal, Hiroshima, and so on. Although this group had excellent intentions and many impressive spokespeople, it was vulnerable to manipulation of its non-humanitarian concerns.

Another specialized group called itself "Generals and Admirals for Peace and Disarmament." At its second meeting in Moscow, only twenty participants attended. They presented a commemorative medal to Mikhail S. Gorbachev for his "great contribution to the prevention of nuclear war." The third meeting in Washington, D.C. discussed preventing war through "mutual respect and cooperation." This suggested moral equivalence between the United States and the USSR and a similar commitment to the resolution of hostilities.

But intransigence at MBFR, the continued occupation of WTO countries, the mechanisms to disseminate disinformation, and so on, should speak for themselves. The Cold War was indeed a serious confrontation between the "Free World" and one that could not lay claim to that title in any respect. With collapse of the Soviet Union, the front organizations disappeared. Without power, support, or funding, there was no longer a "cause" for them to back.

CHAPTER 9

THE "END OF HISTORY?"

In retrospect, the demise of the Soviet Union was no great surprise. Overextended economically, military, and politically, that country faced challenges that neither Marx and Lenin—nor any living expert—could have resolved. The attempt to correct its course, through *perestroika* and "new political thinking," resulted ultimately in disaster. Creation of a successor "Commonwealth of Independent States" (CIS) in December 1991 proved barely successful, even in name. Thus, after seventeen years of the MBFR-CFE talks and the struggle over Solidarity in Poland, the USSR collapsed under its own oppressive weight and inflexibility.

The political fallout from the Soviets' "imperial overreach" is being felt in many countries of the Third World. Ultimately, the "mopping up" operation must be carried out by the United States, the European Union, NATO, and the UN. A country still reeling from its relations with the superpowers is, of course, Afghanistan. Invasion by Soviet troops in December 1979 was only one of some forty-six conflicts in which the USSR was involved since the end of World War II. For the Soviets and the Afghanis, this war broke the camel's back.

Although Hafizullah Amin had "invited" the Red Army into his country, he and his young son were assassinated by a *spetsnaz* group (special forces) soon after Soviet troops had arrived. The thoroughly unpopular "puppet" Najibullah, installed in his place, could not bring order to his country or force it into the Soviet fold. The resulting ten-year war (1979–89) proved a disaster for the "socialist cause" and a clinical study in foreign policy as well as military mismanagement by the USSR.

The invaders were equipped with armored personnel carriers, modern artillery, and helicopter gunships. At the height of the conflict, as many as

100,000 Soviet troops occupied the capital city of Kabul and surrounding areas. Although official sources claimed only the loss of some 15,000 Red Army soldiers in this war (with some 37,000 wounded), in truth the damage was more serious.[1]

The Army had been reluctant to give guns and training to recruits from the Central Asian republics—for fear they might be used against Soviet authorities, instead. Ironically, this proved to be the case in Chechnya years later, where "green" recruits from Russia found themselves confronting Chechens who were Afghani war veterans and former members of *spetsnaz*. The Red Army drew most of its soldiers instead from the Baltic states and "European" Russia. The disproportionately high losses of men from this region (certainly higher than those released by official sources) and the apparent lack of purpose to their fighting put pressure on the Soviet government to withdraw. The fact that the United States was arming and supporting the opposing side (at a time when arms control treaties and economic cooperation were crucial to Soviet stability) revealed the contradictory nature of the USSR's policies. The ruin of Afghanistan itself (more than one million Afghani soldiers and civilians killed, some five million refugees in Pakistan and Iran) made this war unwinnable and untenable. Finally, at Geneva, Switzerland, the USSR representatives agreed on 14 April 1989 to the following:

1. non-interference in Afghanistan;

2. voluntary return of refugees;

3. complete withdrawal of all Soviet forces;

4. U.S. and USSR to act as guarantors of the peace.

The war continued, however, between the Soviet puppet regime of Najibullah and indigenous insurgents, even after the USSR had completely withdrawn its forces on 15 February 1989. The rebels would proclaim victory some two and half months later.

---

1. Anthony Arnold, *Afghanistan: The Soviet Invasion in Perspective* (Stanford, Calif.: Hoover Institution Press, 1985), revised and enlarged edition, pp. 85–111.

Several important army officers from the war would play a role in Soviet/Russian politics. General Boris Gromov, whose picture graced the cover of *Newsweek* as the "last man out of Afghanistan," later figured prominently in the 1991 and 1993 "coups" against Gorbachev and Yeltsin; Gromov is currently governor of the Moscow region. General Alexander Lebed', who resisted both coups, is now governor of Krasnoyarsk province.

Since that time, however, Muslim fundamentalists have continued to penetrate the Soviet Union itself from Afghanistan into Tajikistan. Tajikistan itself then exploded into civil war, with thousands of civilian casualties. It is most probable that the traumatic effect of such protracted conflicts has affected morale of the professional Russian officer corps.

Russia itself provoked a Muslim uprising in the North Caucasus, specifically by the relatively small (1.3 million) group of Chechens. In the course of two wars (1994–96 and 1999 to date) these mountain people have suffered under carpet bombing of their villages as well as "search and destroy" missions by special forces that have decimated the civilian population. Although Chechen independence was nominally the issue of the first hostilities, the current war has taken on a greater significance to both sides.

Seemingly being disregarded are other Muslims in Russia, who total approximately 20 million. It is not inconceivable that Iran and/or Turkey may become the source of volunteers as well as weapons for the insurgents. The Academy of the General Staff in Moscow had projected that such "low intensity" conflicts may result ultimately in about 500,000 combatants and 8 million civilians being killed.[2] In addition, the Russian army has an undefined role in the civil war in Abkhazia (Georgia). In early 2002, there was even talk of U.S. troops being welcomed as peacekeepers.

Eastern Europe

As the war in Afghanistan painfully continued, the Soviet empire in East-Central Europe underwent a series of developments that ultimately led to the Iron Curtain's disintegration. It is worthwhile to review some history. Establishment of the Communist Information Bureau (Cominform) in October 1947 was followed by creation of the Council for Mutual

---

2. Oleg Vladykin, "Ugroza s iuga," *Krasnaia zvezda*, 3 February 1995, p. 2. Note that this date corresponds to halfway through the first war in Chechnya.

Economic Assistance (CMEA) in January 1949 to coordinate political and economic activities throughout the Soviet Bloc. Only Yugoslavia (under Josip Broz-Tito) and Albania (under Enver Hoxha) remained apart from this integration. CMEA was intended as a Soviet response to the post-World War II Marshall Plan in the West. Unfortunately, it became an institution of continuing exploitation over the next forty years.

After the death of Stalin in March 1953, Nikita Sergeevich Khrushchev emerged as the new Soviet leader by 1955 after a power struggle. He called for "peaceful coexistence" with the West.[3] The following year, Khrushchev gave his famous "secret speech" at the 20th CPSU Congress in February 1956, in which he denounced the crimes of Stalin. The Cominform was disbanded two months later.

The first country to undergo *de facto* decolonization also happened to be the largest in East-Central Europe. This was Poland. Demonstrations by industrial workers at Poznań in June 1956 were followed in mid-October by return to the Politburo in Warsaw of the "nationalist" Władysław Gomułka. Within six months, he had obtained cancellation of debts to the USSR, new credits, and permission to abandon collectivization of farms in Poland.

Developments in Hungary included a struggle for power between hardliner Mátyás Rákósi and communist reformer Imre Nagy. After the Soviet accommodation with Yugoslavia and military withdrawal from Austria in May 1955, it appeared that Hungarians might regain their independence. In late October and early November 1956, however, Soviet troops invaded the country in order to crush the "uprising." Approximately 25,000 Hungarians were killed, including Nagy, who was executed. The new regime was headed by János Kádár, and the Soviet empire seemed to be secure again.

The next challenge to Soviet domination arose in Prague, Czechoslovakia, where the local communist regime had two leaders: Antonin Novotny for the Czechs and Alexander Dubček for the Slovaks. The latter won in the struggle for control over the Communist Party of Czechoslovakia (KSČ). In June 1968, the Warsaw Pact deployed troops on Czechoslovak soil for the first time since World War II and remained there after the war games had ended. In mid-August a new draft KSČ statute was released for

---

3. See William J. Tompson, *Khrushchev: A Political Life* (New York: St. Martin's Press/Griffin, 1995), 341 pp.

domestic discussion. It would have abolished the communist party's monopoly of power. To block this, during the night of 20–21 August 1968, Warsaw Pact troops (minus Romanians) began the occupation of Czechoslovakia. The "Prague Spring" of reform was quickly suppressed.

It was the "Brezhnev Doctrine" that reasserted Moscow's control over the Soviet bloc in East-Central Europe. This made clear that military intervention would be exercised also in the future to maintain the status quo. A purge of individuals prominent during Dubček's brief tenure followed. Some 80,000 Czechs and Slovaks fled the country into exile. Nobody was officially executed, however, in contrast with the bloody aftermath of October 1956 in Hungary.

Seven years after the occupation of Czechoslovakia, the 35-member nation Conference on Security and Cooperation in Europe (CSCE) met at Helsinki during July–August 1975. It resulted in acceptance and recognition of *de facto* territorial jurisdictions that coincided with those agreed upon by Roosevelt, Churchill, and Stalin at Yalta in February 1945. In one respect, the Helsinki conference "concluded" World War II. On the other hand, the agreement provided the USSR with undue legitimacy and respectability for its territorial heavy-handedness.

The decade following Helsinki proved to be crucial for the introduction of basic civil and human rights that had been guaranteed by the CSCE agreement. The results included the Charter 77 movement in Czechoslovakia under Václav Havel and the Solidarity organization in Poland under Lech Wałęsa. These two men later became presidents of their newly independent countries. Election of Cardinal Karol Wojtyła at the Vatican to become Pope John Paul II in October 1978 also helped the Poles in their struggle for emancipation. Here, the strength and authority of the Catholic Church came to bear on political and human rights in that country.

Imposition of martial law throughout Poland in October 1981 by General Wojciech Jaruzelski as well as mass arrests could not break the resistance, and the state of emergency had to be lifted in July 1983. Why did the Soviets not invade Poland, as they had done in Hungary (1956) and Czechoslovakia (1968)?

First of all, Poland was the largest country in Eastern Europe, Hungary being the smallest at that time. The Poles are ethnically homogeneous; they have a history of military resistance; and, finally, Soviet leaders probably did not relish a war on two fronts (Afghanistan being the other one).

Another factor that must have played a part in that crucial decision involved the leadership changes in Moscow, which included:

1. the death of Leonid I. Brezhnev in November 1982 at age 76;

2. followed by Yurii V. Andropov (after fourteen months) in February 1984 at 74;

3. then Konstantin U. Chernenko (after thirteen months) in March 1985 at 73;

4. finally, Mikhail S. Gorbachev, selected on 11 March 1985 at age 54.

Thus, three Soviet leaders died within a period of less than two and a half years, suggesting that decisions at the highest level must have been difficult to make during that time. Gorbachev, about two decades younger than any of his three predecessors, realized that the USSR had overextended itself militarily. See Table 12 on selected Soviet and Russian combat operations between 1946 and 2000.

Table 12
USSR/Russia in Local Wars, 1946–2000 (selected)

No.	Country	Dates	Activities; Russian Troops and Advisers
1.	China	1946–49; 1950–53; 1964; 1969	Civil war and borders; 6,695 men
2.	Arabs vs. Israel	1948–49; 1956; 1969–70; 1973; 1982	Advisers; weapons; pilots; operational group; fleet
3.	Western Irian	February–October 1956; 1961–62	2,997 men; Netherlands ousted
4.	Korea, North	1950–53	40,000 air force; 727 advisers; armistice
5.	Algeria	1954–62	10,373 advisers; French withdrew

No.	Country	Dates	Activities; Russian Troops and Advisers
6.	Hungary	October 1956	9,349 troops suppressed uprising
7.	Laos	1960–70	1,840 advisers; French withdrew
8.	Cuba	1962	51,293 troops withdrawn
9.	Yemen	1963–67	1,200 advisers; Egypt withdrew
10.	Vietnam	1964–73	6,359 advisers; U.S. withdrew
11.	Cambodia	March–August 1967	? ; CPDR established
12.	Czechoslovakia	August 1968	14,867 advisers; suppressed independence drive
13.	Chad	1975–94	11,000; CPD established
14.	Pakistan/India	1971	3,561; Bangladesh established
15.	Mozambique	1975–91	4,320; MPD established
16.	Angola	1975–94	11,000; APD established
17.	Nicaragua	1978–90	638; Sandinista victory
18.	Afghanistan	1979–89	100,000, with 14,000 killed; Russian withdrawal
19.	Iran-Iraq	1980–87	8,174; and 90 percent of Iraqi arms from USSR
20.	Iraq/Kuwait	1990–91	No record, although fifteen killed
21.	Chechnya	1994–96; September 1999 to date	100,000, with 3,434 killed and 11,000 wounded since 4 October 1990 (ITAR-TASS, Moscow, 1 November 2001)

Source: Major General V. A. Zolotarev (ed..), *Rossiia (SSSR) v lokal'nykh voennykh konfliktakh vtoroi poloviny XX veka* (Moscow: Kuchkovo pole, 2000), appendix; published by the Institute of Military History at the Ministry of Defense.

Note: This source lists a total of 46 local wars with Soviet or Russian involvement during 1946–2000.

✧ ✧ ✧ ✧

That Moscow did not intervene directly in Poland in 1981 was probably due, in part, to reluctance to move troops toward the West at the same time it was conducting war in Afghanistan. By 1986, war, economic instability, and the need for a new kind of domestic support set a different stage entirely.

At the Reykjavik summit in October, Gorbachev agreed to a complete withdrawal from Afghanistan, which took place two and a half years later. He could hardly do otherwise. In domestic affairs, the new emphasis included *glasnost'* ("openness") and *perestroika* ("reconstruction"). They introduced an atmosphere diametrically opposed to that under Gorbachev's three predecessors.[4] Among other things, for the first time, Moscow had to admit to its past.

Glasnost' led to the admission that the NKVD (predecessor of KGB) had executed 21,857 Polish army officers, civil servants, landowners, policemen, ordinary soldiers, and prison guards at Katyn Forest, the Starobelsk and Ostashkovo POW camps, as well as other locations in the western Ukraine and western Belorussia. These figures had appeared in a secret memorandum, dated 3 March 1959, from KGB chief Aleksandr N. Shelepin to Nikita S. Khrushchev[5] but had always been officially denied.

Once Soviet crimes were revealed, it is understandable that the first two satellites to break the bonds were Hungary and Poland. In May 1988, the Hungarian communist János Kádár was removed from power because of his "nationalist" proclivities. Roughly translated, this meant that enough was enough. The following year, the Hungarian CP admitted retroactively that a national uprising had indeed taken place in October 1956. It then permitted a multiparty system to operate in Hungary. A section of the Iron Curtain with Austria came down in May 1989. This led to a mass flight of East Germans via Czechoslovakia and Hungary to West Germany. In view of such a response, no one could pretend that any country was a socialist ally by choice.

Encouraged, Poland experienced general strikes during that time. The communist regime began negotiations with the Solidarity trade union, headed by Lech Wałęsa; both sides agreed that 35 percent of the lower

---

4. Raymond Pearson, *The Rise and Fall of the Soviet Empire* (New York: St. Martin's Press, 1998), 194 pp.

5. See Brian Crozier, "Remember Katyn," *Hoover Digest*, no. 2 (2000), pp. 171–174, which is based on archival materials at the Hoover Institution.

house (*Sejm*) seats in parliament and all of those in the Senate could be contested. Solidarity candidates won the 35 percent plus all but one for senators in the upper house. During August 1989, the new government in Warsaw was headed by a Solidarity leader as prime minister. Times were indeed changing.

Two months later, on 23 October 1989, the Hungarians declared themselves a sovereign and independent republic. That same month, Soviet foreign minister Eduard A. Shevardnadze announced that the USSR would no longer interfere in the affairs of Eastern Europe. What was happening in Hungary and Poland would soon be duplicated in Bulgaria, Czechoslovakia, and Romania. On 25 October 1989, during a visit to Finland, Gorbachev officially repudiated the Brezhnev Doctrine.

At midnight between 8–9 November 1989, the Berlin Wall was finally breached by crowds of East Berliners. Following so spectacular and symbolic an event, Todor Zhivkov (Bulgaria) was deposed in mid-November and Miloš Jakeš (Czechoslovakia) in December. The couple Nicolae and Elena Ceaušescu (whom Václav Havel described as "Mr. & Mrs. Dracula") were both executed by an army firing squad on Christmas Day in Romania.

This sudden collapse of communist rule throughout Eastern Europe affected many of the republics within the USSR proper. Pioneers in the drive for independence were to be found, first of all, in the three Baltic states; they had been forcibly incorporated by the USSR in June 1940 as a result of the secret Hitler-Stalin pact of the previous year.

Almost half a century later (August 1989), a freedom chain of peaceful demonstrators extended from Tallin through Riga to Vilnius. Earlier that same year, Moldavia (the former province of Bessarabia in Romania) sought independence after the death of the Ceaušescu dictators. The Transcaucasus followed suit: Armenia, Azerbaijian, and Georgia all had been sovereign states during the 1917–1920 civil war in Russia and now demanded that status again.

Only the republics in Central Asia remained quiescent for the time being. However, the Ukrainians were reacquiring their dormant nationalism through an organization called *Rukh* (the Movement). It took longer for such sentiments to take root in neighboring Belarus. Although some 25 million ethnic Russians lived in the republics outside of Russia proper, they could not be counted upon to maintain control over developments that were rapidly escalating in intensity.

The year 1990 was crucial for Gorbachev. In January, he visited Lithuania yet failed to reconcile the opposing factions within that republic's communist party. The following month, he proclaimed *demokratizatsiia*, whereby the CPSU renounced its monopoly and allowed non-communist political parties to operate. Article 6 of the USSR constitution, codifying that monopoly, was rescinded. However, while it was placating its European neighbors, that same month the Russian Army massacred some 150 nationalists who were demonstrating in Baku, Azerbaijan.

Parliamentary elections in the three Baltic republics as well as in Moldavia resulted in majorities for independence. All four proclaimed their sovereignties. Gorbachev then arranged to have himself elected Presidium chairman of the USSR Supreme Soviet (i.e., titular president of the country) in March. He next announced renegotiation of the contractual relationship among all fifteen republics at the CPSU Congress in July. A Soviet secession law of the previous April had established a five-year procedure before independence could be proclaimed by any one of the constituent republics. Too little and too late!

Interestingly enough, Russia had led the way, when Boris Yel'tsin was elected president of that republic's parliament in May 1990. The following month, the Communist Party of Russia declared separation from the CPSU, and the republic's parliament proclaimed its own laws as taking precedence over USSR legislation. During the summer, all thirteen other union republics followed with declarations of sovereignty. Lithuania had already proclaimed its independence, which represented one step beyond sovereignty.

Given escalating events, Gorbachev was permitted the right to rule by decree in September 1990. His foreign minister, Eduard Shevardnadze, resigned two months later in protest "against the coming dictatorship." Some three million CPSU members (14 percent of the total) left the party during 1990. Despite all of the foregoing, Russian troops stormed the television tower in Vilnius (January 1991) as a warning that independence for the Baltic states was unacceptable.

Not with a Bang but a Whimper

In April 1991, at Gorbachev's dacha in Novo Ogarevo, the so-called "Nine plus One" accord was signed. The leaders of nine republics (without the Baltic states) restricted all union functions to a specified list of six defined areas. In July 1991, a new draft union treaty would have converted the inner empire into a genuine federation of voluntary member states. The day before it could take effect, however, a *coup d'état* was launched in Moscow. On 19 August 1991 a so-called Government Committee for the State of Emergency announced its ascendancy. This took place while Gorbachev was vacationing in Foros, Crimea. In addition to Gorbachev's own chief of staff, the conspirators included the vice president, prime minister, five senior KGB officers, the two leading army generals, and other "patriots."

The coup collapsed within forty-eight hours, and Gorbachev returned—to whatever his position was. His fate was now in the hands of Boris Yeltsin, a man whom he had expelled and publicly humiliated four years earlier. An investigation and hearings were conducted by a civilian commission of parliament. The attempt to seize power would have involved approximately 5,000 military personnel, some 350 tanks, and 270 armored personnel carriers, which had been ordered to augment the Moscow city garrison.[6]

Thirty-one generals (10 percent of the total estimated to have been involved) were subsequently relieved of their command positions. Testimony by Aleksandr V. Frolov from the prosecutor's office included the following description of the attemped coup:[7]

- *5 August 1991*. Conspirators, led by KGB chairman Kriuchkov and Defense Minister Iazov, met at a KGB safe house near the Garden Ring Road [a beltway around Moscow]. Decision: to prevent signing on 20 August 1991 of the Union Treaty, which would *de facto* recognize secession of six republics from the USSR.

- *14 August*. A three-member specialized team, including airborne troop commander Colonel General Pavel S. Grachëv, assigned to prepare state of emergency

- *17 August*. A larger group, including Iazov, Varennikov, and deputy defense minister Achalov collectively decided to seize power. They

---

6. Verkhovnyi Sovet, Komissiia po rassledovaniiu i obstoiatelstv gosudarstvennogo perevorota, *Stenogramma* (Moscow, 18 February 1992), pp. 4–5; from the 220-page transcript of hearings in the Hoover Institution archives.

7. Ibid., pp. 111–117.

would replace Gorbachev with his vice president, Gennadii Ianaev, under Article 127 (7) of the Soviet constitution, if Gorbachev refused to declare martial law and postpone signing of the Union Treaty.

- *18 August.* Gorbachev claims he refused to join the conspirators; he was detained at his vacation dacha until collapse of the coup.

The march of troops into the capital commenced at 0400, after Iazov had ordered Moscow military district commanders to transfer elements of two divisions into the city.

- *19 August* (the day before the Union Treaty would have gone into effect). Grachev alerted elements of the 106th Airborne division at Tula to secure Tushino airport outside of Moscow. Movements followed by the 2nd Taman motorized rifle division and the 4th Kantemirov armored division. The 106th Airborne division was next ordered to deploy around key installations within the city of Moscow.

- *20 August.* Iazov ordered elements of the 98th Airborne division to be flown from Bolgrad in Moldavia to the Kubinka and Chkalovskiy airfields near Moscow. A curfew was announced to begin at 2300 (it would have taken ten divisions to enforce that order throughout the city).

Iazov, Achalov, Varennikov, Grachëv, and Gromov met to plan the assault on the so-called White House of parliament, where Yel'tsin and other coup opponents were located. The attack was to include airborne, interior, and KGB units. This meeting also included commanders of *spetsnaz* Group "Al'fa" (Major General Viktor E. Karpukhin) and Group "Beta" (Colonel Boris P. Beskov).

During this session, retired Marshal Sergei F. Akhromeev entered the room. Whether he addressed the group remains uncertain. However, the record does show that Grachëv as well as his deputy (Lt. General Aleksandr I. Lebed') strongly opposed storming the White House, due to the high probability of failure and unwillingness of soldiers to fire on civilians. At this point, Grachëv and Lebed' changed sides.

- *21 August.* At 0800, the military collegium (composed of ranking flag officers) recommended withdrawal from Moscow of all troops to their home bases and cancellation of the curfew. Defense Minister Iazov ordered that this be done, and the attempted seizure of power ended.

After Gorbachev had survived this aborted coup d'état, Yel'tsin soon moved against him. All union republics were now determined to attain full independence. On 1 December 1991, the Ukraine (second-largest republic after Russia) held a referendum on the issue. Some 90 percent supported this course of action.

Eight days later, the leaders of Russia, Ukraine, and Belarus met at Belovezhskaia Pushcha. They formally seceded from the USSR and formed a new Commonwealth of Independent States (CIS). At a subsequent meeting on 21 December in Alma Ata, another eight of the former Soviet republics accepted an invitation to join the CIS. On Christmas Day 1991, Gorbachev resigned as president of the then already defunct USSR. A rump parliament dissolved the Soviet Union.

Yel'tsin gave Gorbachev one day to vacate his office.

The October 1993 Mutiny

Several of those involved in the August 1991 attempt to seize power joined in this plot. After that first experience, Yel'tsin had courted the military by promoting about two hundred (rather than the usual fifty) colonels and navy captains to flag rank. Perhaps because of this, only isolated instances occurred of small groups attempting to join the mutineers who had occupied the parliament building.

President Yel'tsin, as commander-in-chief, was forced to issue a written order before his "loyal generals" would act. It took until 0300 hours on 4 October 1993 before Defense Minister Grachëv moved his main battle tanks into position for shelling the parliament building. The assault itself was delayed until daybreak.[8]

Leaders of the mutiny had neither heavy equipment nor regular armed forces, other than 1,452 men with light weapons. "Defense Minister" Vladislav Achalov ordered all military commanders in Moscow to place their troops at his disposal. None would comply. "Acting President" Aleksandr Rutskoi appealed even to cadets at military schools, also without

---

8. See Boris Yel'tsin, *The Struggle for Russia* (New York: Random House, 1994), pp. 278–79, 287.

success. About 6,000 weapons, later found in the parliament building, could have armed four times the number of rebels.

Surrender came soon after the first salvo of tank shells crashed into the upper floors of the parliament building. A total of 147 persons were killed and 878 wounded during the course of the mutiny. All who could walk filed out of the building and were transported to prison.

On 23 February 1994, the newly elected parliament of Russia voted 253 to 67 (with 28 abstentions) for an amnesty covering all leaders of the August 1991 attempted coup as well as all survivors from the October 1993 mutiny.

The end of the USSR was not a victory for "our side," by any means. The world today must still contend with the enormous stockpile of weapons throughout the Soviet rubble. Given Russia's wretched financial situation, these items may well end up in the hands of the highest bidder. The once mighty Red Army remains embroiled in its war with the tiny mini-state of Chechnya, with no end to hostilities in sight. This involvement jeopardizes its relations with all of its Central Asian neighbors and brings instability to an already fragile part of the world.

CHAPTER 10

BACK IN "GOD'S COUNTRY"

Based on what had been learned in Vienna, I sent a final report to Secretary of State George Shultz (see Appendix); I organized two conferences subsequently at the Hoover Institution which resulted in the publication of books.

The first to come out under my editorship was titled *Arms Control: Myth versus Reality* (Stanford, Calif.: Hoover Press, 1984). I also contributed the preface and one of the chapters as well as overseeing the publication itself. We drew on the work of experts from the U.S. government and in academia, who attended the conference. They made thoughtful and valuable presentations on this subject.

The list of participants read like a "Who's Who" in this field: our guests came from R&D Associates (Samuel T. Cohen); IRT Corporation (Joseph D. Douglass, Jr.); U.S. Arms Control and Disarmament Agency (James L. George); National Institute for Public Policy (Colin S. Gray); General Advisory Committee on Arms Control (William R. Graham, Charles M. Kupperman, and Harriet Fast Scott); Rand Corporation (William R. Harris); defense legislative assistant at the U.S. Congress (John G. Keliher); U.S. Information Agency (Robert E. Kiernan); Systems Planning Corporation (Charles Burton Marshall); Harvard (Richard Pipes); Office of Secretary of Defense (Mark R. Schneider); Lawrence Livermore National Laboratory (Edward Teller and Gough C. Reinhardt); Fletcher School of Law and Diplomacy (W. Scott Thompson); University of Southern California (William R. Van Cleave and Robin Ranger); Foreign Policy Research Institute (Nils H. Wessell); and University of Kiel (Werner Kaltefleiter).

The second conference following MBFR involved a volume entitled *Public Diplomacy: USA versus USSR* (Stanford, Calif.: Hoover Press, 1986). Contributors of papers and discussants were once again recruited from academia as well as the U.S. government. In addition, Part Three of the book included papers that had been delivered by scholars and/or government officials from Austria, France, Great Britain, Italy, and the Federal Republic of Germany. Concluding remarks at the conference were delivered by former U.S. Ambassador Philip Habib, then a scholar in residence at the Hoover Institution, and these were incorporated as well.

Contributors of papers included James H. Billington (director, Woodrow Wilson International Center for Scholars); Lisa Jameson (senior commentator, Voice of America); Michael A. Ledeen (Center for Strategic and International Studies); Stanton H. Burnett (USIA counselor); Mark Blitz (Senate Committee on Foreign Relations senior staff member); Edwin J. Feulner, Jr. (president, Heritage Foundation); Gifford D. Malone (former senior foreign service officer); Nils H. Wessell (Office of Research director, USIA); Allen M. Peterson (professor at Stanford University); and Richard E. Bissell (editor, *Washington Quarterly*). Our experts from Western Europe were Monique Garnier-Lançon (Paris); Friedrich Hoess (Vienna); Lucio Leante (Rome); Henning von Lövis of Menar and Gerhard Wettig (Köln); and Roger Scruton (London).

That same year, I co-authored a book with William T. Lee, *Soviet Military Policy Since World War II* (Stanford, Calif.; Hoover Press, 1986). It covered such matters as nuclear doctrine, operational concepts, strategic forces, the SALT era, capabilities to perform damage-limiting missions, as well as prospects for the 1980s. This volume was translated into Chinese at Beijing, which resulted in our being invited to visit the PRC. Each of us did this, although at separate times.

In 1986, Jadwiga and I took a United flight from San Francisco to Tokyo, then transferred to a plane for Shanghai. There, we visited the Institute of International Studies. One of its senior fellows, Jialin Zhang, subsequently became a visiting fellow at the Hoover Institution. At one point during our visit, I asked him why he and his colleagues appeared to be so pale. He hesitated, then explained that all of them had been forced to work at manual labor in factories, where there was no sun. Jadwiga and I were taken aback by this answer.

We took the train up the coast of mainland China and finally arrived at Wuxi. Here, a government guide met us. This young lady presented us with tickets via China Airlines to Xian. The plane was a turbo-prop built in Brazil, and it carried a full load of passengers.

At Xian, we stayed in the "Friendship" Hotel. This odd building had been constructed by the Russians out of cinder blocks and had no identifiable architectural style or decor. The hotel could have dated back to the turn of the century, but this was not the case. It was worth the trip to visit the nearby excavation site of the ancient terra cotta warriors, however. This army of lifesize statues, literally hundreds of ancient soldiers and their horses, was most impressive. A guide then took us to the airport and politely but firmly stayed until we had boarded the plane.

Our flight to Beijing was uneventful, despite the fact that the aircraft was of the same vintage as the one that had brought us to Xian. Fortunately, no terra cotta for the wings or wheels! Again, we were met by a guide—this time a young man driving a Mercedes limousine. He spoke excellent English and told us that he had been studying at Beijing's diplomatic academy.

Our meeting with the deputy minister of foreign affairs for the PRC took place in a spacious hall, with a large group of officials standing at the other end of the room. We sat behind small tables, with an interpreter and a stenographer. Between the translating and recording, our discussion proved a bit laborious. At the end of our conversation, the deputy foreign minister escorted us to the exit door. While shaking hands, he said in perfect English, "I wish you a safe journey back to San Francisco."

In 1998, I organized another conference at the Hoover Institution. This resulted in a book, entitled *The Future Information Revolution in the USSR* (New York: Crane Russak, 1988). Twelve scholars contributed papers on the information society and computer education, personal computers, networks and Soviet-style information, computer simulation, manufacturing, and scientific-technical performance. We talked in broad terms about new technology ushering in a third industrial revolution in the USSR. Little did we know that electronic messages and desktop printing would present so fundamental a challenge to Soviet authority. That censorship would soon be all but impossible was surely a reason to institute *glasnost'*.

Thought-provoking papers and predictions were delivered by scholars from Arizona (Seymour E. Goodman and Ross Stapleton), Hudson Institute and Indianapolis Public Schools (Richard Judy and Jane Lommel), USIA (Richard B. Dobson), Georgetown University (William K. McHenry), Duke (Thomas H. Nayler), the Pentagon (John R. Thomas), as well as the

Congressional Research Service (John P. Hardt and Jean F. Boone). What seemed fantastic at that time is already out of date today! Coinciding with the annual meeting of the American Political Science Association, I oversaw a conference on the premises of the U.S. Institute of Peace in Washington, D.C.. This organization had awarded a $15,000 grant for the project, which enabled me to offer to each of those presenting papers an honorarium of $1,500. Since there were ten of them, it worked out perfectly. The resulting book, *United States-East European Relations in the 1990s* (New York: Crane Russak, 1989), was well received, since all contributors were experts in their respective fields. Joyce Cerwin, who had come to the Hoover Institution from SRI in 1986, was of great help in organizing such conferences.

This volume covered political, economic, and military relations throughout Eastern Europe. It provided a helpful overall framework, followed by detailed discussions of the northern and southern tiers and the two "maverick" non-Warsaw Pact members (Yugoslavia and Albania). In all, twenty-one active participants contributed. Our work was published in attractive and simultaneous hardback as well as paperback editions. That the 1990s turned out differently from what we foresaw, however, is no cause to blush. The remarkable cascade of events that led to the end of the USSR could not have been predicted by anyone present.

Finally, the circle turned 360 degrees with a conference volume titled *Transition to Democracy in Poland* (New York: St. Martin's Press, 1993). This book comprised chapters by fifteen American and Polish scholars. The same publisher brought out a second, revised edition in 1998, with several new contributions. Authors of the new chapters included one attorney from Washington, D.C., as well as professors from Harvard, Virginia, Maryland, Israel, Rhodes College, the U.S. Naval Academy, Rutgers, Tulane, Tufts, Rice, and the George Washington University. This book meant a lot to me. I was very glad that in my lifetime I had seen and could write about this new chapter in Poland's history. Finally, freedom and prosperity were becoming established in a country that had suffered so much.

Between these two editions, I myself researched and wrote *The New Military in Russia: Ten Myths that Shape the Image* (Annapolis, Md.: Naval Institute Press, 1996). This book came out simultaneously in paper and hardback editions. It dealt with discrepancies between perceived change and status quo. I covered the military in politics, Russia's "allies," reform of the armed forces, the military-industrial complex, arms exports, "peace-making," the Commonwealth of Independent States, arms control treaties, the national security concept, and projections into the future. Appendix A included biographic sketches from primary sources of eighty-three contemporary Russian generals and admirals.

I continued to write opinion pieces for numerous newspapers and journals. As a result of an almost full-page article by William H. Honan, entitled "Sovietologists... Cope with a New Reality," *New York Times*, 13 March 1996, p. B-7, in which my views were contrasted with those of Professor Mark Hagen at the Harriman Institute, I received an invitation to be interviewed by Jim Lehrer on his national television news program.

Our Hoover public relations officer drove me up to San Francisco, where the link-up with New York would take place. Unfortunately, for some technical reason, I could hear both Lehrer as well as a professor from Columbia University but could not see them. Despite this handicap, I held my own in the debate.

This was not my first such U.S. opinion interview. Previously, Dr. Edward Teller and Professor Peter Duignan (both from the Hoover Institution) had joined me for a full segment, entitled "The United States in the 1980s" (Subject No. 402) on "Firing Line" with William F. Buckley in January 1980. This reached a nationwide audience and publicized the Hoover Institution book under the same title.

Despite all the benefits of life in California, during the years 1997–1999, Jadwiga and I nevertheless took a second leave-of-absence without pay to live in New England. Chancellor John Silber of Boston University had responded positively to my request for scholar in residence status, and I was named visiting research professor. Affiliated with the international relations department, I received a private office as well as a half-time research assistant, who occupied a smaller office one floor above mine.

This new and stimulating atmosphere of academic collegiality allowed me to do extensive research and to write a monograph about the MBFR talks in Vienna. It also provided the opportunity to meet Professor Uri Ra'anan, director of the Institute for Study of Conflict, and his colleagues. The Institute's publication, *Perspective*, appears six times per year, and I was pleased to contribute articles from time to time. Almost every day during my stay, I would visit the Institute to read the Russian newspapers to which it subscribed.

In the spring of 1999, I had the opportunity to co-teach in the department of political science at Duquesne University in Pittsburgh as a visiting professor. The chairman, Dr. Peter Roman, had remembered a lecture I gave there several years earlier and now proposed that the two of us co-teach a new upper division course, "American and Russian Defense Policies." It was organized by subject matter, such as "civil-military relations," with Professor Roman and I alternating our teaching weeks on the same theme. My book *The New Military in Russia* served as one of the texts. The flight from Manchester, N.H. (just as close as Boston from North Andover, although much less congested) lasted only one hour and twenty minutes, and I did not object to the "commute" as part of this very interesting experience.

Even after we had moved back to California, I was asked by Professor Roman whether I would co-teach with him and a third faculty member another upper division advanced seminar on "Comparative Intelligence Systems." My book, *Foreign Policies of the Soviet Union*, became one of the texts. Even though it meant being on campus only every third week, the travel to Pittsburgh and back to San Francisco became a burden. Each one-way trip meant five and a half hours in the air plus the three-hour change in time. However, I did complete the assignment and thanked Duquesne authorities for that privilege. I never accepted any salary for these teaching assignments: the money was instead directed into an anonymous scholarship fund for political science majors.

Back at the Hoover Institution full time, Jadwiga and I purchased a condominium on campus which is located only a ten-minute walk from the office. In addition, both of our daughters live nearby. The younger, Christina, has a family here in Silicon Valley, and the older, Monica, resides in the Pacific northwest. We could visit Christy, husband Bruce, and our three grandchildren (Rachel, Scotty, and Eric) more often than if we had remained on the East Coast. We also see Monica from time to time.

On the other hand, the return to California has limited my possible visits to my two dear sisters. Marie, our savior during the war years, retired in Ann Arbor. Both husband Harold and son Tom are now deceased. Fortunately, Marie has a wonderful friend in Roger Pradel, who resides in the same apartment building. He is of French extraction and a retired professor from the Graduate School of Business at the University of Michigan.

Younger sister Barbara, also retired from teaching, has three grown children (Alex in North Carolina, Debbie in Texas, and Lee in nearby Canton, Michigan) who live close enough for reciprocal visits from time to time. Barbara also looks in on Marie, since they both live in Ann Arbor.

Changing of the Guard at Hoover

California has been called "God's country" due to the climate as well as its polyglot population. I would add to that the absolutely unique research materials at the Hoover Institution. This center for advanced study represents a perfect academic entity, with various political views and no ideological "litmus test" for affiliation.

In January 1990, a new era had begun with Dr. Campbell's retirement and appointment as counselor of the Hoover Institution. His successor, Dr. John Raisian, had been one of twelve prominent candidates for the position.[1] Fortunately, he was a known entity, having served as a senior fellow since 1986 and more recently as deputy director. Previously, Professor Raisian had taught economics and, before that, held important positions in the Bureau of Labor Statistics as well as in the U.S. Department of Labor.

A most congenial individual, Dr. Raisian has been supportive in all of my endeavors. Even though our fields did not overlap, the new director always found the time to listen, has provided me with good counsel, and never turned down any request that I brought to his attention. In addition, the two associate directors, Thomas H. Henriksen (program development) and Richard Sousa (operations) have been wonderful colleagues and outstanding administrators.

Upon returning from my second "double sabbatical" in Boston, I moved into a private office on the second floor of the Lou Henry Hoover Building. Part of the Hoover complex, it is adjacent to the Tower and looks out onto redwood trees and a fountain. Surrounded by scholars, most of whom are doing research and writing on international subjects, I still find life full of adventure and excitement.

Although I have met and been friends with remarkable people over the years, my mentor and role model has always been my father, Alfred. He faced hardship with courage, gave himself wholeheartedly to helping people who needed him, and maintained his curiosity about the world even in old age and broken health. My real "lucky star," of course, was to have been born to him and my mother.

---

1. See Campbell, *op. cit.*, pp. 343–44.

Appendix

APPENDIX A

EXECUTIVE CORRESPONDENCE

To: The Secretary of State

From: Richard F. Staar

Executive Summary

The basic question regarding Mutual and Balanced Forces Reduction (MBFR) talks in Vienna is whether the East really wants an agreement. One must assume seriousness of purpose, despite Soviet rhetoric, although it may be difficult to resolve the problems of data and verification. Would the East be willing actually to take sizable reductions to parity, and will it accept the types of intrusive associated measures?

The outline of an acceptable treaty exists, and the USSR has proposed token asymmetrical reductions (20,000 to 13,000) in the first phase. Verification remains the *sine qua non* of an agreement for the West, and here no progress has been made to date. If a treaty on the right terms is in the national interest of the United States, then it will require a political decision at the highest level and approval by NATO. This cannot be accomplished by technicians in Vienna.

It is suggested that consideration be given to establishing a connection between the MBFR negotiations and the INF talks in Geneva. An offer at the appropriate time to withdraw certain battlefield and/or intermediate range nuclear weapons in return for large asymmetrical reductions (260,000 versus 90,000) and on-site inspection may represent a solution to the current impasse.

21 March 1983

The Honorable George P. Shultz
The Secretary of State
Washington, D.C. 20520

Dear Mr. Secretary:

Upon completion of assignment as United States Representative to the Mutual and Balanced Forces Reduction (MBFR) negotiations in Vienna, Austria, the following thoughts and observations are submitted for your consideration.

Before departure on 30 October 1981, two meetings with my predecessor had been arranged in the Department of State. Subsequently I read a summary of his comments made on 9 October to the North Atlantic Council. He suggested at that time that the talks did not figure prominently in the minds of the public or governments. He seemed optimistic, however, that a modest first agreement could be reached. And he finally noted the requirement for at least small Western moves, in order to alleviate the friction that had developed among allied representatives in Vienna.

Recently I reread the full text of my predecessor's remarks to the North Atlantic Council, and those parts dealing with Eastern intransigence could be repeated today. On the other hand, several important developments have taken place during the past sixteen months. The enhanced visibility provided MBFR by the President himself, active efforts by the U.S. Delegation in Vienna to influence public opinion, and peace movement activities all have contributed to upgrading the attention devoted to negotiations on conventional force reductions.

Furthermore, two draft treaties are now on the table in Vienna. The draft, submitted 18 February 1982 by the Warsaw Pact, is a compilation in treaty form of well known Eastern positions which does not provide for agreed data and is woefully deficient in the area of verification. It should not become a basis for drafting a common text. The Western draft treaty, presented on 8 July 1982, made a major concession in meeting the East's requirements for contractual treaty obligations by all direct participants (including the Federal Republic of Germany) from the outset of an agreement on reductions, limitations, and the implementation of associated measures.

Unfortunately, despite this concession, the East to date has not shown any willingness to make comparable moves on the remaining major problems in the negotiations: (1) the approximately 170,000 discrepancy between NATO and Warsaw Pact estimates of Eastern troop levels in the reductions area and (2) associated measures, i.e., in essence verification of troop reductions and of residual levels as well as confidence-building measures.

On a more positive note, I can report that friction within the Western alliance in Vienna has been reduced. The NATO draft treaty, with its three annexes, has provided the allies with enough work and even some excitement which have made the operation run smoothly as well as more efficiently. It gave the West the high ground.

USSR Tactics. First of all, it should be recognized that the Soviet delegation is in complete control of its allies at the negotiating table. During informals, not infrequently, heads of other Eastern delegations could not explain the meaning of passages they themselves had read. On some occasions, Soviet delegation members would answer questions asked by us of the East Europeans.

Within the USSR delegation itself, the senior military advisor appears to be the dominant figure. During bilateral meetings, the latter at times monopolized the conversation and spoke authoritatively in the presence of his nominal superior, the Soviet ambassador.

In general, the Easterners have attempted to denigrate the Western draft treaty, stating that it cannot serve as the basis for an agreement. They have criticized methodically and comprehensively the NATO proposal in negative terms, while concentrating on their own draft document.

Current Negotiations (January–March 1983). These opened with an Eastern statement which repeated proposals made at the 5 January meeting of the Warsaw Pact's Political Consultative Committee in its declaration at Prague, Czechoslovakia. At the ensuing press conference, the East's spokesman asserted that "the Western draft agreement ... can not be accepted as a basis for a mutually acceptable agreement." On 3 February, a different Eastern press spokesman contended that, since neither side recognizes the other's draft treaty as a suitable basis for discussion, a first agreement could be quickly attained if the Warsaw Pact offer were accepted.

This proposal was tabled by the East two weeks later and called for (1) reduction of armed forces to previously agreed upon equal ceilings of 900,000 men on each side, "regardless of present troop strengths"; (2) an initial step of the USA and the USSR to be taken in 1983, "thinning out" their forces by 13,000 and 20,000, respectively, in Central Europe; and (3) after these token cuts, a freeze on the troop levels of all direct participants until a comprehensive agreement can be reached.

What the East wants, in effect, is the first part of its own 18 February 1982 draft treaty, without any mention of agreed data and the reference to associated measures being unspecified "arrangements for observation." The latter would apply only to the period of withdrawals and not to the residual troop levels thereafter, as Eastern negotiators have stated repeatedly.

One problem with exposing such a ploy involves the necessity for obtaining North Atlantic Council guidance. In the meanwhile, the East will continue to exploit its "new initiative," orchestrating a wide-ranging campaign through official comments, the media, and public demonstrations. This already has been done at the so-called international peace conference held in Vienna from 6 to 9 February 1983. Several hundred delegates from East and West applauded Warsaw Pact proposals to eliminate the threat of war from Europe.

Prospects. How does Moscow perceive the offer of an agreement on MBFR as proposed by the West? Specifically, will the Soviet Union accept our figures on the data discrepancy and our concepts for verification? These represent the two basic obstacles to a treaty.

Apart from admitting that they had lied to us and really do have about 170,000 more troops in the reductions area than announced during the 1980 official exchange of data, the East would be compelled to take asymmetrical reductions. In other words, some 260,000 Czechoslovak, GDR, Polish and Soviet ground troops either would have to be demobilized (the East Europeans) or withdrawn behind their national borders (USSR). The West in turn would reduce its forces only by some 90,000 men.

Such a genuine move toward equal levels of ground troops should not be expected. "Nothing for nothing," characterizes the Soviet attitude. Also psychologically, the peoples of Eastern Europe and the USSR might perceive such an agreement as "unequal" and as an indication of weakness on the part of the new Kremlin leadership.

The other problem—verification—also has psychological overtones. How would on-site inspection, for example, affect the morale of East European and Soviet troops in the reductions area and beyond? The presence of NATO military personnel—American and especially West German—inspecting Warsaw Pact ground and air force installations could be interpreted within indigenous and Soviet armed forces as a sign that their regimes had been compelled to accept a treaty dictated by the West.

What Can Be Done? After a full decade of negotiations in Vienna this coming October 1983, one might consider breaking off the talks. That could have negative repercussions within NATO, however, if the United States were to do so unilaterally and also would provide the East with enormous propaganda advantages. The Austrian State Treaty was not signed until May 1955, a full ten years after the Second World War had ended in Europe. This suggests patience.

Any precedents, established in the other two sets of bilateral talks as well as in the 40-member Committee on Disarmament (CD) at Geneva, should be exploited also in MBFR. CD has an ad hoc working group on verification and compliance for an eventual test ban agreement. On-site inspection is being discussed also within CD for a ban on chemical weapons and at the IAEA in Vienna for nuclear-powered reactors. We did propose emulating INF and establishing a group of experts to discuss data within the MBFR context. No response has been received thus far from the East.

Finally, a personal note on a matter that would have to be raised at the secretary of state or presidential (summit) level. Since it appears that the East will not accommodate the West in resolving the MBFR data dispute in Vienna under present circumstances the possibility of a trade-off might be considered after consultation with our NATO allies.

This might be done by establishing linkage between conventional ground/air force reduction talks and the INF negotiations. If the USSR is serious, such a proposal could lead possibly to asymmetrical Eastern reductions when combined with a withdrawal and/or non-deployment of certain Western nuclear armaments (battlefield as well as intermediate-range). On-site inspection should be made a *sine qua non* as part of the bargain. At present, the MBFR negotiations appear to be at a standstill. If they continue isolated from a broader concept of arms control, they may soon pass into history as a wasted effort.

Sincerely,
Richard F. Staar
Hoover Institution
Stanford University

cc: William P. Clark
    James L. George

Three weeks later, the Secretary of State sent me the following letter:

April 14, 1983

The Honorable
Richard F. Staar,
Hoover Institution,
Stanford University,
Stanford, California.

Dear Dr. Staar:

I read with interest your thoughtful letter on MBFR, based on your first-hand observations as U.S. Representative in Vienna. I have asked that your letter be passed on to ACDA and the concerned bureaus in the State Department, so that your ideas can be considered as we plan our negotiations over the coming months. I appreciate your sharing your views on this issue.

Let me also take this opportunity to offer my warm thanks for your service as ambassador in this negotiation, which over the past two years had been a centerpiece of the Administration's arms control program. You have my best wishes as you resume your academic work. You may be assured that I will continue to welcome your views on current policy issues.

With best regards,

Sincerely yours,
/s/ *George P. Shultz*

Note: The above is reproduced with the kind permission of Secretary Shultz, who is a Distinguished Fellow-in-Residence at the Hoover Institution.

APPENDIX B

OTHER WORKS BY AUTHOR

Major Publications

1. Author, *Poland, 1944–1962: The Sovietization of a Captive People* (Baton Rouge, La.: Lousiana State University Press, 1962), 300 pp.; reprinted by Greenwood Press, Westport, Conn., 1975.

2. Author, *Communist Regimes in Eastern Europe* (Stanford, Ca.: Hoover Institution Press, 1967), 387 pp.; revised editions 1971, 1977, 1982, 1988; translated into Spanish as *El Régimen Comunista en Europa Central y Oriental* by Editorial Jus in Mexico City, 1964; as *La Europa Comunista: Economia y Sociedad* by Editorial Playor in Madrid, 1983; into German as *Die Kommunistischen Regierungssysteme in Osteuropa* by Seewald Verlag in Stuttgart, 1977; into Korean by the International Studies Association at Seoul, 1972 (396 pp.); and into Chinese at Taipei School of Political Warfare, 1976 (475 pp.).

3. Editor, *Aspects of Modern Communism* (Columbia, S.C.: University of South Carolina Press, 1968), 416 pp.

4. Editor, *Yearbook on International Communist Affairs, 1969–1991* (Stanford, Ca.: Hoover Institution Press), 22 vols.

5. Editor, *Hoover International Studies Series* (Stanford, Ca.: Hoover Institution Press, 1978–1985), 23 vols.

6. Editor, *Histories of Ruling Communist Parties* (Stanford, Ca.: Hoover Institution Press, 1978–1988), 12 vols.

7. Editor, *Arms Control: Myth versus Reality* (Stanford, Ca.: Hoover Institution Press, 1984), 211 pp.

8. Author, *USSR Foreign Policies after Detente* (Stanford, Ca.: Hoover Institution Press, 1985), 308 pp.; rev. ed., 1987; translated into Chinese by Li Ming Publishing Co., Taipei, 1986 (296 pp.); updated and expanded version, entitled *Foreign Policies of the Soviet Union* (Stanford, Ca.: Hoover Institution Press, 1991), 357 pp.

9. Co-author with William T. Lee, *Soviet Military Strategy since World War II* (Stanford, Ca.: Hoover Institution Press, 1986), 263 pp.; translated into Chinese by Defense Science and Technology Center, Beijing, 1987 (300 pp.).

10. Editor, *Public Diplomacy: USA versus USSR* (Stanford, Ca.: Hoover Institution Press, 1986), 305 pp.

11. Editor, *The Future Information Revolution in the USSR* (New York: Crane Russak and Co., 1988), 212 pp.

12. Editor, *United States-East European Relations in the 1990s* (New York: Crane Russak and Co., 1989), 327 pp.

13. Editor, *East Central Europe and the USSR* (London: Macmillan, 1991), 264 pp.

14. Editor, *Transition to Democracy in Poland* (New York: St. Martin's Press ; London: Macmillan, 1993), 271 pp.; 2nd rev. edition in 1998 with 298 pp.

15. Author, *The New Military in Russia: Ten Myths That Shape the Image* (Annapolis, Md.: Naval Institute Press, 1996), 248 pp.

Chapters in Books

1. "New Course in Communist Poland," in John H. Hallowell (ed.), *Soviet Satellite Nations: A Study of the New Imperialism* (Gainesville, Fla.: Kalman Publ. Co., 1958), pp. 64–88.

2. "Rusia y Europa Oriental," in Asamblea de las Naciones Captivas de Europa (ed.), *El Regimen Comunista en Europa Central y Oriental* (Mexico City: Editorial Jus, 1964), pp. 87–108.

3. "Eastern Europe," in Marilyn Robb Trier (ed.), *World Topics Yearbook 1966* (Lake Bluff, Illinois: Tangley Books Educational Center, 1966); annual contribution through the 1981 yearbook.

4. "Destalinization in Eastern Europe," in Andrew Gyorgy (ed.), *Issues of World Communism* (New York: D. Van Nostrand Co., 1966), pp. 66–85.

5. "Military Threat to NATO," in *The Crisis in NATO* (Washington, D.C.: U.S. Government Printing Office, 1966), pp. 285–321.

6. "Die Volksrepublik Polen," in Alfred Domes (ed.), *Osteuropa und die Hoffnung auf Freiheit* (Köln: Verlag Wissenschaft und Politik, 1967), pp. 200–203 of summary.

7. "The Warsaw Treaty Organization," in Francis A. Beer (ed.), *Alliances: Latent War Communities in the Contemporary World* (New York: Holt, Rinehart, and Winston, 1970), pp. 158–183.

8. "What Next in East European Intrabloc Relations?" in Aurie Dunlap (ed.), *Readings on National and Regional Foreign Policies* (New York: MSS Educational Publ. Co., 1971), pp. 94–112.

9. "Wladyslaw Gomulka: Poland's Retrogressive 'Liberal,'" in Rodger Swearingen (ed.), *Leaders of the Communist World* (New York: The Free Press, 1971), pp. 330–354.

10. "Superpower-Ally Military Relations: Eastern Europe and the West," in *Centenaire École de Guerre, 1870–1970* (Brussels: Eeuwfeest Krijgsschool, 1971), pp. 106–125.

11. "Czechoslovakia," in Witold S. Sworakowski (ed.), *World Communism: A Handbook, 1918–1965* (Stanford, Calif.: Hoover Institution Press, 1973), pp. 108–115.

12. "Military Constraints in East-West Relations," in Louis J. Mensonides and James A. Kuhlman (eds.), *The Future of Inter-Bloc Relations in Europe* (New York: Praeger Publ., 1974), pp. 49–63.

13. "East-West Perceptions: The U.S. and Europe," in Mensonides and Kuhlman (eds.), *America and European Security* (Leyden: A. W. Sijthoff, 1976), pp. 1–17.

14. "Soviet Union," in Peter Duignan and Alvin Rabushka (eds.), *The United States in the 1980s* (Stanford, Calif.: Hoover Institution Press, 1980), pp. 735–755.

15. "MBFR, Europa und die Sicherheit der Allianz: Die Perspektiven der USA," in *28. Jahresversammlung der ATA* (Bonn: Deutsche Atlantische Gesellschaft, 1982), pp. 20–40.

16. "East-Central Europe and Soviet Foreign Policy," in Milorad M. Drachkovitch (ed.), *East-Central Europe: Yesterday, Today, Tomorrow* (Stanford, Calif.: Hoover Institution Press, 1982), pp. 20–40.

17. "MBFR Europe and Alliance Security: The United States Perspective," in Richmond M. Lloyd (coordinator), *Foundations of Force Planning: Concepts and Issues* (Newport, Rhode Island: Naval War College Press, 1983), pp. 562–573.

18. "Auslandspropaganda," in Hans-Joachim Veen (ed.), *Wohin entwickelt sich die Sowjetunion?* (Melle: Verlag Ernst Knoth, 1984), pp. 220–232.

19. "Confidence-Building Measures," in William T. Parsons (ed.), *Arms Control and Strategic Stability* (Lanham, Md.: University Press of America, 1986), pp. 131–145.

20. "MBFR, Europe, and Alliance Security: The U.S. Perspective," in Richmond M. Lloyd *et al., Foundation of Force Planning* (Newport, Rhode Island: Naval War College Press, 1986), pp. 562–573.

21. "Soviet Deception at MBFR: A Case Study," in Brian D. Dailey and Patrick J. Parker (eds.), *Soviet Strategic Deception* (Lexington, Mass.: D. C. Heath and Co., 1987), pp. 261–272.

22. "The Information Revolution in Soviet Schools," in Alan Heslop (ed.), *Issues in Soviet Education* (Washington, D.C.: U.S. Government Printing Office, 1988), pp. 47–52.

23. "The Soviet Union Abroad," in Annelise Anderson and Dennis L. Bark (eds.), *Thinking about America: The United States in the 1990s* (Stanford, Calif.: Hoover Institution Press, 1988), pp. 153–163.

24. "Soviet Policy: A New Era?" in Donald R. Kelley and Hoyt Purvis (eds.), *Old Myths and New Realities in United States–Soviet Relations* (New York: Praeger, 1990), pp. 97–114.

25. "Poland under Occupation," in David W. Pike (ed.), *The Opening of the Second World War* (New York: Peter Lang, 1991), pp. 137–143.

26. "Évolution des Forces Armées en Russie," in Georges Nivat (ed.), *De la dissidence à la democratie* (Paris: Éditions du Rocher, 1996), pp. 181–192.

27. "Russia in the Islamic Middle East," in Nikolaus A. Stavrou (ed.), *Mediterranean Security at the Crossroads: A Reader* (Durham, N.C.: Duke University Press, 1999), pp. 209–221.

Testimony before Committees of the U.S. Congress

1. Statement on "The Military Threat to NATO: The Warsaw Pact," to the Subcommittee on Europe, Committee on Foreign Affairs, House of Representatives, *The Crisis in NATO* (Washington, D.C.: 89th Congress, Second Session on 7 June 1996), pp. 285–302.

2. Statement on "Soviet Foreign Policy," before the Committee on Foreign Relations, United States Senate, in *The Future of U.S.-Soviet Relations* (Washington, D.C.: 101st Congress, First Session on 19 April 1989), pp. 232–285.

Periodicals

1. *Affari Esteri* (Rome)
   "Riduzioni della Armi Convenzionali nell'Europa Centrale," vol. 14, no. 56 (autumn 1982), pp. 413–419.

2. *Allgemeine Schweizerische Militärzeitschrift* (Zurich)
   "Sowjetische Waffen für die Dritte Welt," vol. 140, no. 1 (January 1974), pp. 14–17.

3. *The American Legion Magazine*
   "Foreign Policy in the Soviet Union," vol. 119, no. 6 (December 1985), pp. 20–21 and 46–47.
   "Arms Control: A History of Soviet Lies," vol. 121, no. 5 (November 1986), pp. 28–29.
   "The Merchant of Lies," vol. 124, no. 5 (May 1988), p. 22.

4. *American Mercury*
   "Ten Years of the Polish People's Republic," November 1955, pp. 133–137.

5. *The American Slavic and East European Review*
   "The Political Bureau of the United Polish Workers' Party," vol. 15, no. 2 (April 1956), pp. 206–215.
   "The Third Congress of the Polish Communist Party," vol. 19, no. 1 (February 1960), pp. 63–73.

6. *Australian Defence 2000* (Kew, Victoria)
   "Military Balance between the Atlantic and the Urals," vol. 4, no. 11 (December 1989), pp. 20–24.

7. *Beiträge zur Konfliktforschung* (Köln)
   "Die Beziehungen der Vereinigten Staaten zur Sowjetunion," vol. 10, no. 1 (1980), pp. 5–28.

8. *The Catholic Historical Review*
   "The Church of Silence in Communist Poland," vol. 42, no. 3 (October 1956), pp. 296–321.

9. *The Central European Federalist*
   "Polish-German Relations: Problems and Prospects," vol. 12, no. 1 (July 1964), pp. 15–18.

10. *Chronicle of Higher Education*
    "The Big Guns Sound Off," vol. 9, no. 9 (September 1985), pp. 57–58.
    "Soviet Nuclear War Politics," vol. 12, no. 10 (October 1988), pp. 22–23.

11. *Chronicles of Culture*
    "East-West Talks in Vienna," vol. 9, no. 5 (May 1985), pp. 22–24.
    "Soviet Nuclear War Policies," vol. 12, no. 10 (October 1988), pp. 22–23.

12. *Communist Affairs*
    "Gomulka: Head of People's Poland," vol. 3, no. 6 (November–December 1965), pp. 17–26.

13. *Current History*
    "Profile of Poland," vol. 44, no. 261 (May 1963), pp. 257–264.
    "How Strong Is the Soviet Bloc?" vol. 45, no. 266 (October 1963), pp. 209–215.
    "East Europe in Flux," vol. 48, no. 283 (March 1965), pp. 154–160, 179–180.
    "The Hard Line in Poland," vol. 52, no. 308 (April 1967), pp. 208–213.
    "Poland: Myth versus Reality," vol. 56, no. 332 (April 1969), pp. 218–223.
    "New Course in Communist-Ruled Poland?" vol. 60, no. 357 (May 1971), pp.269–275.
    "Poland: Old Wine in New Bottles?" vol. 64, no. 381 (May 1973), pp. 197–201.
    "Poland: The Price of Stability," vol. 70, no. 414 (March 1976), pp. 101–106, 133–134.
    "Soviet Relations with East Europe," vol. 74, no. 436 (April 1978), pp. 145–149, 184–185.

"Soviet Policies in East Europe," vol. 77, no. 450 (October 1979), pp. 119–123.
"Soviet Policy in East Europe," vol. 79, no. 459 (October 1980), pp. 75–79.
"The Opposition Movement in Poland," vol. 80, no. 465 (April 1981), pp. 149–153.
"Soviet Policies in East Europe," vol. 80, no. 468 (October 1981), pp. 317–320.
"Soviet Relations with East Europe," vol. 83, no. 496 (November 1984), pp. 353–356, 386–387.
"The Warsaw Treaty Organization," vol. 86, no. 523 (November 1987), pp. 357–360.
"Poland: Renewal or Stagnation?" vol. 88, no. 541 (November 1989), pp. 373–376.
"Transition in Poland," vol. 89, no. 351 (December 1990), pp. 401–404.

14. *Dickinson Magazine*
"Mutual and Balanced Force Reduction Negotiations," vol. 60, no.1 (February 1983), pp. 1–3.
"Legacy of Revolution," vol. 67, no. 3 (October 1990), pp. 9–13.

15. *East Asia Quarterly* (Taipei)
"Ideological Basis of Soviet Foreign Policy," vol. 2, no. 2 (fall 1970), pp. 1–14.

16. *East Europe*
"Warsaw's Quiet Congress," vol. 13, no. 8 (August 1964), pp. 2–6.
"What Next in East European Intrabloc Relations?" vol. 18, no. 11–12 (November–December 1969), pp. 19–28.

17. *East European Studies* (Kwang-ju, Republic of Korea)
"Confidence-Building Measures as a Problem in Arms Control Negotiations," vol. 1, no. 1 (November 1984), pp. 149–170.

18. *Emory University Quarterly*
"Revolts in Hungary and Poland," vol. 15, no. 4 (winter 1959), pp. 220–227.

"Selling Freedom behind the Iron Curtain," vol. 16, no. 4 (winter 1960), pp. 211–220.
"The Three Berlin Crises," vol. 17, no. 4 (winter 1961), pp. 206–231.
"The United States Response to the Common Market," vol. 18, no. 4 (winter 1962), pp. 229–238.

19. *Est-Ouest* (Paris)
"Soviet Strategic Force Prospects for the 1980s," vol. 4, no. 28 (March 1986), pp. 5–19.
"Les relations américano-soviétiques: une ère nouvelle?" vol. 21, no. 3 (September 1990), pp. 5–21.

20. *Hinter dem Eisernen Vorhang* (Munich)
"Gomulka hält die Stellung," vol. 10, no. 9 (September 1964), pp. 9–12.

21. *Insight* (Washington, D.C.)
"On the Paper Trail of POWs in Russia," 23 November 1992, pp. 17–18.

22. *Intellect*
"Unity of the Left," vol. 106, no. 1 (January 1978), pp. 145–149, 184–185.

23. *Issues and Studies* (Taipei, Republic of China)
"The USSR: Neither Renewal nor Revolution," vol. 6, no. 1 (October 1970), pp. 1–3.
"Future of Red China: After Mao What?" vol. 8, no. 12 (September 1972), pp. 31–40.
"Moscow-Peiping Competition in the Third World," vol. 14, no. 1 (October 1978), pp. 42–58.

24. *Journal of Central European Affairs*
"The Secretariat of the PZPR," vol. 15, no. 3 (October 1955), pp. 272–285.
"The Central Committee of the PZPR," vol. 16, no. 4 (January 1957), pp. 371–383.
"The Political Bureau of the Central Committee of the PZPR," vol. 22, no. 3 (October 1962), pp. 206–215.

25. *Journal of Politics*
    "The New Course in Poland," vol. 20, no. 1 (February 1958), pp. 64–88.

26. *Journal of Public Law*
    "The Polish-German Boundary: A Case Study in International Law," vol. 11, no. 1 (spring 1962), pp. 156–174.

27. *Kultura* (Paris)
    "Strategiczne możliwości ZSSR," no. 12/267 (December 1969), pp. 77–88.

28. *Marine Corps Gazette*
    "Soviet Comments on Vertical Envelopment," vol. 45, no. 9 (September 1961), pp. 44–47.
    "Soviet Political-Military Strategy," vol. 49, no. 10 (October 1965), pp. 20–26.
    "Strategic Power of the USSR," vol. 53, no. 6 (June 1969), pp. 32–38.
    "A Soviet's View of the USMC," vol. 54, no. 12 (December 1970), pp. 15–16.
    "Mainland China after Mao," vol. 56, no. 10 (October 1972), pp. 18–26.
    "Soviet Weapons for the Third World," vol. 57, no. 12 (December 1973), pp. 14–22.

29. *Mediterranean Quarterly*
    "Military Balance between the Atlantic and Urals," vol. 1, no. 1 (fall 1989), pp. 33–46; summary in *Australian Defence 2000*, vol. 4, no. 11 (December 1989), pp. 20–24.
    "The Russian Military in a Union of Sovereign States," vol. 3, no. 1 (winter 1992), pp. 49–59.
    "Russia's Army in Transition," vol. 5, no. 2 (spring 1994), pp. 1–24.
    "Russia and the West: Changing Course?" vol. 6, no. 4 (fall 1995), pp. 63–79.
    "Russia and the Middle East," vol. 7, no. 2 (spring 1997), pp. 163–175.
    "Why NATO Should Expand," vol. 9, no. 3 (summer 1998), pp. 25–33.
    "Russia Reenters World Politics," vol. 11, no. 4 (fall 2000), pp. 23–39.
    "Decision-Making in Russia," vol. 13, no.2 (spring 2002), pp. 9–26.

30. *Michigan Alumnus*
    "Modern Russian Poetry," vol. 62, no. 14 (25 February 1956), pp. 106–108.

31. *Midwest Journal*
    "Written on Human Parchment," vol. 7, no. 4 (winter 1955–1956), pp. 308–314.

32. *Midwest Journal of Political Science*
    "Elections in Communist Poland," vol. 2, no. 2 (May 1958), pp. 200–218.

33. *Military Review*
    "Military Potential of Communist Poland," vol. 36. no. 4 (July 1956), pp. 41–47.

34. *Moderne Welt* (Düsseldorf)
    "Osteuropa im Wandel: Eine Bestandsaufnahme," vol. 8, no.3 (1967), pp. 258–278.

35. *Nationalities Papers*
    "The Opposition Movement in Poland," vol. 9, no. 1 (spring 1981), pp. 35–44.

36. *NATO's Fifteen Nations* (Brussels)
    "USSR and Red China in the Third World," vol. 25, no. 3 (June–July 1980), pp. 81–88.

37. *NATO Review*
    "U.S.-Soviet Relations in the 1980s," vol. 28, no.6 (December 1980), pp. 18–23; translated for Dutch, German, and Italian editions.

38. *Naval War College Review*
    "The USSR in Historical Perspective," vol. 16, no. 5 (January 1964), pp. 1–14.
    "Current Soviet Military Strategy," vol. 18, no. 5 (January 1966), pp. 1–23.

39. *The New Leader*
 "Poland Steps Backward," vol. 42, no. 47 (21 December 1959), pp. 12–14.

40. *The Officer*
 "Soviet Foreign Policy Shift Affects U.S. and NATO Relations," vol. 7, no. 8 (August 1989), pp. 1–5 of insert.
 "Seasick Summit Reduces Passions," vol. 8, no. 1 (January 1990), pp. 1–6 of insert.
 "The '90 Summit: Was It a Success or a Failure?" vol. 8, no. 7 (July 1990), pp. 1–5.
 "The Armed Forces in a New USSR after a Failed Coup and Possible Dissolution," vol. 8, no. 10 (October 1990), pp. 1–4.

41. *Okay America* (Warsaw)
 "W Bastionie Antykomunizmu," no. 6 (November 1991), pp. 5–7.

42. *Orbis*
 "The MBFR Process and Its Prospects," vol. 27, no. 4 (winter 1984), pp. 999–1009.
 "Moscow's Plans to Restore Its Power," vol. 40, no. 3 (summer 1996), pp. 375–389.
 "A Russian Rearmament Wish List," vol. 43, no. 3 (fall 1999), pp. 605–611.

43. *Österreichische Monatshefte* (Vienna)
 "Abrüstung aus der Sicht der USA," vol. 36, no. 6 (June 1982), pp. 219–222.

44. *Osteuropa* (Stuttgart)
 "Weltkommunismus: Ein Überblick," vol. 74, no. 426 (April 1978), pp. 184–185; annual survey, published through 1989.

45. *Perspective* (Boston University)
 "Russia Expands Its Military R&D," vol. 7, no. 4 (March–April 1997), pp. 1, 6–8.
 "Russia's National Security Concept," vol. 8, no. 3 (January–February 1998), pp. 1, 5–8.

"Corruption in the Higher Ranks," vol. 9, no. 2 (November–December 1998), pp. 1, 5–7.
"Funding Russia's Rearmament," vol. 10, no. 1 (September–October 1999), pp. 1, 7–10.
"KGB and Other Buddies in Putin Apparat," vol. 10, no. 4 (March–April 2000), pp. 2–5.
"Toward a Police State?" vol. 11, no. 3 (January–February 2001), pp. 1, 7–10.
"Russia's New Politburo?" vol. 12, no. 2 (November–December 2001), pp. 1, 10–14.

46. *Policy Review*
"The Bear versus the Dragon in the Third World," no. 7 (winter 1979), pp. 93–105.

47. *The Polish Review* (New York)
"Further Prospects for Poland," vol. 43, no. 1 (1998), pp. 3–11.

48. *Il Politico* (University of Pavia)
"La Sovietizzazione di un Popolo Prigioniero," vol. 26, no. 2 (June 1961), pp. 337–357.
"Il Consiglio per il Mutuo Aiuto Economico," vol. 30, no. 2 (June 1965), pp. 272–281.

49. *Polska w Europie* (Warsaw)
"Poczet Prezydenta Putina," vol. 32, no. 2 (June 2000), pp. 80–86.
"Kto kogo?—Wladimira Putina," vol. 34, no. 4 (December 2000), pp. 78–84.
"Ku Państwu Policyjnemu?" vol. 36, no. 2 (June 2001), pp. 85–91.

50. *Problems of Communism* (USIA)
"Checklist of Communist Parties and Fronts" (March–April issues, 1981–1990); *ca.* ten pages each year.

51. *Proceedings* (of the U.S. Naval Institute)
"The East European Alliance System," vol. 90, no. 9 (September 1964), pp. 26–39.
"Russia's Navy Remains in Decline," vol. 124, no. 8 (August 1998), pp. 45–48.

52. *Revista del Estudios Politicos* (Madrid)
"El Movimiento Anticlerical en la Polonia Comunista," no. 127 (January–February 1963), pp. 131–142.
"Los Satelites del Este Europeo," no. 135–136 (May–August 1964), pp. 151–170.

53. *Revue d'Études Comparatives Est-Ouest*
"Les forces stratégiques Soviétiques," vol. 17, no. 1 (March 1986), pp. 5–19; co-authored with William T. Lee.
"Les rélations américaine-soviétique: une heure nouvelle?" vol. 21, no. 3 (September 1990), pp. 5–21.

54. *Slavic and East European Studies* (Montreal)
"Legislative Foundations of Contemporary Poland," vol. 6, pts. 1 and 2 (spring–summer 1961), pp. 62–75.

55. *Southwestern Social Science Quarterly*
"Regimentation of Youth in Satellite Poland," vol. 37, no. 1 (June 1956), pp. 7–19.

56. *Studies on the Soviet Union* (Munich)
"The Communization of a Captive Nation: Poland, 1944–1947," vol. 11, no. 4 (1971), pp. 310–320.

57. *Strategic Review*
"The High-Tech Transfer Offensive of the Soviet Union," vol. 17, no. 2 (spring 1989), pp. 32–39; reprinted in *Australian Defence 2000*, vol. 4, no. 9 (October 1989), pp. 22–26.
"Russia's New Blueprint for National Security," vol. 26, no. 2 (spring 1998), pp. 31–42.

58. *Taurus European Quarterly*
"Status of World Communism," no. 1 (1982), pp. 24–27.

59. *Temoinages* (Marseilles)
"Congrès Paisible à Varsovie," no. 39 (September–October 1964), pp. 14–19.

60. *USA Today*
 "Communism at the Crossroads in Eastern Europe," vol. 117, no. 2528 (May 1989), pp. 46–47.

61. *Vital Speeches of the Day*
 "Sino-American Relations: Retrospect and Prospect," vol. 29, no. 15 (15 May 1963), pp. 468–473.
 "United States Relations with the USSR," vol. 46, no. 19 (15 July 1980), pp. 597–599.
 "MBFR, Europe, and Alliance Security: The U.S. Perspective," vol. 48, no. 23 (15 September 1982), pp. 709–713.
 "Arms Control: Myth or Reality?" vol. 50, no. 6 (1 January 1984), pp. 171–173.
 "The USSR in the 1990s: Threats and Opportunities," vol. 53, no. 16 (1 June 1987), pp. 487–490.

62. *Die Wehrkunde* (Munich)
 "Sowjetische Stimmen über Umfassung aus der Luft," vol. 11, no. 2 (February 1962), pp. 98–101.
 "Semper Fidelis: Die amerikanische Marine-Infanterie," vol. 11, no. 5 (May 1962), pp. 252–257.
 "Probleme und Aussichten des Warschauer Paktes," vol. 13, no. 3 (March 1964), pp. 119–126.
 "Sowjetische Strategie," vol. 18, no. 6 (June 1969), pp. 282–288.
 "Die Zukunft Rochinas: Was kommt nach Mao?" vol. 21, no. 10 (October 1972), pp. 497–502.
 "Die Wettstreit zwischen Moskau und Peking in der Dritten Welt," vol. 27, no. 9 (September 1978), pp. 444–450; renamed *Europäische Wehrkunde*.
 "Die Weltweite Entwicklung des Kommunismus, 1975–1980," vol. 29, no. 6 (June 1980), pp. 287–293.

63. *The Western Political Quarterly*
 "Theory of a Polish People's Democracy," vol. 9, no. 4 (December 1956), pp. 835–849.

64. *The World and I*
 "Should the West Help the East Modernize?" vol. 3, no. 8 (August 1988), pp. 31–35.

"Nonreformers: The Other Eastern Europe," vol. 4, no. 7 (July 1989), pp. 97–101.
"The U.S.-Russia Relationship," vol. 11, no. 9 (September 1996), pp. 38–43.
"Can Putin Pull It Off?" vol. 16, no. 12 (December 2001), pp. 38–43.

Newspaper Articles

1. *Akron Beacon Journal* (Akron, Ohio)
   "The USSR and Disarmament," 6 May 1987.

2. *The Asian Wall Street Journal*
   "Communist Party's Growing Membership," 3 April 1981.

3. *Berkeley Tri-City Post*
   "A Look at the Communist World, 1987," 18 October 1987. Also in *San Francisco Chronicle*, 21 October 1987.

4. *Buffalo Evening News*
   "Slaughter of Polish Officers by Stalin is not Forgotten," 23 October 1988.

5. *Chicago Tribune*
   "Let's Lay Down Law to Soviets," 3 January 1981. Reprinted in the *Congressional Record*, 6 January 1981.
   "The Next Coup Attempt in Russia," 12 November 1992.

6. *Christian Science Monitor*
   "Moscow's Escalating Espionage," 26 December 1979.
   "Your Move, Warsaw Pact," 22 July 1982.
   "Retooling Russian Schooling," 11 March 1988.

7. *The Cincinnati Enquirer*
   "Moscow's Espionage Challenge," 7 July 1980.
   "Moscow's Active Ties to World Terrorism," 7 June 1981.

8. *Corpus Christi Caller Times*
   "Polish POWs Were Shot in Back of Head," 26 October 1988.

9. *The Daily Advance* (Lynchburg, Va.)
   "Worldwide Communism Makes Major Gains in Latin America," 13 October 1979.
   "Kremlin Succession: Danger or Opportunity?" 27 November 1979.
   "Expanded Soviet Espionage: What Can Be Done?" 12 June 1980.
   "Poland: Will It Live?" 4 March 1981.

10. *The Evening Sun* (Baltimore)
    "Don't Blame the Moscow Mess Entirely on the Marines," 22 April 1987.

11. *Herald Examiner* (Los Angeles)
    "In Defense of the Corps," 19 April 1987; same in *State Journal* (Lansing, Mich.), 19 April 1987; *The State Journal-Register* (Springfield, Ill.), 22 April 1987; *The Evening Sun* (Baltimore), 22 April 1987; *The Times Herald Record* (Middletown, N.Y.), 22 April 1987; *Morning Call* (Allentown, Pa.), 27 April 1987.

12. *Houston Chronicle*
    "After Brezhnev, Get Tough," 15 December 1980.
    "Who Would Benefit, Lose What in a Mutual Arms Agreement?" 11 November 1984.
    "Americans in the Gulag," 6 September 1992.
    "Moscow May Not Long Control Greater Russia," 11 November 1993.
    "Russia's Military Manifesto Is Frightening Reading," 1 June 2000.
    "Signs of a Return to the Bad Old Days in Russia," 6 November 2000.
    "Putin's Choice of a 'Civilian' Reins in Russia's Military," 1 April 2001.

13. *Houston Post*
    "Who Would Benefit, Lose What in a Mutual Arms Agreement?" 11 November 1984.

14. *Hoy* (La Paz, Bolivia)
    "Diplomacia i terrorismo," 16 October 1986; same in *El Pais* (Montevideo, Uruguay), 21 October 1986; same in *Impacto* (New York), 6–12 November 1986.

15. *Impacto* (Bolivia)
    "Diplomacia y terrorismao," 6–12 November 1988.

16. *Impacto: The Latin News* (New York)
    "Preparando el encuentro USA.-URSS," 19–25 September 1985.

17. *Indianapolis Star*
    "Viewpoint," 10 May 1985.

18. *The Intelligencer* (Wheeling, W. Va.)
    "Danger or Opportunity for U.S.?: Soviet Leadership Changes," 3 April 1981.

19. *Izvestiia* (Moscow)
    "Byvshii Sovetskii Soiuz imeet izbytok zerna," 22 January 1992; translated into Russian from the *Wall Street Journal* (European edition), 17–18 January 1992, with deletion of the key paragraph.

20. *Journal Inquirer* (Manchester, Conn.)
    "Will 'Glasnost' Extend to Katyn Massacre of Polish Officers Held in Soviet Union?" 25 November 1988.

21. *Los Angeles Times*
    "Worldwide Terrorism: The Soviet Union is at the Bottom of It," 1 May 1981.

22. *Morning Call* (Allentown, Pa.)
    "Marine Guards in Moscow: A Witness for the Defense," 27 April 1987.

23. *El Mundo* (Caracas, Venezuela)
    "Un vistazo al mundo comunista," 14 December 1987; also in *El Mundo* (El Salvador, San Salvador), 14 December 1987; *La Prensa* (Tegucigalpa, Honduras), 14 December 1987.

24. *El Mundo* (San Salvador)
    "Los comunistas que no quieren reformas," 2 September 1989; also in *La Prensa* (Buenos Aires, Argentina), 2 September 1989.

25. *Neue Zürcher Zeitung*
    "Präsident Putin: In der Denktradition des KBG? Wenig Interesse am Aufbau demokratischer Institutionen," 2–3 September 2000.

26. *New York Times*
    "Soviet Arms: Out of Control," 19 August 1991.
    "The Fate of Wallenberg," 30 July 2000.

27. *The News World* (New York)
    "Quantitative, Qualitative U.S. Military Picture is Dim," 11 September 1980.
    "Block Moscow in the Third World,"2 October 1980.
    "The Status of World Communism in Early 1981," 15 March 1981.

28. *Oakland Tribune*
    "1979 Communist Party Grew 5 Percent Worldwide," 15 May 1980.

29. *The Orange County Register*
    "The State of the Nations on the Marxist Party Line," 17 August 1987.
    "Soviets Lag in Age of Computers," 6 March 1988; also in *The Register* (Santa Ana, Calif.), 6 March 1988.

30. *Outlook* (Santa Monica, Calif.)
    "The Choice is Moscow's," 10 December 1980.

31. *The Peninsula Times* (Palo Alto, Calif.)
    "How to Deal with the Kremlin in the 1980s," 13 December 1979.

32. *Pittsburgh Tribune Review*
    "Solidarity's Marian Krzaklewski: Betting Is that He Will Be Poland's Next President," 24 March 1998.

33. *Port Arthur News* (Port Arthur, Texas)
    "Soviets Must Admit Katyn Massacre," 20 March 1989.

34. *Record* (Columbia, S.C.)
    "The Sovietizing of Captive Poland—I & II," 12 July 1962.

35. *The Register* (Santa Ana, Calif.)
"The Soviet Union and the Third World," 30 September 1980.
"Soviet Terrorism: Fiction or Fact?" 20 March 1981.

36. *Rzeczpospolita* (Warsaw)
"Wiek XXI będzie wiekem Rosji?" 10–11 August 1996.

37. *Sacramento Bee*
"Change in Command in Russia Will Confront U.S. Leaders in 1980s," 25 November 1979.

38. *Sacramento Union*
"A Realistic Approach to Relations with the Soviets," 8 December 1980.
"Soviet Concept of Coexistence Examined," 14 August 1983.

39. *St. Louis Post Dispatch*
"Who Will Succeed Brezhnev?"3 December 1979.

40. *The San Diego Union*
"World Communism, 1977–78,"19 February 1978.
"Lithuania Has Struggled Long for Liberty," 18 March 1990.

41. *The San Francisco Chronicle*
"The Soviet Military Factor,"5 January 1980.
"Soviets Fail to Follow Spirit and Letter of CFE Treaty," 16 July 1991.
"Russia's New Military Doctrine Deserves a Read," 15 December 1999.

42. *San Jose Mercury News*
"Why the Soviets Did Not Invade Poland," 12 April 1981.
"West Retooling Soviet Military Machine," 22 February 1987.
"Leaders' Failure to Build Support Helped Doom Coup," 25 August 1991.
"Be Wary of Putin's Russia," 26 March 2000.

43. *San Martin News* (Washington, D.C.)
"Soviet Propaganda Aims at Third World Countries," 20 July 1984.

44. *Scottsdale* (Arizona) *Progress*
   "Soviets Vary Global Propaganda Tactics," 8 September 1984.

45. *Le Soleil* (Quebec)
   "Quand les ideologies et le commerce s'entremelent," 6 January 1986.

46. *Stamford Advocate* (Stamford, Conn.)
   "Facts Give Lie to Soviets' Denial of Terrorist Links," 5 May 1981.

47. *Stanford Daily*
   "Questions for President Gorbachev," September 24, 1990.
   "Russians Call for Bread: Boris, *dai khleba!*" 14 January 1992.

48. *State Journal* (Lansing, Mich.)
   "The Marines: Embassy Mess Blame Goes beyond Guards," 19 April 1987.

49. *The State Journal-Register* (Springfield, Ill.)
   "Don't Blame it all on the Marines," 22 April 1987.

50. *The Times Herald Record* (Middletown, N.Y.)
   "In Defense of Marines," 22 April 1987.

51. *Tribune Review* (Bethany, Okla.)
   "The Soviets ... and the Information Age," 16 August 1988.

52. *Tribune Review* (Greensburg, Pa.)
   "America Pays High Price for U.N. 'Peacekeeping,'" 17 April 1994.

53. *USA Today*
   "An Annual Summit Would Be Terrible Idea," 19 November 1985.
   "Moscow is Just Playing Games," 24 March 1986.
   "This Ploy by Soviets Too Good to be True," 4 March 1987.
   "Soviet Flim-flam puts Europe, USA at Risk," 21 April 1987.
   "Don't Take This Step, It'd Undermine NATO," 2 September 1987.
   "Treaty and Summit Give Away Too Much," 21 September 1987.

54. *Wall Street Journal*
   "Sergei's Propaganda Is Showing," 6 May 1991.

"UN Peacekeeping Costs Are Exploding," 22 December 1993.
"Boris's Belligerent Backers," 12 June 1996; reprinted by *WSJ-Europe*, 17 June 1996; quoted in *Le Monde* (Paris), 27 June 1996.

55. *The Wall Street Journal Europe*
"The Former USSR has Grain in Abundance," 17–18 January 1991. Reprinted as "Russia Has Lots of Grain—Just Ask the Army," *Wall Street Journal*, U.S. edition, 21 January 1992.
"U.N. Peacekeeping Costs Are Exploding," 22 December 1993.

56. *The Washington Times*
"Whatever Happened to That Grain?" 11 February 1992.
"The Lost Yanks in the Gulag," 20 October 1992.
"Russia's Network of Secret Cities," 3 June 1993.
"Round after Round of Secessions," 10 December 1993.
"International Peacekeeping Perils and Prizes," 18 April 1994.
"United States and International Peacekeeping," 19 April 1994.
"Risks and Costs That Come with the Duty," 10 January 1996.
"The Power in Lebed's Arms," 30 July 1996.
"How the Mob Moves in on Moscow...," 27 November 1996.
"Russia and the Middle East Islamic States," 4 March 1997.
"Toxic Weapon Warning Signals," 28 August 1997.
"Tarnished Big Brass in Russia," 20 December 1998.
"Russia's New Plan to Rearm," 30 September 1999.
"Russia's Next President," 23 March 2000.
"Russia's New Concept of National Security," 16 July 2000.

57. *Waterbury Republican* (Waterbury, Conn.)
"Soviets Can't Preach Glasnost, Keep Katyn a Secret Too," 9 November 1988.

58. *Woonsocket Call and Reporter* (Rhode Island)
"Propaganda Masks Future Aims of Soviet Union," 23 May 1984.
"Foreign Policies of the Soviet Union," 16 October 1984.

NAME INDEX

A

Allen, Richard V., xiii, 50, 67, 68, 81, 88
Almond, Professor Gabriel, 30
Amin, Hafizullah, 153
Andropov, Iurii V., 82, 87, 88-89, 120, 121, 122, 124-26, 158
Arbatov, Georgii A., 123, 150
Ault, Professor Stanley, 8
Austin, Vice Admiral B. L., 44

B

Bacchetti, Fausto, 99
Baker, Patricia, 59
Barutcu, Ecmel, 100
Barghoorn, Professor Frederick C., 29, 46
Bark, Dennis L., 51
Baroody, William, 48, 49
Beatty, Warren, 56-57
Bell, Jr., Professor Whitfield, xiv, 24
Belmont, Allan, 53, 59
Bernard, Noel, 40
Bernstam, Mikhail S., 58
Bidzhan, Ivan (John Bittson), 54
Bishop, Dr. William, 24
Black, Shirley Temple, 78
Bor-Komorowski, General Tadeusz, n16, 17, n18
Borcherdt, Wendy H., xiii, 68
Borda, William F., 25

Boss, Walter, 99
Bretton, Henry, 34
Brezhnev, Leonid, I., 82, 85, 87, 94, 111, 124, 141, 158
Brodie, Professor Bernard, 30
Brown, Professor Edward S., 34
Brundtland, Dr. Gro Harlem, 140
Burress, Dr. Richard T., xiii, 54, 59-60, 63
Buss, Professor Claude, 60
Bush, Vice President George, 88

C

Campbell, Dr. W. Glenn, xiii, 44-50, 52-54, 55-56, 68, 173
Carney, Congressman William, 139
Ceausescu, Nicolae, 40
  and wife Elena, 161
Cerwin, Joyce, 170
Chase, Brigadier General Harold, 62
Chernenko, Konstantin U., 82, 124, 158
Cizmaresco, Mihai, 40
Clark, Jr., William P., 69
Conquest, Dr. Robert, 48, 51
Cranston, Senator Alan, 69
Curtiss, Conrad M., 13

D

Dean, Jonathan, xiii, 69, 100
Deaver, Michael K., 69

Dornan, Congressman Robert K., 139
Doying, Louise, 50
Drummond, Jack, 3
Dubcek, Alexander, 91, 156
Duignan, Dr. Peter, 48, 59, 171
Dwan, Jack, 30

E

Eden, Anthony, 18

F

Fifield, Professor Russell H., 34
Filley, Professor Walter O., 34
Fox, Professor William T. R., 29
Freeman, Dr. Roger, 49
Friedman, Dr. Milton, 44

G

Garrett, James, 30
Garvey, Anne, 47
George, Dr. James L., xiii, 134, 135
Georgescu, Vlad, 40
Gingrich, Dr. Newton L., 43
Goddard, Dr. A. N., 9
Goldberg, Colonel Sherwood D., 27, 93
Gomulka, Wladyslaw, 156
Goodpaster, Lt. General Andrew J., 46
Gorbachev, Mikhail S., 82, 89, 94, 120, 124, 151, 155, 158, 162-65
Grachev, General Pavel S., 164-65
Green, Andrew Wilson, 26
Grigory, Margit N., xiv, 50-51
Grinevsky, Oleg A., xiv
Gromov, General Boris V., 155, 164
Gromyko, Andrei A., 120, 121, 121-123, 129
Groza, Octavian, 119

H

Habib, Philip C., 144
Haig, Jr., General Alexander M., xiii, passim 27, 70, 85, 88, 93

Handler, Captain Bruce, USNR, 62
Harper, Jr., Colonel James R., 61
Hatch, Senator Orrin G., 139
Havel, Vaclav, 157, 161
Hazelhof, Erik, 40, 42
Henriksen, Dr. Thomas H., 51, 173
Hepler, Professor John, 24
Hilsman, Roger, 30
Himmler, Heinrich, 14
Holland, Dr. Lynwood M., 42
Hounshell, Professor Charles D., 43
Hoxha, Enver, 93, 156

J

Jakes, Milos, 161
James, E. Pendleton, 69
Jaruzelski, General Wojciech, 87-9, 110, 157
John Paul II, Pope, 88, 157

K

Kadar, Janos, 156, 160
Karch, Dr. John, 137-38, 139, 142, 143
Keller, Richard O., 44
Kelley, General Paul X., 63
Kennedy, Professor David M., 139
Kennedy, President John F., 29, 132, 134
Kennedy, Richard T., xiii, 69
Khrushchev, Nikita S., 29, 93, 156, 160
Klebofski, Laverne, 50
Kriuchkov, Vladimir I., 126, 149, 163
Kuklinski, Colonel Ryszard, 88
Kutovoy, Evgenii G., 101-102

L

Lassner, Dr. Franz, 52
Lawrence, Ruth, 11
Lebed', General Aleksandr I., 125-26, 155, 164
Ledogar, Stephen J., 140
Leoni, Professor Bruno, 44
Leser, Krystyna, 12
Lobanov-Rostovsky, Professor Andre,

Name Index

33
Lyman, Dr. Richard W., 59

M

Meese, III, Edwin, xiii, 66-67,
Meisel, Professor James H., 34, 35
Mikhailov, Valerian V., 100, 110, 120, 127, 128, 129, 130
Mitchell, Professor R. Judson, 54
Molloy, Molly, xiv
Myers, Dr. Ramon H., 48, 51

N

Najibullah, 153
Nathan, Dr. Reuben, 41
Nitze, Paul, 127, 129
Noyes, James H., 51
Nutter, Dr. Warren, 46-47

P

Paszkiewiczowna, Janina, 8
Pawlowski, Professor Felix W., 8
Pell, Senator Claiborne, 70
Pilsudski, Marshal Jozef, 1, 5
Perry, William J., 104
Peterson, Agnes, 48
Politis, Constantine G., 100
Pollock, Professor James K., 33, 41-42, 46
Pradel, Professor Roger, 172
Preuss, Professor Lawrence, 34, 37
Przygodski, Stanislaw, 101

R

Ra'anan, Professor Uri, 171
Raisian, Dr. John, xiii, 173
Ratliff, Dr. William, 51
Rautenstrauch, Professor Walter, 8
Ray, Lt. Colonel Charles A., 103
Reagan, President Ronald W., 58, 63, 65-66, 69, 70, 81-82, 83, 85, 88, 94, 125
Reece, David C., 101-02

Reddy, Leo J., 102
Rentz, Dr. George, 48
Roman, Professor Peter, 171-72
Roosevelt, President Franklin D., 19, 157
Roscoe, Colonel John, USMCR, 62
Rostow, Professor Eugene V., xii, 68, 95, 134
Rowny, Lt. General Edward L., 127
Rudder, Dr. Catherine E., 43

S

Savage, David A., 19
Scaife, Richard, 53
Shevardnadze, Eduard A., 161, 162
Shopov, Lubomir, 102, 119
Shultz, Professor George S., xiii, 63, 94, 167, 177-82
Siekierski, Dr. Maciej, xiv, 49
Simons, A. Murray, 99
Sledz, Father 13
Smirnov, Leonid V., 121, 122
Smith, General W.Y., 103
Solzhenitsyn, Alexander I., 55-58
Souza, Richard, 173
Stalin, Joseph, 17, 156, 157
Stanczyk, Zbigniew, xiv
Squire, Paul, 11
Staar, Agnes, xvii, 1-4, 6, 19-20, 34, 39
Staar, Alfred, 1-9, 20, 24, 31,34, 39, 173
Staar, Barbara, xvii, 3, 4, 6, 19-20, 20, 34, 172
  and family 172
Staar, Christina, 32, 39, 40, 47-48, 172
  and family 172
Staar, Jadwiga, xiii, xviii, 27, 31-32, 34, 42, 43, 44, 55, 56 ,60, 68, 78, 95, 97, 99, 101, 102, 104-106, 124, 131, 137, 140-41, 168-69, 171, 172
Staar, Marie, 1, 3, 4, 6, 7, 8, 20, 31, 34, 39, 172
  husband Harold 4, 20, 172
  son Tommy 20, 172
Staar, Monica, 32, 34, 38, 47-48, 172

Stratton, Pamela, xiii
Sworakowski, Professor Witold S., 45, 48, 50, 54

T

Tacosa, Dr. Corliss A., 52
Teller, Dr. Edward, 171
Thatcher, Margaret, 58
Thompson, Professor Ewa M., 55
Tierney, Dr. Jack, 134-35
Tims, Dr. Richard, 38
Tito, Josip Broz, 93, 156
Trent, Darrell, 66
Triska, Professor Jan F., 60
Trotsky, Leon, 54

U

Ustinov, Dmitrii F., 120, 121-22

V

van Steenwijk, Baron Willem J. De Vos, 99
Vandegrift, Colonel A.A., USMC, 61
Ventura, Deborah, 54
Vernadsky, Professor George, 29
Vucinich, Professor Wayne S., 48-49
Vuilleumier, Dean Ernest A., 24, 25

W

Walch, Elsbeth, 25
Warfield, Dr. Gaither, 10, n 11,11, 20, 22, 23, 24, 27
  daughter, Monica 11
  Memorial Scholarship, 27
  wife Hania, 10, 11, 20, 22
Walesa, Lech, 86, 89, 157, 160
Weinberger, Caspar, 88
Wickenden, Dr. W., 8
Wick, Charles Z., 137
Wieland, Dr. Hella, 101
Wilcox, Dr. Stanley, 37-38,
Wing, Jr., Professor Herbert, 24
  and son Gilman 26
Wolfe, Dr. Bertram D., 49
Wolfers, Professor Arnold, 29
Woolsey, Jr., R. James, xiii

Y

Yel'tsin, Boris N., 162, 153, 16-65

Z

Zablocki, Congressman Clement J., 139
Zhivkov, Todor, 161

Subject Index

A

Abkhazia, 155
ACDA (see U.S. Arms Control and Disarmament Agency)
Afghanistan, 83, 153-55, 157, 159, 160
ambassadors, 78-79, 100, 140
American Association for Advancement of Slavic Studies (AAASS), 45
American Enterprise Institute (AEI), 48, 49,
American Political Science Association AOSA), xiv, 42, 43, 170
American Red Cross, 13
Armia Krajowa (see also Home Army), 6, 12, 18
arms control, 70-79, 85, 147, 182
Arms Control Export Act of 1976, 132
arms sales, 115
Azerbaijan, 161-62
and Transcaucasus, 161

B

Berlin Wall, collapse of, 161
Brezhnev Doctrine, 157, 161
BBC (British Broadcasting Corporation), 15

C

Central Intelligence Agency (CIA), 51, 82, 88, 127, 143, 145
Charter 77 movement, 157
Chechnya, 112, 154, 159, 166
China, People's Republic (PRC), 158, 168-69
Chinese Staff College, 60
Cold War, 93, 111, 151
Commonwealth Club, 139, 142
Communist Party of the Soviet Union (CPSU)
    Politburo (see also Kremlin), 87, 88, 120, 130, 144, 162
    Arms Control Commission, 120-24
    Central Committee, 143
    Foreign Propaganda Commission, 147
    Ideology Commission, 147
    International Department, 143
Conference on Disarmament in Europe (CDE), 74-5,
Conference on Forces in Europe (CFE), 111, 128, 130, 140, 153
    TLE (Treaty-Limited Equipment), 111-112, 113, 114, 115-17
    subterfuge, 113
    verification of, 113-15
    violations of treaty, 112
Conference on Security and Cooperation in Europe (CSCE), 157
Cosmos Club, 65, 66, 69
Council for Mutual Economic Assistance (CMEA), 86, 155-156
Cowell Foundation, 53
Czechoslovakia, 87, 91, 92, 123-24, 156, 159

D

Defense Language Institute, 60
demokratizatsiia,162
Dickinson College, 23-7, 28, 93
disinformation (see also propaganda) 89, 126-7, 146-151
dissertation, 35, 39
Duquesne University, 171

E

Ecole de Guerre, 51
Emory University, xvii, 32, 42-43, 46, 61, 67
Eucom, 103
European Union, 153

F

Federal Bureau of Investigation (FBI), 53, 69
Front Organizations 85, 147, 148, 149-51
    Dartmouth Meetings, 150
    Generals and Admirals for Peace and Disarmament, 151
    International Physicians for Prevention of Nuclear War, 150-51
    World Peace Organization, 148, 149

G

Georgia (Republic of), 112
German Democratic Republic (GDR), 91, 92
Gestapo, xvii, 7, 8, 10, 11, 12, 14, 17, 18
glasnost', 147, 160, 169
Government Committee for State of Emergency (coup), 155, 163-65, 166
Gulf War, 115

H

Helsinki International Radio Service, 141-42
Hitler Jugend, xv, 14
Hitler-Stalin Pact, 87, 161
Home Army (see also Armia Krajowa), 6, 16, 17-8
Hoover Institution, xiii-xiv, xvii-xviii, 43, 44, 45, 46, 47, 48, 49, 52, 55, 57-8, 60, 65, 67, 68, 94, 105, 140, 172, 173, 182
    International Studies Program, 50
    Visiting Fellows Program, 54, 168
Hoover Institution Press, 45, 54, 59
Hungary, 91, 92, 156, 159, 161

I

ILAG VII-Z (see also Laufen camp), 19
INF (Intermediate Range Nuclear Force Treaty), 74-75, 78, 127, 129, 130, 177
Institute for International Affairs (Stockholm), 141
Institute for Study of Conflict (Boston), 171
Institute of USA and Canada (ISKAN), 123-24, 143, 150
International Political Science Association, 41

J

Jewish Combat Organization (see also ZOB), 16

K

Kappa Sigma fraternity, 24-5, 26
Katyn Forest massacre, 160
KGB, 57, 88-9, 125, 130, 145, 160, 163, 164
Kremlin (see also CPSU Politburo), 81, 83, 94, 95, 127, 180

L

Laufen camp (see also ILAG VII-Z), xvii, 11, 14, 15, 16, 19
Liebenau camp, 20
Lithuania, 6, 7, 161-62
   and Baltic states, 161-62
Lubyanka prison, 9

M

MAD (Mutually Assured Destruction), 82
Military Council of National Salvation, 110
Moldova (Moldavia), 112, 117, 161, 164
Mont Pelerin Society, xvii, 44
Mutual and Balanced Forces Reduction talks (MBFR), 68, 69, 70-79, 82, 90, 97-102, 111, 119, 122, 135, 137, 138, 140, 143, 153, 177-82
   Ad-Hoc Group, 98
   associated measures, 107, 109-110, 111
   budget, 97
   chiefs of mission, 99-100
   data disputed, 108-9, 111, 179
   Eastern negotiation strategy, 110-11, 119, 128-32, 179-80
   inspection issues, 73
   inter-agency meetings, 127
   name change, 111
   parity/equality, 107
   trilateral meetings, 97-9
   verification, 72-5, 107-8, 177, 179-80,
   Western negotiation strategy, 76-7, 107-8, 109, 132, 177, 181

N

National Intelligence Estimate (NIE), 90
National Security Directive 77 (NSDD), 81-2, 85, 137, 142-43, 144

Special Planning Group (SPG), 142-43
National War College, 46, 62, 138, 139
NATO, 46, 71-8, 82, 83, 90, 93, 106-10, 114, 115, 124, 139, 153, 177
   and CFE, 111
   naval armaments, 117
   new members, 115
   troops stationed, 106, 107-8
Naval Air Station, Moffett Field, CA., 62
Naval Officers' School, USMC Reserve Training Center, 61
Naval Postgraduate School, 60
Naval War College, 61
"New Political Thinking" policy, 89, 110, 147, 153
"Nine Plus One" treaty, 162
nuclear weapons, 75, 83, 92, 107, 124, 131, 150, 166, 177

O

October Mutiny (coup), 155, 165-66
Omnibus Diplomatic Security and Anti-Terrorism Act, 103
"Operation Barbarossa", 8
"Operation Ryan", 125-6

P

Pawiak prison, 12, 16
Pentagon, 82, 106, 169
perestroika, 153, 160
Phi Beta Kappa society, 26,
Poland's losses in World War II, xvi
Polish crisis, 77, 86-89, 101, 111
Peaceful Nuclear Explosions Treaty, 73
Presidential Legion of Merit, 63
publications:
   Arms Control: Myth versus Reality, 167
   Aspects of Modern Communism, 45
   Communist Regimes in Eastern Europe, 45, 50-1, 60
   Future Information Revolution in

the USSR, 169
Histories of the Ruling Communist Parties, 51
Hoover International Studies, 51
New Military in Russia: Ten Myths that Shape the Image, xiv, 170
Poland, 1944-1962, 35
Public Diplomacy: USA versus USSR, 168
Soviet Military Policy Since World War II, 168
Transition to Democracy in Poland, xiv, 170
United States-East European Relations in the 1990s, 170
Yearbook on International Communist Affairs, xiv, 50-51, 54
Pugwash Committee, 141, 150

R

Radio Free Europe (RFE), 39-41, 42, 94
Radio Liberty, 40, 94
Rand Corporation, 167
Research Analysis Corporation, 47
RAF, 7, 18
Red Army (see also Soviet Army), 6, 7, 8, 9, 17-18, 29, 31, 87, 93, 153-55, 162, 166
Romania, 124
Rukh, 161

S

SALT, 168
Sandia National Laboratories, 47
Scaife Family Foundation, 53
SDI (Strategic Defense Initiative), 83, 125, 127
Senate Foreign Relations Committee, 69-78
Sino-Soviet conflict, 95
spetsnaz, 153-54, 164
START, 78, 127, 130
START-II, 95

Solidarity Movement, 83, 86, 88-89, 101, 110, 153, 161
Soviet Army (see also Red Army), 17
Soviet Military Doctrine, 92, 123
Soviet propaganda (see also disinformation), 9, 85, 94, 128, 130, 137, 143-47, 150
Soviet Union
  collapse of, 89, 115, 116, 151, 166, 170
  Commonwealth of Independent States (CIS), 153, 165
  crisis in leadership, 82-83
  economy, 82, 95, 110, 116, 166
  espionage, 94, 129
  local wars, 158-69
  oil, 82, 95, 110
  republics and independence, 116, 162, 165
  response to CFE requirements, 113-17
  troops:
    Afghanistan, 83, 154-55
    post-World War II, 90
  Union Treaty, 163-64
Stanford Research Institute, 32
Stanford University, 45, 48, 53, 57, 58-9, 139, 168
Sun Microsystems, 32

T

Taipei, 60-61
Tajikistan, 155
Third Reich, 6, 19, 28
Third World, 83, 84, 94, 95
Tittmoning, xvii, 12, 14, 17
transition team, 65-68
Treblinka camp, 16

U

underground railroad, 6, 7, 8
United Nations (UN), 153
University of Georgia (U.S.), 43
University of London matriculation examinations, xvii, 13, 15, 19, 23

University of Maryland overseas programs, 41
University of Michigan, 3, 32-35
    father on engineering faculty, 3
    sister as graduate, 4
University of Warsaw, xviii
U. S. Air Force, 13, 19,
U.S. Arms Control and Disarmament Agency (ACDA), 68, 70, 95, n100, 127- 28, 132-35, 142, 167, 182
    budget, 133-35, 167
U.S. Department of State, xvii-xviii, 9, 35, 37-38, 51, 69, 70, 79,104, 106, 127, 144, 182
    INR (Intelligence and Research), 55
U.S. Department of Defense, 47, 69, 127, 167
    International Security Affairs (ISA), 47
U.S. Information Agency (USIA), 137-38, 167, 168, 169
U.S. Marine Corps, 61-63, 68, 69, 104-5, 135
    Command and Staff College, 62, 68
    Educational Center 61
U.S. Naval War College, 43, 44, 46
U.S. Navy Reserve Politico-Military Affairs Company, Treasure Island, CA., 62
U.S.S.R. (see Soviet Union)

V

Vienna talks, xvii, 90, 97, 106-110, 127-8, 140, 178
    deadlock, 73

Congress of Vienna, 98, 104
    security, 103-106
    "vodka diplomacy", 131
Voice of America, 94, 168
Volksgericht, 8

W

Waffen SS troops, 16, 17
Warsaw
    city of, 3, 5,6
    destruction in, 18
    ghetto, 16, 17, 18
    life in hiding, 10-11
    uprisings, 16-19
Warsaw Treaty Organization, 71, 77, 90-2, 106-10, 114, 178
    and CFE ,111
    delegation, 97
    disintegration of, 111
    groups of forces, 91
    preparations for war, 92
    Romanian non-participation, 157
    Soviet naval armaments, 117
    troops, 91-92, 106, 107-8, 180
Wehrkunde, 140
Wehrmacht, 6, 9, 15, 31
Wriston Report, 38

Y

Yale University, 28-30, 68

Z

ZOB (Zydowska Organizacja Bojowa), 16

ABOUT THE AUTHOR

Richard F. Staar has served as an intelligence research specialist with the U.S. Department of State in Washington, D.C., and as American ambassador to the conventional arms reduction talks in Vienna, Austria. Between these two assignments, he taught political science at Emory University as well as at two U.S. war colleges.

A prolific writer, Professor Staar's books and articles have appeared in Chinese, German, Italian, Korean, Polish, Russian, and Spanish translations.

The author received degrees from Dickinson, Yale, and the University of Michigan. His first *alma mater* also awarded him an honorary doctorate in political science. Professor Staar has lectured in Austria, Belgium, Finland, Germany, Hungary, Norway, Poland, Romania, Russia, South Korea, Sweden, and Taiwan and was sent by the U.S. Information Agency on a speaking tour of east-central Europe.

The former principal associate director for twelve years, Dr. Staar is currently a senior fellow at the Hoover Institution on War, Revolution, and Peace of Stanford University. He received the presidential Legion of Merit after twenty-one years of service as an active reserve officer in the U.S. Marine Corps and retired two years later with the rank of colonel.